A TRAIL OF TRIALS

A Trail of Trials

JAMES W. TRIMBEE 1884–1972
WITH JEAN TRIMBEE McKENZIE

The Pentland Press
Edinburgh – Cambridge – Durham – USA

© Jean Trimbee Mckenzie, 1995

First published in 1995 by
The Pentland Press Ltd
1 Hutton Close,
South Church
Bishop Auckland
Durham

ISBN 1-85821-302-9

Typeset by Carnegie Publishing, 18 Maynard St, Preston
Printed and bound by Antony Rowe Ltd, Chippenham

Dedicated to the family
of
JAMES WILLIAM TRIMBEE
in his memory

Contents

Preface

My Father wrote this, his autobiography, unknown to anyone until after his death in 1972. Editing his story has been to me truly a 'labour of love', stirring up my interest in tracing the Trimbee family 'roots'. I would like to thank cousin Ethel Trimbee McEvoy for lending the family photo album and for her help in details and dates. Also, my deep thanks to Paul Fini, husband of my niece Martha, for his aid in assembling the material. Finally, to Elsie Butler of Surrey, England, for her help and support in promoting the idea of publication in England.

Jean Trimbee McKenzie

BOOK I

On the morning of 1 November 1884, I made my arrival into this Vale of Woe. The place was the little village of Upham, seven miles south of the city of Winchester, Hampshire, England.

It was a cold, drizzly day and, although I was expected, no bands or welcoming committees were there to greet me. No twenty-one-gun salutes proclaimed my birth and the only ones present were my parents and the old midwife, Granny White, who was one of the finest of her profession. The older children in the family were in bed, unaware until later that they had a new baby brother. The doctor, who lived four miles away, was a secondary consideration in these matters and would be along later to check on us. This was the usual procedure in those days, as there were few hospitals and most of the births were in the homes under conditions similar to mine. My birthplace was a room in the old farm house but, luckier than most in those long-gone days, it had an open fireplace which helped to keep out the cold and dampness up to a point. For the birthings, the old midwife was the most important person and Granny White was the champion of them all, having had many years' experience and possessed the confidence of all who were able to obtain her services. She was loved by everyone and, at that period, such women were held in as much respect as the doctors themselves by the folk of the land.

So my introduction into this world was really very quiet and simple, with little fuss. Having arrived safely and gone through the usual preliminaries, it took me a few weeks of quiet contemplation and observation to understand what was going on around me. By the following spring, the different sights and sounds began to have meanings for me. I realized that I was most fortunate in having the two best parents in the country for my own. They were doing their best for me in all ways, which was not an easy matter in their poor circumstances, as the flock was already too large for the incoming forage.

As yet, there was only one breadwinner and his earnings only amounted to fifteen shillings per week. My arrival complicated things but, according to Dad, one more would not make any difference. Outside of what we ate, the clothes that we needed were mostly hand-me-downs from the older ones.

I was learning the different ways to get attention from those around me, which meant that I was taking an interest in this new world of mine. On looking around, I noticed other ones who were not very large either. These were my older brothers and sisters. They would come up and speak to me at times and we learned to accept each other.

Summer followed Spring and conditions changed, for now we were going to be living outside in the fresh air for a lot of the time. I was going to sleep outside, play outside and have rides down the village lanes in the old perambulator. I found it nicer than lying in the house and my interest in the new surroundings increased. I was just beginning to enjoy life. While watching the activities of not only my Father and my Mother but also those of my brothers and sisters, I began to get curious about all the things around me.

The next two years of my life were repetitions of the first, a time of growing and learning, and, oh, how I learned! I was trying to ask for things that I saw and finding out that, with very little effort, I could slide from one part of the kitchen to another, caring not that it was a cold, red-brick floor covered with coconut matting. It may not have been very warm at times, nor sterile clean, but it was the room in which we did most of our living.

An accident in the Winter at this time left me marked for life. My mother, who unfortunately was hard of hearing, had left me in the high chair in front of the kitchen fire to keep warm, while she made the beds in the morning. Somehow, I must have fallen forward into part of the kitchen range, and I received several bad burns before she found me, as she was unable to hear my screams while she was upstairs in the bedrooms. It took a long time for these burns to heal, leaving me with scars above my upper lip so that, upon maturity, I grew a moustache to cover them.

The fireplace to which I refer is worth description. There was an opening in the wall about six feet wide by three feet deep, with the so-called stove fitted into the centre of this opening. The stove consisted of an open-grate fireplace about eighteen inches wide, with an oven on the side. The chimney going up from this was large enough for the sweep to go all the way up to clean it, but as there were six doors in this kitchen leading off to other parts of the house and outside, I think the chimney was pulling more cold air from below than it was discharging smoke. Alas, in those days we did not know any better and so blundered through for several years with these conditions, having no means at that time to consider changes for improvement. My mother, in her younger days before

1. *Walter and Sarah, James's parents.*

marriage, had been a school teacher, and in many ways she began to instil in me the things necessary to growing up, such as obedience, cleanliness, thankfulness, cheerfulness, and many like things. She also taught me observance of the scene and sounds around me.

And so, through sickness and through health, of which I am unable to remember all, of course, I arrived at the age of three. Those first three years consisted of growing, feeding, and learning to take instructions from my elders and there were several of these as I was the seventh, and there were eventually to be twelve. One of my older sisters died very young, so the grown family resulted in eleven children. During that period, I had not only two major domos, my Father and Mother, but also those five lieutenants, my brothers and sisters, on guard to teach me the do's and do-not's, the wrongs and rights, the ups and downs, the ins and outs, the rights and lefts. If I should start protesting, I would be told in no uncertain terms to stop. While being taken for an outing in good weather in the old pram, they told me of the different birds, such as the cockatoo. They also showed me where all the wild flowers grew. We all had fun and, except for the bad burns and some children's sicknesses, those first three years passed quickly. The family had taught me many things and now I was ready for further education in the outside world. Thus, at three years of age, I was sent off to school, as was the custom then.

I was most fortunate in one way, as the school was right across the road from our home. This was the beginning of my first adventure. By now, another child had arrived in the home to take my place as the youngest of the family and, from now on, I would have to be satisfied with secondary consideration and attention.

Here I think I should digress for a moment and describe the school. At this time of writing, 1968, the idea across the land seems to be that we require palaces in which to educate the young. This school which I attended was built with flint stones that had been gathered off the land locally 100 years previously. It had a slate roof, was whitewashed inside when needed, and I believe that the school is still in use. My first class in the infants' room was composed of boys and girls below the age of five. I can still see the inside of that room and, at eighty-four years of age now, I can still re-live the instructions, scenes and surroundings therein.

From now on, I began to record in my mind what was around me, and why. I was just beginning to learn realities and why these things were necessary in our growing-up years. From the beginning, this period was very important. I often wonder how many people realise just how important, as it is at this point in time that the foundation is built into the little individuals that is to carry them upward until the end.

2. Photo taken of Annie in uniform while 'in service'.

Now I was not only not the youngest in the family anymore, with less attention given to me than before, but I was now attending school, where I would have to do more thinking and learning to help myself. In this way, life began to have more meaning and interest. Being part of a family, I had to learn to give and to take – but not what belonged to the other fellow. Now I was out in the world with many other little children of the same age, who were also starting to learn the rules of life – the whys and wherefores.

We were taught the ABCs, the small sums and so many other things to do with reading and writing. Left, right, left – it took quite a while to grasp that one. I often felt like marking the wall in the classroom so that I could be sure!

The first year went by and now it was time to pass from the infant classroom to the proper classroom of first class, where more was expected from us. Here, we were to learn under tougher supervision. In this department, the Principal's wife taught the first four classes. During these four years, she was very strict but fair as she guided us through our grades.

Now I had reached the age of discretion, having been taught honour, loyalty, obedience, respect, integrity, fair play and other factors pertaining to the foundation of life. I was beginning to assimilate and store in my mind many things of my new environment. At school it was reading, writing, arithmetic, geography, history and the many other different lessons that were taking us in our minds to so many other parts of the world which, at that time, were all so new to us.

As a little stranger among all this, my interest was fast awakening because now, as well as schooling, I was getting instructions in many other matters. I was now around the age of six or seven years, and learning to be useful around my home in many ways before and after school. At that time, there were few electrical appliances, of course, on earth. There was absolutely none at all in the small villages such as ours, which meant so many things had to be done by hand. For example, let me tell you about the heat and water. Every afternoon, one of us little ones would have to chop and prepare a load of dry, small firewood and lay it beside the kitchen range ready for the elders to light the fire before they could even get a cup of tea in the morning. This was done seven days a week. On Monday mornings, one would have to get up earlier than ever to get the copper boiler going in the wash house, requiring much more wood than usual. This had to be done before we went to school. Coal-oil lamps or candles were our illuminants. Our house was located on high land which therefore required a deep well for our water supply. This deep well was from 80 to 100 feet deep, six feet across and lined with large flint stones, no two alike, and had been there for over 100 years. You could only see the water by focusing a looking glass down when the sun was just right.

The well house was part of the overall structure of the farmhouse but the real interest lay in the method we had to use to obtain our water. The equipment used was a twelve-foot treadwheel with a twelve-foot spindle, fifteen inches thick, which ran six feet high across the well. The rope was two inches thick, number one material. The well bucket, as it was called, was of heavy oak with a heavy iron handle to which the rope was affixed with proper splicing. The procedure used to get a bucket of water was as follows: grasp the spoke of the wheel, close all the lids to allow the rope to work back and forth on the big spindle, grasp the pole which was a young tree eight feet long, three to five inches in circumference, slide it under the outside of the wheel, resit it upon your shoulder and steady the momentum of the outfit. Then, as you realised the bucket was in the water and full, you stepped into the inside of the wheel and grasped a strap on the wall as you began to walk uphill. If you could have another person to pull down on the spokes, it was a great help. In any case, when you did get the water up, you had earned it − sparkling as it was. It was not polluted at that depth but the men would not go down to clean it before dropping down a caged canary to prove that it was free of gas.

There were three similar outfits for water like ours in the district. One was also hand-operated, another had big dogs trained for the wheel, and the third was operated by donkey power. I know now of at least one of these still in existence.

Now life was beginning to get more serious and the next three or four years were busy ones, as there was a lot to learn and a great many questions to ask in this new world of mine. Living on a farm, we were in the middle of Nature and I found that this took up limitless space which included many different things. Sometimes, when I asked questions of the older ones, I did not always receive the right answers. For instance, when very young, I asked how they grew the *Polyanthus*, commonly known now as primrose. For quite a long time they informed me that if I planted the primrose upside down, it would come up as *Polyanthus*! There were some jokers among the young lads even in those days. I received many answers like that one but I think it sharpened me up and caused me to be more wary.

I was now in the schoolroom of the Principal, who taught up to Standard Seven. After about seven years of age, school attendances would begin to be 'spotty', because if there was a chance to earn a sixpence at the cost of losing half a day at school, you lost it, as the sixpence was always needed at home. As one grew older, more and more time was lost from school. This was a farming community and the methods used in those days required all the extra labour available.

I was beginning to ramble farther from home and my interest in so many things was developing at a furious pace. There were all the different people to meet and try to understand what they were doing and why. I found that this was going to take a long time, as there were so many ways and means of obtaining a living to keep a roof over their heads and food in their mouths. I now realised that, by keeping my eyes and ears alert and my mouth shut, I would learn that life was not all roses.

Just a few, the upper classes, had life easy in this period of the 1890s. The lower-class people were kept in that position through no fault of their own. Wages were around nine to twelve shillings a week for all farm help, if you were fortunate enough to obtain work. You were supposed to salute, bow or curtsy to all above the village schoolmaster, such as the minister, farmer, squire, lord, earl, doctor, lawyer, officers of all ranks and many others, for the slightest reason. Yes, in those days the little fellow was really small.

Our attention was now drawn to many things other than school, namely the great outdoors. The animal kingdom was unfolding before my eyes. Being born on a farm, I had had animals around me since my first recollections and now, at the age of seven to eight, I began to learn of the different classes. The horse kingdom was held in high esteem at this time for, other than some steam power and a little water power, they were the only other source of power known to man. Power was referred to as so much horse power, whether it took one horse or ten horses to move a certain object. We had the heavy horse for the very heavy hard work, the medium-built for the lighter, faster haulage, the carriage horse and hunter class for the upper class trade, the cob, a young horse, and pony for the light delivery or pleasure driving, with the donkey to follow up for other small detail work or pleasure.

Then there were all the other domestic animals with which to acquaint myself, such as the cows and the bulls. I wanted to know why they were there, their purpose in being there, where they came from and how they were reproduced, what feed and conditions they required. These questions and many more were answered before I was satisfied.

Over the fence in the next field were hundreds of sheep. The same questions were asked about these over the following months. Then it was on the enquiries about hogs or tame rabbits. All the time, I was researching for answers to many questions.

Also, there were the wild animals I wanted to learn things about, such as their habits, their usefulness to mankind, if any, and their distrustfulness, and all facts pertaining to them. Each day I felt myself gathering and storing knowledge of wonders about me. It seemed like a wonderful world that I had started through, and I was happy.

I soon found that there were other marvellous things around us calling for my attention. For example, there were our feathered friends, of which there were many, from the turkey down to the little Jenny Wren. Around our barnyard, and our neighbours', were the different varieties of domestic fowl, including turkeys, geese, ducks, peacocks, guinea fowl, domestic chickens in the different classes. The owners required some specialised knowledge of each to be able to handle them successfully and profitably. The acquisition of this knowledge took many years, after which one had to keep up to date on the information pertaining to all such matters, even husbandry.

By now, I had learned of many things around me regarding Nature and her ways, registering them all in my mind for future use. I was beginning to love Creation and, the more I studied it, the more I realised there was always something else to learn. Now as I started to travel the highways and byways, lanes and paths in Spring, I noticed that this Creation seemed to be bursting out all over. The ground plants were trying to beat each other in developing their glorious colours mile after mile over hill and dale. All this was accompanied by the sounds of thousands of song birds. I thought to myself many times what a marvellous place I was living in, for as soon as the snow disappeared, I began to hunt for red moss cup, a little red fungus. The next week or so, I would find the primrose in selected spots, followed by the violets in different colours and scents. There were also the cuckoo cups, wild narcissus, wild hyacinth and dozens of other little beauties of the flora world which seemed endless in succession.

While seeking out the flora, the song birds and others seemed to call for our attention. I would run for miles in the hope of finding the skylark's nest and that would lead me on. The linnet, goldfinch, yellowhammer, bullfinch, blackbird, thrush, blue jay, dove, sparrow and starling would all keep me on my toes for hours, hunting for their nests. We must not forget also the tomtits, wrens, robins, cuckoos and others. Each one had its own ideas, locations and structures for nest. Never will I forget my delight in finding the one and only long-tailed caven's (raven's) nest that I ever saw. The location was in a yew plantation within a clump of *Mahonia*, the prickly-leaved plant. The construction was marvellous, consisting of a deep, oval nest with a very small hole in the top side. The material used from top to the bottom was the lichen growing on the tree trunks around the area. The inside was lined with horse hair. I handled this find reverently, and showed it to no other children. I searched often for the nest of our other little pal, the nightingale, and although year after year you could listen to it in the same location, I never found it. Now, at the age of eighty-four, I can lean back and visualise those birds piping their songs.

These years of my life were careless, free time for most of the time, interest unlimited in all around me with everything new and beautiful. My growing up continued till now I had reached the age of eight, in the year 1892. By now, two more little ones had enlarged the family. My parents felt that it was time for me to take on more responsibility than ever around home, so more duties were assigned me before and after school. This would gradually bring me into the scheme of things surrounding me, to learn what life's road was all about. Little did I know then what a long road I was embarking on!

Each year, school was getting more exacting and more demanding, while I was also being called on for more and more help from others. By now we were receiving quite a bit of religious instruction, which at this time was taken very seriously. Although in Sunday School, when reciting the Lord's Prayer, emphasis would be given to the lines 'Give us this day our daily bread', outside on earth we learned very young that we would be expected to put forth our best effort in order to obtain that daily bread!

In these next four years or so, I would be called upon frequently for chores that would take me away from school. There might be a message to be run to Bishop's Waltham, three and one-half miles each way, and I would be expected back for school in the afternoon. Or maybe I would have to take a cow or sow up to Tommy Hounshan's for service, two and one-half miles each way walking, and again would be expected to be back for afternoon school. Another reason to miss school was that some neighbour would need assistance for a few hours. Poppa knew how to handle his family as much by a look as by the word. He knew that idle hands made mischief so that the majority of our spare time from school was mapped out with different jobs to take up the slack, and many a seven-mile journey I had to take at this time. This resulted in losing one-half day in school, all for a sixpence which went into the home to help out. Sometimes, a whole day's school would be lost if the job so required. Along with the school learning, I was getting educated around the garden and farm. The garden was walled, full of varieties of fruits, nuts and vegetables. The front garden was for flowers.

In summer, you were required to help with the haying, harvest and sheep-shearing. At eight or nine, you would have to lead the horses or the wagons as they were driven one ahead of the other to each stook or pile of hay. We might also have to drive the old horse on to the elevator, a machine used in those days to take the material up, as they built the stacks. There, you would follow the horse around in a circle for ten or twelve hours a day. For this, you would receive the magnificent sum of sixpence, and your meals. Each year, as you grew older, you were advanced to the heavier jobs.

The sheep-shearing each year was quite an event. There was a flock of 800 sheep on the farm where I was born, which required nearly a week for the shearing operations. To prepare for the event, my father, who was chief factotum, and the head labourer would have to spend two or three days brewing a batch of beer for the workers. This place was still run in the old-fashioned way whereby, instead of giving the workers double pay for overtime, they fed them and found them in beer, made mostly out of material raised on the farm for that purpose. This resulted in a lad of nine or ten running around on the shearing floor with a big pewter jug of beer and a couple of horns from which to drink. These were made from the horns of cows with a bottom fixed in, and they lasted for years and were not easily broken. The shearers were a group of men who came from a certain district in the country and travelled from farm to farm over so many weeks in the early summer. It was all done by a pair of hand shears, as at that time there were no power tools. These men took great pride in their work and if one got a little ragged, he was soon brought to heel, as they returned year after year. They worked long hours but in the late evening, they usually finished up with a singsong. As a lad, I looked forward to these times and now, with nearly eighty years passing since then, one old ballad still haunts me as I relive those scenes. It went like this:

For the old man said unto his wife
My love, we soon shall part this life,
After tonight, the workhouse door
Shall part us, love, for evermore.

This was very appropriate at the period, for the workhouse was the only, and last, resource for the poor and disabled – a pretty sorrowful outlook.

Even with all the busy events and work building up all round us, I made time to disappear when I could, to commune with Nature, as I was feeling even more strongly how much there was to see and learn upon investigation. It seemed that the more one learned, the more there was to further this learning. An example of this would be in the fact that the older lads would take a delight in telling us young gaffers all sorts of tales of the different places around the area. Nearly every corner, field, chalk pit, farm, bush or weed had its own name, such as Shepherd's Field Dell. This was a discarded chalk pit in the middle of a farm that had not been used for over 100 years. The deep part was all overgrown with bushes and trees with a walk-through, the roots overhanging from the top, dangerous, of course, to traverse. The big lads would encourage us, the young ones, to hunt all through this top for squirrels and for owls' eggs.

Another time we would go down to Bouldean's to get the young rook or hazel nuts, up to Durwood in the fall to hunt for sweet chestnuts, over to Rowage or up to Greenhill for mushrooms, down to Blackdown for early narcissus. These trips were typical of dozens of others we took, placing a different value on each one. I found much in my expanding world to seek and investigate.

Then out of the blue, at the 'old' age of nine, I was called to the forefront of things. The rector's wife sent out an order for so many of us boys to attend a meeting in the Rectory, as she wished to try out our voices to see which were suitable for training for the Church Choir. I passed the test and was in the Choir for many years following, and this may have been one of the finer things I found along life's way. I have no regrets of the many hours I spent in the different choirs in which I sang.

Winter followed Summer and Fall and, with it, came extra responsibilities, for as well as our regular jobs to be done daily before and after school, we lads would be called upon to act as beaters for the shooting parties. Our own village was practically surrounded by large estates and, throughout the winter, shooting parties were held that sometimes lasted a week. We lads were needed to walk about two and a half to three miles to the estate, then walk all day over hill and dale to flush out the animals. For this, we left home before seven in the morning and would return after seven in the evening. As recompense, we would receive a chunk of bread and cheese and a drink of tea at noon, plus one shilling for a day's pay. I was now one of a large family and Dad's pay was just fifteen shilling weekly for seven days a week, as well as often quite a bit of overtime for no extra pay. With a family his size to look after, he had to stay put.

To recompense him for extra work, his employer would occasionally give him a few pounds of rusty, fat pork that had been in the brine for perhaps two or three years. When he brought it home, Mother would soak it for several hours, then place it in the pot on the side of the stove, letting it boil slowly for hours. With vegetables added, it would be our dinner meat, not a stretch of lean in the whole lot, as they used to kill the pigs in those days when 700 or 800 pounds. Of course there were times when the youngsters would hesitate to tackle their dinner because of the salt pork. When this happened Dad would quietly tell them that if they did not eat now, it would be their supper, with pepper and vinegar. Then they surely tried to put it down! The liquid in which it had been boiled would be put by to cool, after which perhaps about one inch of fat would have set on top. Mother would use this for cake and pastry making. She was a good cook and nothing was wasted in our home.

In our large, walled fruit and vegetable garden, Dad was an expert grower. The crop gained from this was a big help in supporting the food for the table. It also meant a lot of work for us lads, which was a means of keeping us out of mischief that might have resulted from seeking out entertainment. The only entertainment then was the school concert or the village pub after you reached the age of eighteen.

It was around this time that the phonograph was invented, although it was years afterwards before it appeared in our village. One of the social gentry kindly demonstrated it to the schoolchildren. I well remember the occasion as it was a red-letter day and, as I am writing, I can picture in my mind the gentleman with the pointed beard exhibiting the wax cylinders and the big horn. Events such as these and training for the district choral festival were things to remember for ever. For fun and recreation, we had to improvise quite a lot. Boys would have their 'wars' at the chalk pits or 'Hare and Hounds' at lunch, resulting in arriving late back at school, dirty and dishevelled. We would then have to line up to get a strapping by the schoolmaster, with a lecture added. Did we go home and tell our parents? Not likely, as it would have meant another punishment! The schoolyard, so called, was an angled piece of land between three roads in front of the school. In those days, an old wagon or cart would be all the traffic on those roads while we were at play. We also played rounders and jugglecat, two games which were the foundation of American baseball. More games we enjoyed were marbles, hopscotch and skipping up the lane a bit. In season, we played field hockey. For our sticks we went to the hedges and searched for a stick with the right curve, and cut it. For pucks, we used a small ball of some kind. I remember using an ivory billiard ball awhile and, when you got hit with that, you certainly knew it, as we used no guards of any kind. Wounds were frequent and expected, so taken in their stride. Those times are unforgettable.

As we had no school work to do at home, we had some spare time on our hands, though little, after the chores were done. In the dark evenings after supper, outside of reading by the light of the coal-oil lamps, any other recreation had to be improvised, and it took on different forms. For instance, there was a game called 'Tick of the Spider', where several of the youngsters would get together with a spool of thread, a pin and a button tied to the thread in a certain way. The thread would be attached to the wood on a window, carefully and quietly, of a local householder. The thread was then taken back a safe distance behind the hedge or wall, where the operators would start their ticking . . . so many ticks, then wait. We would carry on in this way until the householder became suspicious and appeared at the door. This meant then pulling the pin and departing for fresh victims. It meant quite a lot of running to get clear of the latest victim. Thus the evening would go by, then home to bed.

Other evenings, we would congregate at the corner of the road and wait for some folks to drive by with a pony or donkey. Two or three of us would go and lie down across the road. It would be very dark and as soon as the animal approached us, it would stop dead until the occupant got out to investigate. Then again we would have to do some fast disappearing. Sometimes, the old fishmonger would come out from the farmhouse where he had had his mug of beer, and as he got on the seat of his wagon to drive on, he would see his old nag looking soulfully up at him. Some smart youngster had reversed the horse in the shafts. For variety, we would go round and arouse folks after they had gone to bed. When they poked their heads out of bedroom windows to know what was the matter, they were advised to take in their chimney pots as we were likely to have a frost. You can just imagine what followed! In those days, we made our own spice of life but we never did anything that would put us in trouble with the Law. We were growing up and had to learn that, outside of our home and the main highways, you would be liable to prosecution if you wandered on to private property for any reason. To learn this, was as vital as learning the Lord's Prayer for, when you were of the lower class, it was well to remember that and act accordingly.

Of the hundreds of children that passed through the school in my days, only three, that I knew of, went forward to higher or grammar school. They were the teacher's sons, and his nephew. In fact, I think that most of our schooling and college education was of a practical nature – learning by doing. The schooling that we were able to obtain, in between jobs, could be adding a little salt to your vegetables. It added to the salt of life, too, or at least gave us enough to become more inquisitive regarding all the things around us. We knew how to read and write, which opened unlimited possibilities. With these two gifts, we had the world at our fingertips. Using this foundation at hand on which to build, the heights were unlimited, provided we watched the materials we used, and the workmanship. We learned to look before leaping. Mistakes made then meant another lesson had been learned, which was to avoid making the same mistake twice.

My earliest recollection of trouble in the home happened late one summer evening. On entering the house to go to bed, I heard quite a commotion in the back kitchen. It was my elder brother, Ernest, receiving punishment from my Father for a foolish mistake he had made. It seems that he and another lad were bringing up the cows from the lower meadow, and started playing with two of the cows' tails as they wandered up the road. Whether intentionally or not, the ends of the tails locked. As soon as the animals realised what had happened, they became scared and tried to pull free of each other. The result was that one animal lost the end of its tail, and as these animals were under my Father's charge and his responsibility, he was extremely annoyed and hurt as he realised the suffering the animals must have endured. Although my Father was a kindly, quiet man, he was also very strict, which I realise was necessary in bringing up eleven of us. His word was law and, although I know we often did things which made him angry, I never heard him swear. If he was speaking to Mother at the meal table of any matter rather private, he would look round and say to us that if any of the conversation came back to him from outside, we would all know what to expect. When Mama would send us down to meet him coming home from work, should we meet one of his friends and they start to talk, Father would look around at us and we knew we had to wander up the road, out of hearing, and wait for him. No word needed to be said. The only material thing he had for a lifetime of work was a large family, but we all revered him and still respect his memory.

In those early years, we had all the usual varieties of pets, such as rabbits, which would keep us busy after school. We hunted the highways and byways for food for them in the early summer, with an old perambulator and two or three sacks. It took lots of effort but we were doing something useful. There were also tame doves, hawks, pigeons, squirrels, white rats and mice, chickens and cuckoos. I could write a book about these animals alone but time does not permit. Nevertheless, I must enlarge upon one little chap. He was Little Joe, the Seven Sleeper mouse. These little fellows were pretty hard to find and observe. They are supposed to sleep for seven days and then be awake for seven days. They are small, reddish-coloured mice with a slightly bushy tail, and as sharp as a needle. My brother and I were gathering nuts one fall and disturbed some in their nest. This was a beautiful piece of construction of woven dead grass. It had a small hole on the top side, fixed securely up in a hazelnut bush six to seven feet high. Being young and sharp, we managed to catch Little Joe, as we then named him. By the following year, he was so tame that we gave him the freedom of the garden, where we had a large filbert nut tree growing. This was where he made his home. If we tapped the tree, he would scurry down and play all over us. By handling and rearing such different kinds of creatures, and the cattle, we knew by the time we had reached ten how life was created and carried on. Our 'college' education was enlarged as fast as we could grasp it.

It was around this period of time, in the 1890s, that my Father returned home from a stay in a convalescent hospital, after a siege of illness. As we youngsters all sat round the kitchen table by the light of the coal-oil lamp, he started to tell us of the wonderful light he had seen while away. His words were, 'Oh, I have seen the most wondrous sight! It was so bright that you could see to pick up a pin from the floor.' This was our first introduction to the world of electricity. Little did we know then that by its unlimited use in the next fifty years, it would advance the world around us more than it had moved forward the preceding 500 years, perhaps too fast for the human element to keep up with. It has opened up such a tremendous amount of knowledge, I am wondering where it will eventually lead us.

In the above period the Boys' Choir, of which I was a member, was taken on a yearly outing. We visited Portsmouth Dockyard one year, which was an outstanding plant for those years. Even then, all the machinery was steam-driven. I remember one great steel wheel four to five feet high, connected to the main shaft that ran all through the plant with hundreds of smaller shafts offset from it, to handle all the differnt operations needed. Electricity was very scarcely used in plants for power as yet.

To broaden our minds a little, we received the local weekly newspaper, which took us a little beyond the village boundary but usually caused little commotion upon arrival. What did excite our little heads to great imagination were the 'Penny Dreadfuls' that appeared in print at this time. That was the name my Mother gave these little paperbacks! One set was about the airplanes fighting the Apaches in the Western States. There were no planes in those days or for many years after, but the pictures of the planes in those books were exactly the same as the one of the present day. Obviously, someone was able to visualise what the future would unmistakably bring.

About the same time, Jules Verne was busy with his *Forty Leagues Under the Sea* and there were no submarines invented then, either, but that also came true. These authors, and other like them, kept our minds active. They also kept Mama in action, too, burning them as soon as she got her hands on them, because she did not approve of them for us! I remember buying a few 'Vivid Pictures' of the Italo-Austrian War. We thought that they were really something special but they displeased Mamma when she found them. She continually did her best to keep us on the line by her example and good advice. God bless Her!

With all these things going on, time seemed to slip by too fast and, before I realised it, my early youthful days were lost, which meant more work, less school. Each year now, I would be called upon for heavier work and more often. It might be that Harry Garnett would need me at seven in the morning to help him kill some pigs before I went to school, or maybe Farmer Targett wanted me for work for the whole morning. Other jobs came before school, too. I still treasured my free moments, though they were less and less, to slip off to the bush and study Nature. Old Mother Nature was kind and taught me many things. Eighteen ninety-five still stands out quite vividly as that was the year I reached eleven years of age, and my last fairly free year. That harvest time, I was hired out to one of the farm labourers for one shilling a day from four in the morning till dark! I was to assist him in the harvest operations for this sum. He would cut the wheat with a scythe and lay it alongside the uncut. My job was to gather it up and lay it aside for his niece, who would take so many heads of grain and tie up the loose bundle. In this way, it would be stooked up to dry, awaiting the wagons.

That was the usual procedure, but during harvest time that year, the Massey Harris Binder was introduced into the district. Our employers, not wishing to jump in the dark, made arrangements with the company that owned the machine to come in and cut at so much per acre. They came but, even using four horses on the machine, they were unable to handle the crop, which was finally cut by hand. Good straw was worth money and cutting it with the binder sacrificed the length. They did have other machines then that would cut the barley, oats and rye. Occasionally you would see a family harvesting with hand hooks. This was just the start of the labour on the grain. It then had to be picked up and loaded on the wagons, to be drawn either to the barn or to the stack, where it would have to be handled often four times before it was in the position required by the men, who knew their work and did it well. If it should be in a stack, the thatchers would be called in as soon as possible to thatch the stack to protect it from the elements until the thrashers could be hired. In the meantime, the rats and mice took charge of the stack and, by the time it was thrashed, there was often quite a loss. The same amount of help was needed to take it apart and put it through the machine, from which the returns would be discharged through the many openings. It was not all number one grade, either, but then again, the number one would have to be thoroughly cleaned by manpower to await a favourable market. It would be drawn to the market by horse and wagon, to compete with cheaper grain from the Colonies. Under such methods, it is not hard to understand why the farm labourer's wages were ten to twelve shillings a week.

After all the harvesting operations were completed for the season, we looked forward to what was a yearly event know as the Harvest Supper.

This was a day set aside, after the daily chores had been done, for frolic, games, luncheon, a big supper, and then a singsong. It was one of the old-time traditions carried on year after year, when all about gathered together for the day.

Harvest over, we had to help Mamma with the gleaning of the wheat fields for several days. It meant flour for the winter, and this came in very handy in the home. After that, it was the pig-minding, which meant taking about one hundred of the animals, of all sizes, down some side road or lane to the fields where either oats or barley had been harvested. There, we let the pigs wander over the fields to pick up any heads of grain that had been missed in the harvesting. If a few oaks were on the boundary, it added to their feast, for they loved acorns. The trouble with pigs was that they all had the idea they were individuals and could go their own different ways. As a lad of eleven, I was interested in gathering a few hazel nuts or blackberries from the hedges, and sometimes forgot about the pigs for a moment. Then I would take count again and find that I was maybe three short, which resulted in a long search for the missing ones. Attentiveness was another lesson learned, for I had to return home with the orginal count. You were given responsibilities, and through this you felt your elders had a certain amount of faith in you. You were given a chance to show what you could do, if left on your own. This pig-minding job would last perhaps three weeks, after which it would be time to return to school and carry on as usual.

The hunting season would have started by now and, after doing the required jobs at home, I would have to take my Dad's supper down to the stable, as he was too busy to take time out to come home for it. While he cleaned and fixed up the horses, I would go into the tack room and busy myself on all the steel, straight steel – not stainless. This had to be thoroughly cleaned and stored away carefully until needed. This sort of job was for love, to help Dad. There was no money in it at all for me.

There was a routine we followed for pocket or spending money from my Dad. After our Sunday dinner at home, two or three of us small ones would go down and wait at the stile at the back entrance of the Manor Farm. Any man who did Sunday work on the farm was provided with a Sunday dinner at midday. Dad, being one of these workers, found us waiting for him when he came out. If times had been good, he would take out his chamois leather money bag to give us a penny between us, or perhaps even a halfpenny each. Our anticipation must have been obvious! The only way he could afford to be so generous with us was because he was also the village barber in his minimal spare time. He charged twopence for a haircut, adding slightly to his other income, but every bit helped. He was well known for his knowledge in animal husbandry, and so earned the occasional shilling helping his neighbours with their sick animals.

If we had been lucky enough to receive some money from Dad, we would then go down to old Granny Cooper, who made candies, and each of us had our own lots made up separately. I remember my little sister, Lottie, going in one time and asking for a farthing's worth, and could she please have that in three lots. Of course she was told that it was just a little too much to ask for, and she received one bag only. Spending money was very scarce and treasured when made available.

Just before Christmas that year, we were told that my favourite sister, Elizabeth, was to be married on Boxing Day. We all loved her so very much. She had started working in service at the age of eleven years, and had always done all she could to help out at home, with the result that she often went without herself. One year when Dad was ill, I remember that she sent home a Christmas pudding. In it, she had mixed a half sovereign, a five shilling piece and a half crown. This was just one of the many ways in which she aided us.

We were all naturally very excited about the coming event. Her intended husband, Arthur Freemantle, was an artificer in the Naval Yard at Portsmouth, and it was decided that, after I graduated from school, I would go and live with them to receive a higher education there. As a youngster, eager for more learning, I was naturally thrilled with the prospect of this chance to obtain more knowledge. I read all the books obtainable and was a keen student. The only openings in those days in Upham were for farm labourers or the Army at one shilling a day, so it seemed I was about to have a chance for something better. My elder brother, Ernest, was in the British Navy and my brother Harry, the next one in the family above me, was considering the same future. I was reading more than ever now so I was excited at the possibilities awaiting me. In the meantime, I carried on with my everyday duties.

Christmas was now drawing near and, when Elizabeth came home to prepare for the wedding, she made two requests of me which I shall always remember. One was for a nice little Christmas tree and the other was for a big bunch of mistletoe. These would be used to decorate the house for the wedding day. There was much of each within walking distance, but it was as much as your life was worth to be caught taking either. Both grew on private property, and we sure had no encouragement from Dad about taking anything belonging to others. However, I scurried off alone quietly very early one Saturday morning, and found a nice little yew tree, which I carried home without any trouble. I believe it was the only Christmas tree we ever had in my Dad's home.

3. *Lottie, the youngest of the family, married in Canada to Charles Boulton from New Zealand. In the early 1920s they settled in California, where she died in 1978. A son, Edward, lives in Sacramento, California.*

The mistletoe was hanging by the dozens of big bunches in an old apple tree, probably about 150 years old, and at least seventy-five feet high, but the tree was in the Rectory garden. Thankfully, it was not too close to the house, as the garden was quite large. Just at this vital time, there was no one in the Rectory, so one moonlight night I slipped down to the tree. As the trunk of the tree was so large, I had quite a job to reach the first branches to scale. By the time I did reach the mistletoe, nerves and fear had nearly mastered me. When I started to gather the mistletoe, out flew a flock of starlings. I nearly dropped out of the tree from fright but somehow stuck it out for my sister's sake. The little bit of mistletoe that I took for her would never be missed for there was a wagon-load left on the tree.

We all enjoyed the wedding festivities and the happy couple departed for their home. Little did we know that it would be the last time we saw our sister alive. In the following March, a telegram arrived asking Mother to go down to Portsmouth as soon as possible as Elizabeth was very ill. She never recovered, and her loss was felt very deeply by all. The aftermath for me personally was hard to bear, for not only had I lost my favourite sister, but had also lost forever my chance for higher education. The year was 1897, and I was twelve.

I had passed my twelfth birthday in November of 1896 and schooling was being decreased – and work increased, but I did manage to keep to school until the following Spring, when we had our May Day celebrations. The first of May was Garland Day, when all the school children made their garlands and went round the village homes that looked prosperous enough to give a penny. As they did, they sang May Day songs. One went as follows:

The first of May is Garland Day,
The Chimney Sweepers' Holiday.
Please Ma'am, please Ma'am,
What will you give me
To see my fine garland?

On the morning of May the first, at breakfast, my Father informed me that, after we were over our May Day celebrations, I was through with school and would be starting steady work, This, of course, took the joy from my May Day celebrating as I longed to stay in school, but in those days we were taught never to question one's elder or his reasoning. I was to report to the Manor Farm to take over the Indoor Boy's job. This was from 7.00 a.m. until 5.00 p.m., so my schooldays were definitely over. The job was seven days a week, so that my freedom time was reduced.

One of the duties was cleaning boots of all varieties, from farm boots to dress and hunting boots, and if they were not cleaned to pefection they were returned to be done again. I was also to clean the tableware which was of straight, not stainless steel. This had to be cleaned with brick dust, so called, and rubbed on a board until you could see your face in it. If this job was not also done up to the mark, it was returned to be redone.

It was my job to fire up the baking oven once or twice a week. This was a large brick oven fired with wood. The big wash boiler also had to be fired up and ready for the washerwoman when she arrived for work on washdays.

I was required to feed the dogs and chickens, gather the eggs, assist the maids in the house if necessary, and pluck any poultry or game used. Sometimes the game birds were so high that most of the feathers would leave them with a good shake. Then they would be blue or green (the birds, that is) when you took them back to the house. Hares would be hung until they were half decayed, before being used for jugged hare. I kept the flagstones clean of weeds around the back of the house, helped with the fruit-picking in season, worked in the pleasure grounds, cut the tennis court grass, and had many other duties too numerous to mention. For this seven days a week, I was paid three shillings and sixpence.

The job carried many responsibilities and there seemed to be so many people to please. During one period, someone must have complained to my Father that I had not been doing enough work. He gave me a little black book and told me I had better keep a diary of what I did each day. Dad was strict, so I did as I was told. I started out all right, but it would take the evening to record all that I had done in the day, thereby making the job even longer. The life of the diary was short!

4. Elizabeth, who married Arthur Freemantle. She died in 1897, only three months after her marriage.

5. *Arthur Freemantle, sister Elizabeth's husband.*

I was growing up in more ways than one and, after eighteen months of that treatment, I decided that if I was to advance in my 'College of Life', I had better ascend one grade somehow. This was not easy in those days because if you lived in the employer's house, he thought he owned the whole family. Dad was living in his employer's house and, if I went to work for someone else, it could mean that I might have to leave home to live elsewhere. When I told Dad I was thinking of making a change, he informed me that he would expect me to get another job right away as he was in no position to keep me around home if I could not pay my own way.

The only local opening of any kind was a job under the shepherd, so I was told to consider this. The next phase in my College of Life's education was under the shepherd's teaching. This should round out my 'agricultural college' experience, as I had already been working among all the other farm stock and fowl. It would also give me another chance to understand the many matters pertaining to the welfare of the land, and the methods used to keep it productive, year after year.

I had now turned thirteen, and needed to look forward in life. My older brother, Harry, who was already a shepherd, obtained a dog for me and off I went to my new job with the flock that consisted of eight hundred ewes. Part of my duties in the summer season was to take them up on the South Downs. This was next to the part of the farm where different parties were allowed to graze on certain portions of it. Sometimes I would take them to other places on the farm to graze, while the head shepherd would bring forward the hurdles, a temporary enclosure, for a new fold for the coming night, to which the sheep would be returned. My dog and I enjoyed many hours together in our duties. Alas, before many weeks passed, the head shepherd told me that, as the ewes were in lamb, my collie dog was too fast to work around them and I had better change dogs for a while. His was an Old English Sheepdog with hair hanging down over his eyes and face, so that you would think that he could not see anything. He was as slow as molasses but he did teach me many things, and caught for me many a rabbit dinner. He did not need speed, making up of it by using his brain. We would be following the flock home late in the afternoon down one of the old lanes with the high banks topped by hedges, when Old Jim, as I called him, would hesitate for a moment, look up, and take a couple of sniffs. I would remark, 'Well, boy, come on.' Down the lane apiece, I would see a weak part of the hedge on the bank, look down at Jim and say, 'Now Jim, go and get it!' He would go up on the high side and, moments after, tumble down the bank behind me with a rabbit in his mouth. This meant a little extra for dinner at home, to help out with the old salt pork and make for a tastier meal. However, for me, there was not much joy in taking home the rabbit for when Mother would ask for it to be paunched, Dad would call me out to the back kitchen. There I would be questioned as to where and how I obtained it and should I have, as it did not belong to me, and would there be a chance of me getting into trouble because of it?

All this from a man who told us that, when he started out in life, he had to board himself on twelve shillings a month. From this, he would have to grocer put up his sugar in four one-half pound lots, tea in one-pound lots and other food likewise, to allot his food through the next month while he was ploughing and working on the farm. How he kept such high ideals about honesty all through his life, I will never know, but he always did.

However, Jim, the dog, and I still had fun as we understood each other, and we continued to take home the odd dinner. By being with the sheep, I was all over the Estates. I saw many things and retained them in my mind for future use, at the time, unknowingly. I was to learn that sheep can be very temperamental, yet things seemed to go smoothy. As a youngster, of course, I made none of the big decisions. I was to do the best that I knew how. Nevertheless, one sorrowful day will always be with me. On a rather drizzly day in the month of October, I was ordered to take the flock down to a certain section of land where there were two different crops grown. My orders were to walk back and forth between the two crops and keep the sheep on the part upon which they were to graze, which I did. On the other side was a rather steep hill. Between this hill and land was a farm road, from which the head shepherd was watching. As the afternoon wore on, the weather became worse, with an east wind coming up and the drizzle increasing. There was a second crop of clover in the field, so the sheep should have been moved at once. In my innocence, I did not know this and, just before the time when we were to remove them to their right field, I saw some of them on their backs. I yelled for the head shepherd but, before we could get them on the move, eight ewes had died, bloated with a combination of second-growth clover and east wind. My 'college education' was remaining practical, with each lesson deep enough to be remembered. I had to carry on and no two days were alike. Here, the sheep were kept outside all winter and daily had to receive certain attention, according to the weather. You could hardly call it a soft job by any means. For this six and a half days' work weekly, in all kinds of weather, I was paid six shillings. Lambing season arrived about the end of February or early March and that was another anxious time. Often, I had to jump down from my perch on the hay bales, maybe four or five times during my lunch time, to help a ewe or try to make her comfortable.

This year was not to be forgotten as, hardly were we through the lambing season, when I was struck down for the third time with measles. Unfortunately, I left my sick bed too soon, with the result that I caught a chill and was unconscious for three days and not expected to recover. I did recover, but eight other children in the district died from measles that Spring. I felt that I had been given another chance in life and, before going forward, did a lot of thinking. All the neighbours and friends had been so kind to me in my illness that it made me feel perhaps the world was not such a bad place after all. After due time, I picked up the crook again, whistled the dog and returned to work. Now the grass looked greener, the flowers brighter, the birds sang more sweetly, and all Nature seemed more glorious then ever around me. I realised what I had nearly lost forever, and rejoiced. I was soon back in the swing of things, with summer just around the corner. I was improving daily healthwise, and enjoying life and my surroundings.

In the country, every time you turned you head you would see something interesting and beautiful, if you would just take the time to look. It is still the same. All around, for me then, there were so many scenes and sights to take in. It kept me in wonder, there was so much of it all. The earls, lords, squires and other rich folk owned all the land about me, but I was getting more daily from it all than they were. I could appreciate all the things pertaining to nature which they only accepted as possessions. Their minds were seldom open to the glorious beauty of it all.

We lads had little time for fun and frolic now, but we made the most of what time we did have. On Sunday afternoons, we would wait until the older lads came out from the pub, about 2.30 p.m. It was open from 12 noon until 3.00 p.m. After the leaves were off the trees, we would make for the bushes and shrubs, hunting red squirrels. Upon starting up one or two, we would hunt then for the balance of the afternoon or until we had to leave to go to work. Our hunting material was the flint stones that were all around us. We seldom hit them, just kept them moving until we tired or until the gamekeeper arrived – when we in turn were the hunted. This went on for years until my oldest brother, Ernest, came home on leave from the British Navy, in which he was training to be a gunner. He brought home with him a little one-shot pistol that fired a bullet. It was tried out in the hunt and, by the following weekend, there were three or four different varieties of cracking pistols away at the squirrels. How they were obtained I do not know, as the laws were very strict about such things. Only a week or so later, one of the youngsters gathered outside the Church door, waiting to be the last to go in for the evening service, was fooling around with one of these pistols and accidentally put a bullet through the centre of his hand. Next day, the police moved quickly and the pistol-hunting was finished as suddenly as it had started. The Gamekeeper told us later that, after we youngsters quit hunting the squirrels, he hardly ever saw one. They just seemed to disappear.

On other Sunday afternoons, we would make for another bush that had a different growth. There we would play like the later-appearing Tarzan, swinging from tree to tree to see how far we could go in this way. The game resulted in many bad tumbles, but we took them all in our stride. Of course, we naturally assumed that, as soon as we started to work steadily, we were too big for Sunday School.

That year, I did manage to supplement my wages a little in the harvest. I would go stooking after supper until dark. Later, I did some stone-picking until dark, for a while. Some of the fields were heavily loaded with flint stones of all sizes, which were used to keep the roads in good shape in my time there. These stones were very hard, the same kind as were used by our forefathers for arrow heads. They would come to the top as the sheep folded, or with a shower of rain.

Through all this period, we had still been busy with the sheep but now Michaelmas'[1] 29 September 1898, had come round again, and after some serious consideration, I felt that the time had also come round once again for further study of this great world. After some serious consideration, I knew I should change my 'college of learning'. The same rules were still in force at home – no hanging about without a job. This time, my search for higher education did mean leaving home, as I was reaching Man's Estate, nearly fifteen years old, and I would have to assume more of a man's responsibilities. Thus, I went off to a large estate a few miles from home, to be the assistant in their large dairy.

[1] Feast of St. Michael

I worked seven days a week as there was milking to do each day. My working hours were from 7.00 a.m. until 5.00 p.m., for ten shillings weekly. Here I realized that my education would be expanded more rapidly than ever before. Although I had a fair knowledge of cattle and milking, which of course was then all done by hand, my experience in butter-making was very limited. Around my village home, the knowledge of butter-making in the winter was limited. I had known of the different little dairies and farmers working from 7.00 a.m. until 9.00 p.m. before they gained their butter from the start. The method used was to pour the milk into big pans and wait until the cream set. Then it would be skimmed off and built up enough to make a batch of butter. No one had a separator as they were only just being introduced but, in my new job, things were to be different. I had everything to do in the work to the point of churning, washing and leaving the butter in the churn of a specified size.

Here I also learned that it was possible to find a better way of doing things, if you will only search. This had helped me all through life, and still does. The lady supervisor on the butter division was, without doubt, the most demanding, strict, domineering, intelligent, particular and critical person you could ever find. You could not love her but you had to respect her and follow her orders implicitly. She was a Somerset lass and unbeatable in butter-making, but she was an extremely hard woman to work for, as a lad of fifteen. In the middle of winter, you were required to have your butter ingredients ready for her in twenty to thirty minutes. I read in the paper some time later that she had been awarded prizes as the best butter-maker in all of Britain, so I considered myself lucky to have trained under her guidance. I felt that if I had learned nothing else there (although I did), it had been time well spent.

Up to then, life had been rather passive but now, before we could get under way with a little faith in the future, times changed. We had lost our Queen and gained a King. Upon Queen Victoria's death, her son Edward VII ascended to the throne of Great Britain. We had also lost our peace, which was worse, as now we were at war with the Boers in South Africa. In different ways, this would affect the lives of many of us.

I now had not only my elder brother Ernest but also three brothers-in-law — Robert Bible, my eldest sister Annie's husband, my late sister Elizabeth's husband, Arthur Freemantle, and sister Rose's husband, John Hitchcock, all in the British Navy. The War caused a lot of disputes among the people. Some were for the War while others were against it. In my limited experience, this was the first incident to agitate the whole world in a big way. The Boer War was certainly not approved of across the world, and Britain was harshly criticised regarding this. Why this war had to be was questionable and the people were very unhappy over it. This naturally left us children and young people wondering. We were just beginning to live, and had a number of uncles who had been in some of the earlier wars and they would tell of the bad times they experienced. So, even as children, we were unhappy about this war. The only news we received was from our weekly paper, as there were no other news media then, such as radio or television. In different parts of the world, men were working with and on the new element, electricity, but it was in very little general use then. Every horse and mule obtainable was shipped off to South Africa for war transport work. It was tough on man and beast. Then, of course, along came the songs, with their lyrics penned to keep up the spirits of the nation. One was 'Goodbye, My Bluebell', and there were many others.

Going home for a visit one Sunday afternoon, I met an old school pal named Button Vine, son of the proprietor of the village store. This storekeeper was also the village baker. Button had joined the Seaforth Highlanders Regiment and, as he swung his kilt, he was the envy of all the lads. War fever was beginning to penetrate our blood, so in the following week I took a day off work and walked the ten miles to Winchester to enlist. At headquarters, I added a year to my age but was informed that they were taking no more men, so back I walked the ten miles to return to work. The war was having a very disturbing, unsettling effect on the youth of the land, and spread to other lands abroad. As mentioned before, this was a very unpopular war, with the people showing little support for it, that support decreasing as it continued longer than anticipated. One member of our family was to be a victim of it in due course. Then, the soldier's pay was one shilling per day and the sailor's very little more but, for thousands of our youth, it was the only work for them when they reached maturity.

The schooling that I was receiving at my job in the dairy was still as exacting, with no let-up. I am certain that if the lady in charge there had

6. Annie, Robert and Robert Jr Bible. Robert Jr died at 18 months.

7. *Annie Bible.*

8. *Robert Bible, Annie's husband.*

been sent to take charge of the Boer War, instead of General Roberts, it would have been over far sooner than it was! Her husband, poor old Theo, as she always called him, although a well-built man who had travelled during his youth in the United States, could not call his soul his own. Sometimes he would take me up to town with him in the evening, if supplies were needed, and upon his return home he would have to report on every halfpenny he had spent. She would question him as to where, why and if needed. His answers were all booked at once and usually a few reprimands given. He would also be questioned as to whether he had really needed that pint of beer. Although we never had many earthly possessions, we had not been brought up to be questioned like this as adults.

After learning my course here thoroughly, I decided that perhaps it was time again to advance to the next college of practical learning, and began to enquire about the best move.

This time, I found a position on another estate in the opposite direction from home. It was a chance to work in the gardens and so, when Spring came, I was delighted to make the move. It was familiar ground, as I had worked there as a boy beater for the hunts while at school. My duties this time were to help with a few cows and to work in the garden. There,

9. Upham around 1900 – Church shown in background.

in a few weeks, I was able to impart to them the knowledge I had gained regarding butter-making, as I found that they were still fifty years behind the times in this matter. At this period of my life, having moved from post to post furthering my knowledge, I was able to take advantage of my learning. Now, before the age of sixteen, with what I was able to show my new employer about the butter-making, my stock went up tremendously with him and, in turn, I knew I must keep on learning.

It was not long before I was sure that working with Nature was what I had been seeking and the chance came to be fully employed in horticultural work here. From my earliest recollections, I had always been drawn to all Nature's living things, from the trees down to the smallest flower. Now, working in and among all these things, the drudgery was gone and pleasure replaced it. I was beginning to realise what a wonderful, gorgeous outlook the flower kingdom had to offer to those who would seek to learn. This consisted of unlimited possibilities for interest, research, fun and comradeship. I felt that the Creator, when he turned over creation to man, left it in such a way that, as long as man can remain interested, he is permitted to go on and improve all living things. So, as long as man lives, his interest in Nature should thrive. I had now found a new lease in life, a new and lasting interest, and was satisfied with the world into which I was born.

A few weeks after I started on the new job, my employer's second daughter was married. He was the father of four beautiful daughters and one son. As a youngster, I had already attended the wedding of his first daughter, being a member of the Boys' Choir that had sung at the service. Also, in the same capacity as a choirboy, I had been present at the funeral of his father, whose body had been brought to the Church on a timber wagon drawn by two heavy horses. At that time, while I was standing at the Church door, the funeral pall had been handed to me to hold while the coffin was removed from the wagon. Their family vault was in our churchyard. Having been included in all these family happenings, I felt that I was getting to know them fairly well. This family was one of the oldest, most respected ones in the district.

The marriage of the second daughter, to which I refer, was celebrated not only by the nobles of the area but by all the help and tenants. There was a big supper, and an evening's enjoyment with the head folks amongst us throughout it all. This was my first big night and I never forgot it.

The estate family home lay in a big valley with extensive woods all about. On the high side, the majority of the land was given over as a shooting perserve. The farm land of the estate was on the outskirts. The squire of the estate was the Master of Hounds for the district. As I gave more and more thought to my surroundings, it occured to me that it was not reasonable or sensible for most of the land to lie practically useless in a fertile country like England, when so much of the food that was needed had to be imported. Yet an ordinary individual could not buy an acre of land to develop, to save his life. These conditions prevailed throughout the land, not just in my own area, but in those days we had to think silently and keep our opinions to ourselves.

I was now drawing twelve shillings a week for my labour from 7.00 a.m. until 5.00 p.m. I walked two and one-half miles to and from work but I was young and no thought of complaint about those hikes ever entered my mind. Along the road I walked, there were three little covers where the nightingales would stop you in your tracks with their lovely song. I hunted for their nests many times, but never did find them. There was always something, near or far, to catch you attention, and you could go along the road with a song on your lips or whistling some gay tune, over the hills and dales, through the fields, over the stiles, along the hedgerows and through the bush. There were, of course, times in the winter season when the walk seemed unpleasant but, even then, side attractions eased the way.

Now I not only worked hard on the job but had my own batch of Fall chrysanthemums at home, besides other flowers. That autumn, after supper, by the lights of the moon and a lantern, I built my Mother a nice rose garden, as she was as keen on flowers as I was. At the same time, my older brother Harry was calling me foolish for doing it, but it gave her pleasure for several years, until my Dad died and she had to leave the house. She and I worked very closely together on the flowers for the next three years. We would put our pennies together to buy big flower pots in which to grow chrysanthemums for the Fall and, in the summer, we would pull up lots of water by the big treadwheel, just to water our flowers. It took us about a half-hour to bring up an oaken casket that held around eighty gallons, from a depth of ninety feet. You simply had to love your plants to put in that kind of work. In the proper season, on my walks to and from work, I would take along some rosewood, then stop to bud any promising briar for standard roses. I would do a few at a time, and other times would gather some of the dried sheep manure to feed the 'mums' at home. I was learning that if you do have an interest in life, you should try to further it. In doing so, you find that every move has a meaning for good or ill. As I grew older, it was necessary to watch each move.

On my daily walks, I also watched the farm crops started, developed and harvested. All nature was unfolding as each season came round. I could see for many miles in different directions, and the world looked well. If one took the time to ask, the old men would answer many questions about the things around us, so that the learning process continued forever on.

On my job things were never easy as everything was done by hand. I think perhaps the hardest job was the pumping. It took two of us on a heavy force pump to raise the water up to the top of the mansion, two storeys high. An hour and a half each morning was all you were capable of doing. After about eighteen months of that, the single-cylinder internal combustion engine was introduced in Britain, and our employer purchased one. It was a very simple engine and would putter on all day and pump on very little coal oil. This was a good investment for him, and a great relief to us. Another heavy job was the lawn mowing. There were many acres of lawns to be mowed continuously, which incuded the numerous banks and terraces, and the equipment was heavy in those days, so it was often a matter of one pushing, another pulling with a rope. On the level land, we had a donkey to help with the mowing but only those who have used donkey power for such work would have any idea of what a job that was. It was all hand-digging in the garden, too, with everything moved by wheelbarrow, so there was no chance of getting rusty waiting for a job to be done.

While the other lads played in their off time, I worked and read. I soon began thinking of the world that went far beyond the horizon, questioning anyone I met who had travelled afar. I think that maybe we grew older more quickly in those days, and took life more seriously. Still working at the same job, the day arrived for the coronation of King Edward VII. Our local celebration was held on the adjoining estate, paid for by the two overlords. While attending, I visited a pavilion for emigrants representing New South Wales, Australia, from which I collected pamphlets to take home. Wanderlust was probably in my bones, and I discussed this with my older brother Harry. He had tried out for the Navy and the Army but had been refused because of flat feet, but he was to make one more effort, for the stokers in the Navy and, if refused again, we would make tracks for New South Wales. This time he was accepted, which left me high and dry and very unsettled as to the future.

A few weeks later, while looking through our weekly paper, an advertisement caught my eye. This told of a need for young men for apprentices in the Merchant Navy. I answered the ad and, with very little correspondence, was told to report at once. Then I had difficulty in leaving my job as, of course, they tried to dissuade me. I said I would leave a week's wages in lieu of notice, which was accepted, and I was on my way. This apprenticeship was to lead up to be a captain of your own ship. This seemed then to be a great thing, as at that time the outlook around me for the future was not very bright. I now think of the old proverb that says, 'Do things in haste – repent at leisure', which still holds good to this day. It did not take long for those words to sink in!

I was to report at once, because the ship was waiting in Cardiff, Wales, so off in the morning I went, bright and early. I had a seven-mile walk to the railway station, then sixty-six miles to London by train, where I was to go for examination and investigation. I went through all the preliminaries there, and then boarded a train for Cardiff, arriving at around 7.30 p.m. The first mate was there to meet me and took me aboard, where they gave me supper. This was followed by a short tour of the ship, ending with the location of my bunk. The ship was bound for Barcelona, Spain, and I was bound by indenture for the next five years.

By this time, I was very tired but, now that I was aboard, the ship already loaded, they had to be on their way. No rest for me yet, as I had to jump in and help until we were well away, after which I was sure glad to jump into my bunk and slink down. I had hardly settled down when the first mate was at the companionhead yelling to be, 'Timber!', my nickname. Said he, 'You will go on this first watch.' I had to dress at once and go forward for the first two hours, and then back on the bridge for the next two hours. Only after that could I get friendly with my bunk and then just for four hours, after which I was out on watch again at 4.00 a.m. By eight o'clock, my stomach was so upset that I was in no mood for breakfast but no mercy was shown. I was given a bucket of sea

10. James, 1901 – Taken in his Merchant Navy uniform at Cardiff, Wales, before his first trip to sea.

water and a scouring brush and told to scrub out the charthouse. This
was on the top deck under the bridge, and got very dirty every time the
ship was loaded. I had never done any scrubbing before and just then,
being so seasick, was not in shape or humour for such a job. However,
I started it, though I think my head was on the floor as much as the
scrubbing brush. They kept me at it until they knew it was useless. I
think I spent the rest of that day in my bunk, suffering great miseries. It
gradually passed off and, by that time, I was beginning to miss the hills
and dales plus the green fields of home. No time for self-sorrow was
given. We were kept busy swabbing decks, painting or cleaning paint,
taking-off old varnish on the companion tops and doors with caustic soda,
which turned my finger nails rusty (and took years to grow out). We
were also kept busy chipping decks with a sledge hammer and a chipping
hammer, followed by scraping down to the clean steel on which we
applied a coat of red lead for a start.

After a few days out at sea, we were passing through the Bay of Biscay,
a place I had often sung about but never expected to see. One early
morning, we passed four becalmed sailing boats on the beam. They called
for direction from our ship, which was given by the first mate. I never
again saw so many at one time, only the odd one now and then. The
next day, we were passing through the Straits of Gibraltar, with North
Africa to our south. At last I was beginning to see new lands. By working
with the sailors, I was also beginning to acquire a knowledge of seamanship,
although this was not easy for, apart from the officers, cook and steward,
they were of nationalities other than British and I, coming from an inland
village, had no experience with foreigners. However, we soon understood
each other to a certain extent and they wanted to know what position I
held on the ship. I explained that I was an apprentice. They gave me the
laugh, and explained what the game the shipping company was playing
with the likes of me. The shipping people were after cheap labour and
with me they certainly had it, as I had signed up for five years at the
'marvellous' rate of four pounds for the first year, six pounds for the
second, eight for the third, ten pounds for the fourth year, and twelve
for the fifth. The crew told me that, if I stayed, at the end of the fifth
year I would be just a seaman, and certainly not an officer. These seamen
were elderly men, so I listened intently. They were decent men who had
nothing to gain by lying to me. Another little gaffer had been roped in
with me, but he was younger and an orphan. He was made mess boy,
and was company for me.

The steamship to which I am referring was the *S.S. Rosewood* and she
was well up the Mediterranean by now. The first port of call was Barcelona,

where she was to discharge her cargo of Welsh coal. One afternoon before her arrival, the first mate called me aside and gave me orders to take so many of the crew down to the chain lockers to bring up certain hawsers and ropes, which would be needed on our arrival in port. All went well until we were in the lockers. Being the green kid, I had no idea what we were supposed to fetch, but I had to put up a bluff. As I was an apprentice, the seamen began to argue, while I tried to keep the upper hand. All the while, the mate was overhead looking down, listening and enjoying the whole scene. I came out of it fairly well and he at least saw that I had put up a certain amount of fight. Upon receiving an order from your superiors, you had to repeat it to make sure you understood, and by this time I had learned that there were no back answers and no back doors through which to escape your duties.

We were into the month of June now and well up the Mediterranean, so the weather was building up to quite a heat in the day. Coming along the deck one morning, I saw one of the Spanish firemen sitting in the shade of the galley. There was a trickle of water running from him down to the scuppers, and he was soaking. I turned to the steward who was standing by, and asked him if this man had fallen overboard. The answer I received was, 'No, you God-damned young fool, that's sweat,' Not having been aboard long, of course I had not learned all there was to know about stoking the boilers and, on that ship in that heat, it was a terrible job. There were no electric fans yet and the only air they got was what they could coax down the air funnels if there was a breeze. I often felt so sorry for those fellows but somehow they kept us moving, and finally we reached Barcelona.

After dropping anchor, I had my first glimpse of the great statue of Christopher Columbus, which stood out boldly as you gazed towards the city. Also, I saw street cars without horses drawing them, running across the front of the city. Upon inquiring from my friend the steward about them, his gruff answer was to point and say, 'You damn fool, don't you know what they are? They are electric street cars.' Those were the first I ever saw, as there were none in England then. The ones I was seeing there in Barcelona had been installed by a group of men from Toronto, Canada, and were still owned by them.

The next thing was to prepare to transfer the cargo. There were no docking facilities here, so a heavy cable was brought out to the ship from somewhere inland, back of the shore. The loose end was fastened to the ship's mast and heavy bucket-like contraptions were sent out to the ship. My job was running one of the steam winches which raised and lowered these buckets from the cable to the hold, where a group of Spanish men loaded them for transport ashore. I think the power for transporting may have been electric. All in all, it was a rather slow process.

During the lunch hour, I was put on watch for the first half hour to guard against pilfering, then allowed to have lunch. I was soon disliked by my shipmates for carrying out this job, but orders were orders.

The trouble was that the boys had not been on the ship long enough to make a draw on their pay, which was only about fifteen shillings and eightpence a week. They wished to go ashore but had no money to spend while off the ship, so anything that was moveable was likely to be picked up to bring in a few pennies on shore. The people in Barcelona, or the majority of them, at this period were very poor. One woman sold cognac on the ship for one penny a glass. Soap was strongly sought after by the Spaniards. In our berth were the cook, the donkeyman, who was German and disliked the British, the ship's carpenter who was Russian-Finnish, the other apprentice, and myself. Hurrying down for my lunch after guard duty, the men gave me a tongue-lashing, calling me a spy and other harsh words. It was a little tough for a few minutes but I had to carry on. It took several days to unload with the method used.

On the Sunday afternoon, I went ashore with several of the seamen to tour the city. The monument to Columbus was a terrific piece of work but the filth all around the base was disgraceful. From there, we wandered on up through the city, passing one large hotel. A large herd of goats were entering the courtyard to be milked, as was the practice then. Further on, we came to the Bullfighting Ring, which was readying to start operation for the afternoon. The boys passed until we reached the wine shops, one of which they finally entered, and after testing several varieties they settled down with their choice. Bread and cheese as well as the wine were very cheap: the bill for all was less then four shillings. After this, we were pretty well broke so we made our way back to the ship, where I received a reprimand for going ashore without leave.

Then I was given my first letter from home – and what a letter! In it, Mamma had gone all out, beginning by writing that they missed me at home. Some years before, she had had brothers of her own who went to sea and so in the letter she opened her heart and soul to explain all the dangers ahead. She wrote of the consequences that could happen to a young fellow, of stepping out of line, what would happen to his body and soul. Things that she had felt unable to tell me, she wrote in her letter. That was a letter I have never forgotten.

After discharging our cargo, we turned back towards Gibraltar and, having passed it, we turned up a river which was the boundary between Spain and Portugal. As we proceeded slowly up the river, a sentry was walking back and forth. There were little houses set apart and women down by the river bank were washing clothes on the rocks. It was harvest time here, and the people were gathering and thrashing the grain. The method used here was to throw the grain on a large sail cloth and then have four or five scrawny little bullocks walk around on it, knocking the grain out with their feet. I had read of such a way in the Bible, but never expected to see it done. As the terrain was very uneven and hilly, they were using every available piece of land for cultivation, some of the pieces no bigger than a back garden. Existence was barely possible in this place but the temperate climate was in their favour.

We finally arrived at our loading destination, where we were to take on a load of copper ore. There was a limit to this as we had to cross the bar at the river mouth. Slipping ashore after supper, we found ourselves out in the country, where corn and grapes were growing by the acre. We helped ourselves to just a few grapes as they were not yet ripe. On our way back to the ship, we saw people bedded down along the sidewalks and in other positions outside. That is where they slept in the summertime. The next morning the police came aboard to find the ones who had stolen the grapes. We were warned to avoid a repetition of this, and we did. The loading was completed and we went back down the river, followed by a large flotilla of loaded barges of copper ore, which was to be loaded on our ship after we had crossed the bar. At this point, they formed four endless chains of Portuguese, two on either side of the ship.

They proceeded to pass up the copper ore to be dumped into the ship's holds in baskets made of rushes. The ore was very heavy so only a shovelful at a time could be lifted, but with enough people who kept moving, much was accomplished. I was put on as watchman again while the operation continued. The work seemed to be going quite smoothly when all of a sudden a terrific commotion developed among the loaders. The next thing I saw was the first mate wading into them, swinging a big shovel. It appeared that the trouble had started when the Portuguese found out that a Spaniard had somehow mixed in with them. When the loaders realised this, they were out to get rid of him as there was no love lost then between the two nations. The mate quietened matters down and the loading was completed. This was at the town of St. Cethareal, on the River Guadiana.

We made our way back into the Mediterranean and continued on to the Island of Madeira, where we were to pick up bunker coal, that being a coaling station. The approach was very interesting, for we arrived there in daylight to an advantageous view from the harbour. The closer we came in, the more sights revealed themselves to our eyes. Starting near the base, the whole mountainside had been terraced and planted with grapes. No one was allowed to land, as we were to be there only a few hours, but from the ship it surely looked like a lovely place. The Captain went ashore on business and brought back with him two bunches of green bananas, which obviously grew there.

We were on our way as soon as loaded but, early the next morning, we had a little surprise. Who should appear on the top deck but our friend the Spaniard, of the earlier escapade. Some of the Spaniards in the stoke hole had befriended him and kept him out of sight until we had passed Madeira. Otherwise, had the Captain known that he was aboard, he would have put him off there. After receiving a thorough tongue-lashing, he was put to work chipping deck and painting for the rest of the way across the Atlantic. By then, it was July and, being on our way to Georgia, U.S.A., we were going through the heat line, so that the Spaniard had a very hot job. I named him Pomarao as he had come from somewhere around that town. We worked together from then on. My 'college education' was broadened continuously each day, and by now I was getting along well with the officrs and crew, from whom I learned much about seafaring. This knowledge I stored in my mind. I could converse well with two or three of the crew, but of course I was still the youngster. One day, the skipper advised me to get a shave before we reached port, so I was maturing in more ways than one. The old ship was doing seven or eight knots per hour, and I was learning to steer by the stars. I had my first glimpse of flying fish as we were sailing into warmer waters. We had a fairly quiet crossing with few bad storms.

I do remember two bad storms, though. It was interesting to watch them coming towards the ship and wonder how violent they would be when they struck. In the large expanse of the ocean, you were able to see the elements at play. When the storm did strike, the work aboard still had to be carried out, even under those adverse conditions.

One morning, the first mate called me aside and handed me a pail of tar and a handful of waste material, with the order that I was to proceed to the top of the rope ladder on the mast. There, I was to start at the top and give the ladders a good dressing of the tar, using the waste for application. I repeated the order, and climbed up. I started the job but the ship's mast started weaving from side to side with the ship's progress. One time, I was over the seas and the next, over the ship. I had worked my way about halfway, when Mother Nature asserted herself, and I had to come down in a hurry. I don't remember finishing the job but my perfomance beforehand gave the boys quite a laugh at my predicament.

We were now nearing the Sargasso Sea with all its mysteries and legends. I had read many stories of the old sailing ships being becalmed in it and unable to release themselves, but never expected to go through it myself. It was also known for its carpet of weeds and its millions of jelly fish of all sizes, ranging from the size of your thumb to that of a large frying pan. The flying fish would rise around the ship like a pack of starlings at night, occasionally dropping aboard, where you could examine them to see what they really looked like up close. My inquisitive mind was being kept packed full with all the new sights. This was all to the good, as it left little time for self-pity.

In a few hours, we were through it and nearing the next port to discharge our cargo. Rising on the seaboard coast of the United States was the State of Georgia. Arriving there, we proceeded up the mouth of a large river, where we finally tied up at a wooden dock. This was the terminus of a two-to three-mile railway built to connect to drier land, as all the way to it was either swamp or cypress. The railway was built on the top of thousands of large pilings, driven into the mud from the mainland out to the unloading docks. These were eight to ten feet above the mud. When we were there, the mud was loaded with millions of small crabs.

The unloading here was done by the black people, some of whom were very large and very strong. Working on one knee, we had to haul the copper ore up from the hold by our own winches, driven by the donkey engine, to load the railway trucks. This was a very interesting operation to watch, and the loaders all seemed to be happy people. On the way there, I had made an agreement with one of the younger seamen to the effect that, while we were laid up, we would slide off and disappear inland. He had been around much more than I, so using his experience, he was to make the plans. He was a cross between a Greek and a Negro and I, an English lad, but we got along well together. I trusted him, so gave him what little cash I had saved to enable him to finalise our escape. For me it was another lesson learned: he was the only one who left – with my cash!

On arrival, the Captain had strict orders not to let the Spaniard stowaway off the ship. It was not long after the Spanish-American War in Cuba and the Americans had not yet opened their doors to them. However, the Spaniard also quietly disappeared while we were in port.

We tried collecting some of the larger crabs for a feed but the mud was too deep. We only tried one time, with such difficulty that we gave up after that. When we had a few hours off, we made one trip to the end of the trestle to the mainland. There, we became acquainted with an old Scotsman, who ran a coal and wood yard. He had been there a long time and told us quite a bit of history of that part of the country. On his property, he kept a tank full of young alligators, which he lifted out and passed to us. Another singular experience for me, for that was the only time that I ever handled alligators. One morning before daylight, I was aroused by the old nightwatchman, who told me I was to go with him at once. Our mission was to take the rowboat downstream to a big lumber yard and there pick out two long timbers thirty feet in length, ten inches by six inches, and bring them back to the ship. Whether previous arrangements had been made or not, I do not know, but the river police were absent at the time and we completed our mission without mishap. On the voyage to our next destination, the ship's carpenter and I worked these planks down with a double-handed plane about three to four feet long. This type of plane was the only one I ever saw or helped to use, and it was hard work.

In a few days, we were again on the move, this time south, to Fernandina, Florida. As we were now one seaman short, I had to assume more duties. Steering by the stars was interesting in calm weather but as our ship was all hand-steering with no steam help, at times it was a real man's work. Sometimes in very rough weather, it required two men to manoeuvre. The change of water in different ports would sometimes play havoc with your stomach.

The food offered us was certainly not very palatable. At 6.00 a.m., we received a cup of coffee which was half chicory. To drink it, I dumped half overboard and then filled the mug with water from the ship's pump. That enabled me to get it down somehow. After this, we swabbed down the decks till 7.30 a.m. Breakfast usually consisted of cracker hash, which was broken sea biscuits that had been soaked overnight. In the morning, the water was squeezed out, after which the hash was placed in a dish with a few slices of salt pork on the top, then put in the oven to warm up. Dinner was soup made out of salt pork or salt beef, which might have been in barrels for years. With this, was served some sort of vegetable and maybe a boiled pudding. In port, we received perhaps some fresh meat for a change. The soup pot held about six to eight gallons and was kept on the side of the stove at all times and replenished with the odds and ends of leftovers from the meals. Supper was usually wet hash made from the leftovers from lunch with bread added. The food became so bad that the seamen nearly mutinied. At last they formed a committee to meet the Captain to complain about the so-called food on which we were expected to live and work. The potatoes were from the previous season, and had sprouted several times until they were shrivelled little specimens. After reaching the United States, we were fed on sweet potatoes every meal, and it didn't take long to get sick of them, receiving them that often.

After the little debate at Barcelona over my job as the watchman, the Captain had the ship's carpenter fix up a couple of bunks in the charthouse, which was on the top deck, for we two apprentices. This building was constructed of sheet steel and the doorway leading into it was a small oval affair over which, at the base, you had to step about fifteen inches to enter. This was to keep out the sea water when the weather was rough. So now to get my meals, I had to go forward in the storeroom, sit on a box and use a pork barrel for a table.

One of my duties each morning was to go forward on the foredeck, remove a brass plug in the deck, lower a rope and pail to fill with sea water for the Captain's bath. After losing two or three pails in the process at the beginning, the Captain showed me how to tie a proper knot, one I never forgot, and of course I learned many other things after that.

Our journey down to Fernandina, Florida was fairly uneventful, except for the fact that we were all sick again with the change in drinking water. Arriving there, we proceeded up the river till we reached the loading station, where we filled up with phosphorous rock. Here the loading facilities were good but very, very dusty. The population here seemed predominantly black and, as in Georgia, seemed to be happy, enjoying their dancing and singing in the evenings. We were not there long but did manage to get ashore a few times before getting under way again. This time when we pulled out, we had a cleaning-up job to do as the ship was covered from top to bottom with dust from the loading docks. This job kept us busy for several hours at least. We were now making our way to the nearest coaling station for bunker coal. This was located at Newport News, Virginia, which we reached without mishap in a few days. Here we encountered no delays and soon were on our way back to a home port.

On my ocean travels, I learned much from my fellow seamen. The first thing was that I had been roped-in as cheap labour. If I put in the five years required in my indenture, the future would still then look bleak. The pay of the second mate was only thirty shillings a week and jobs were hard to obtain. I wanted out badly and the seamen told me that the only way out possible was to swear that the seafaring life was injurious to my health. This would all have to be settled the first time we reached a British port, otherwise I would be held to my contract. I had explained my desire to my parents in letters written and mailed to them from the various ports of call. By the time we reached Newport News, the Skipper had been informed of what was on the move regarding me. After we

were under way home, he called me over one morning with the remark,
'I hear, Timber, that you don't like a life on the ocean wave with the
hum of the rolling deep?'

'I am afraid not, sir,' I answered.

'Well,' he said, 'I have put in many years at it and I am still around.
So you figure to go back to the farm and settle down?'

'I sure do,' I answered.

'Well,' he said, 'I am willing to bet a sovereign that if you get out of
this, and you may have trouble doing so, you will not be in England in
a year's time.'

He was a wise old skipper, whose frank talk I appreciated. I carried
on with my duties, awaiting our arrival home in England. I had no reason
to be annoyed with anyone aboard the ship. The city slickers, the smart
ones, lived ashore and when the showdown came in the office there, I
would have to be ready to pit my wits against those who had talked me
into this. I had made one more mistake on the forward trail of life, which
I must now try to amend, even though the Skipper did not offer much
hope.

As the season was getting late, our millpond disappeared. No more
flying fish were seen, although now and then a whale was sighted. This
helped to break the monotony. We were getting into rough seas and, on
awakening early one morning, we heard the rush of water in our berth.
Investigation revealed a foot of water in with us. Every time the seas
dashed up on the deck, water was pushed up between the base and the
door into our berth. For the rest of the voyage, we moved our straw
mattresses down to the storeroom and slept among the barrels and boxes.
As the weather deteriorated, more care was needed and it was interesting
to watch how marvellously the ship handled herself. One time she would
be down in a deep valley of the ocean and, within a few minutes, she
would be right up on top of a giant wave, with the propeller racing away.
I was told that sometimes on such occasions the propeller was lost, and
that it was quite a job to replace one at sea, so we carried a spare one in
case this happened. The rough seas stayed with us and on a Saturday night
when we sighted the south of Ireland, we nearly lost a seaman overboard.
He saved himself by grabbing the lifeline we had threaded around the
upper deck for safety.

Within a few days, we were in the Mersey river, pulling into the docks
at Garston, Liverpool, Here we were, back in my home country, ready
for unloading once more, and I could expect to know my fate in the
next few days. The crew were all paid off except for three or four of the
most senior officers. The Skipper and the first mate received their wives

aboard. I was appointed ship's cook, and the other apprentice general roustabout. As the others went ashore, we were left to carry one. One morning, the first mate dropped into the galley to see how things were. I was still keeping the big soup pot on the go. He advised me to dump the contents overboard and replace them slowly, as there were less of us aboard. Then we had a heart-to-heart talk. He told me he did not blame me for trying to get out of my contract, as he himself had obtained his Master's papers ten years before, and was still unable to get his own ship. He said that, unless you had someone with all the proper influences, it was a near impossibility to gain a command. He advised me that if I could not get my realease legally, I should wait until we were ready to leave port again and then just disappear, but to take nothing with me. It was as much as his job was worth to be telling me this and I really did appreciate his advice.

In a few days hence, I was taken to the Shipping Federation offices in Liverpool to appear before a Board of Inquiry. There I was questioned, threatened, badgered, and promised another ship if I would stay. I fought back to the best of my ability to hold my own, and then returned to the ship. I told no one but somehow by now I was beginning to like the life of the seas, but on quiet consideration it looked like a waste of time, especially with the information imparted to me by the seamen and the first mate. Three days later, I was again called to the head office and informed that my parents would have to forward so many pounds to pay for the expenses the company had put out on my behalf, and so on. Of course, the work that I had done had no value as far as they were concerned in their financial statement. They could not allow me anything for that and, as they were the stronger of the two parties, the company naturally came out the winner. It would take at least all I could save in the coming year to pay for this phase of my 'college education', in which I had learned the 'Dangers of the Deep'. But this was probably the best course I could have taken at that period of my journey through the world because, as I have already said, there were no back doors and no back answers. One carried through the orders given, good or bad, and in doing so, learned respect and obedience. If matters annoyed you greatly, you merely had time to consider them. You could not go out for the night and get drunk to drown you sorrows, if that way inclined. Instead of all that, you just had to bite your lip and carry on. Maybe a term such as I had just gone through would be of help to many another youngster around the same age because, until you have learned to obey, you are not fit to command. I have since thought that this was the period in which I established a deep foundation for my life.

My seafaring life was over and settled amicably, and I had to pack and make for home. Packing was a light job. All they had supplied me with was a jute bag, a peak cap, two shirts, two pairs of dungarees, two pairs of socks, a pair of cheap boots, and two red handkerchiefs. I also had two sweet potatoes, two cobs of corn, one dried flying fish and my cage containing a bird I acquired in Barcelona. Now I was ready to obtain my railway ticket for home, from Liverpool to Winchester, which was the closest station to Upham. My arrival in Winchester was followed by the seven-mile walk with my bag in one hand and the bird cage in the other. I finally reached home late one November afternoon, a sadder but wiser lad.

Then it was necessary to listen to a certain amount of condemnation from my elders on the foolish move I had made, and advice that they hoped that I had learned a good lesson for the future. Little did they know that it was probably the best lesson of my life, though many more would follow. No one realised that once the tie was broken, many changes could follow – but the old Skipper knew! I had told him that once I was out of the Navy, I would be content to remain in England, but I was wrong again!

In a little while, the threads that had been broken when I left, were mended and I was back at work at my old job in the garden that I had left so suddenly. I was a little wiser and had to live down my mistake. I also had many more things to think about than before, and wonder over. I had seen my first electric street cars running in Barcelona. I had viewed Christopher Columbus's monument there and many other sights, such as the bullfight rings. During my stay in the Merchant Navy, I had experienced a host of adventures.

Life went on as before now that I was back in the gardening job. The standard roses that I had budded in the hedges were now also in some of my neighbours' gardens. They had seen and claimed them when the leaves fell in the fall, so they had the last laugh after my labours. Mom and I carried on with our flowers, and I was kept busy.

Motor cars were now beginning to appear. Otherwise, outside of keeping in touch with Nature and her different ways and whims, there was not too much excitement in or around the village. I had seen and learned of other lands, and carried maps of the different places in far-off lands in my head. The words of the Skipper would often come out of the void: 'If you get out of this, Timber, you will be out of England in a year.' I tried to forget those words.

Now I was old enough to visit the pub occasionally for a pint of beer, priced at twopence, a game of darts, and a singsong. I could not go very often as I had little money to waste and also Mamma disapproved of those visits. The pub, though, was the only place to gather and find a little fun and diversion with your cronies. They would come in from the different farms and estates from miles around. They came to the pub more regularly than they came to church! Usually, in all the times we met, they were a fairly happy lot. Of course there were sometimes suspicions as to how different ones managed to find the money to spend at the pub so often. Poaching was suspected as the main source. Rabbits were plentiful, and would fetch eightpence to tenpence – enough to buy four to five pints of beer. Also, there were lots of pheasants on the estates, and they would bring in a higher price even than the rabbits. Many gamekeepers were employed by the owners of the estates, but they could not be everywhere at once. One uncle of mine, a gamekeeper, had his head split open with a spade when he tackled a group of poachers, and was never again to regain his health. Some of the poachers were pretty rough in those days because, if caught, heavy sentences were meted out.

This was a way of life at the time: a case of one man pitting his wits against another to get something for nothing. As the months passed in this kind of environment, the call from far places became more insistent, and I began to consider emigrating to Canada. I was reading more all the time and felt that the future here was not promising, but this time I confided in my parents before making the leap. Had it not been for Father, I would have been on my way to Canada before the year's end. He advised me to wait a little longer and give it more thought this time, which I did.

I had been welcomed back to the job I had left to enter the Merchant Navy, and realised that I had better jump in with both feet if I expected to make the grade. I was keenly interested in the work and, by now, had realised that there was no limit to horticulture in all its ramifications. For the next two years, I worked and studied all the time, and I made headway.

Then some old gardener friends of mine advised me to move further afield, and try to find employment on a larger estate in Britain, where I would have the opportunity to broaden my knowledge considerably in the various lines of horticulture. In those days, at the turn of the twentieth century, if you could get the right recommendations, certain seedhouses and nurseries would accept you into their establishments to work, while waiting for an acceptable job in you own line. They paid enough for your board and maybe a little more but not enough to encourage you to want to stay with them. This I considered a splendid arrangement. I went up to Veitches in Chelsea, London, to their greenhouse plant, to await my opportunity.[1] To me, this was a good plan, and could be put to use in Canada. I personally accepted the second offer, which was up in the county of Norfolk on the estate of the then Lord Amherst. This was Didlington Hall.

I arrived there in February 1902, to begin my job as second journeyman inside the greenhouses. The estate, which was seven miles in extent and

---

[1] The method used was that you would have the chance of three refusals of jobs offered as they came in and, if none were acceptable, you were supposed to pull out and fend for yourself to give others the same opportunity.

took in several villages, had been a gift to Lord Amherst's ancestors from the Crown, given in appreciation of their services in helping General Wolfe defeat the French in the battle for Canada, many years before.

There was a considerable amount of glass in the form of vineries, peach houses, a pineapple house, plant house, and special houses just for certain plants, as the family in the past had been great collectors of such specialities and even had plants named after them.

The fruit and kitchen gardens were also quite extensive and produced many foods to supply the mansion. For the house, stables and gardens, a small army of servants was retained the year round. The big features of the place were the artificial lakes and pleasure grounds, created over a number of years in front of the mansion, with underground boathouses. There was also a deer park to the west of the home. As water overflowed from the lakes, it worked a ram which pushed the water up to the top of the tower connected to the mansion. This, in turn, supplied running water for the needs of the mansion, stables, gardens and pleasure grounds.

There were also two large museums connected to the mansion because, at this time, His Lordship was the main person backing the search for Egypt for curios. He was the backer before Lord Caernarvon took it up, and later was behind the search and discovery of the tomb of King Tutankhamun. There was a great number of very interesting finds in these museums. Outside of these, there were numerous other things pertaining to horticulture, such as a long herbaceous border on the pleasure grounds one-half mile long and twenty feet wide, which was a sight to behold. The rose gardens were extensive, as were many other features, and each one had its own maintenance staff. This was such a large estate that, even though the staff employed were many, they were all put to good use.

The housekeeper headed up the inside staff, with eight or nine man-servants, plus many maids. Besides them, there were eight men working in the stables, twelve in the greenhouses and gardens, with extra men brought in when required. As the head gardener was also the forester, the estate maintained its own work crews, such as bricklayers, carpenters, painters, glaziers and other construction staff, with a general overseer. It also had its own steam engine and trucks for long hauling.

His Lordship's private secretary had an office on the estate, while the head office was in London. His nephew managed the estate for him. Most of it was rented out to farmers in various-sized lots of land, and I was told that they were all treated well. Everyone in the district spoke highly of Lord Amherst. He had his own home farm, where a large number of prize stock was raised.

Each month, His Lordship paid out over £200 in old age pensions, a deed unheard of in those days. This, then, was the place in which I had settled, and it was now up to me to increase my knowledge as fast as possible. Here on this estate was more of eveything pertaining to my calling than I had ever worked on or with before.

Changes had occurred recently in the greenhouse section where I was employed. The new foreman had not yet arrived and the head gardener was away up in Scotland, attending his mother's funeral. Within a few days, everything was brought back into balance when the two men assumed their jobs. Then began a period of each feeling the other out, with a usual queries – where have you been employed, what is the extent of your knowledge, and so on. The new foreman apparently had been on many large estates previously and, as I had been taught to look up to my superiors, I naturally expected great things from him. As time went by, he did teach me many things. February arrived, and Spring followed shortly afterwards and, thus, in the horticultural line, things began to move quickly.

In the greenhouses, there were vines, fruit trees, vegetables, plants and flowers in great abundance from all parts of the world. The family's great interest in horticulture tended to keep us growers more alert than ever. There was always lots of work to do as, apart from the growing, the place had to be kept like a new pin all the time. The mansion was decorated with flowers when the family was in residence, and there was extra table work with lavish decorations for all special events. Cut flowers were shipped twice weekly to Lord Amherst's two married daughters' homes. It took a great deal of effort to keep things going smoothly all the time. Spring was virtually bursting out all over, with so much new all around me.

The family had their own church on the estate, and I was asked to join the choir. The two maiden ladies of the mansion had been highly trained in many ways and were gifted musically, even composing new hymns and tunes. I would occasionally be sent for to try out the new compositions. They were lovely, charming ladies and I did not mind helping them a bit. The village church also asked two of us to help out with their evening service. It was either the church or the pub, as there was no other form of outside interest, and the church appealed to me more. In this way, time passed peacefully by.

My first-remembered distress came on the day I saw the traction engine coming up the land with two truckloads of what turned out to be a special Suffolk yellow loam. On enquiring, I was told that the traction engine had gone seventy to eighty miles all the way down to Suffolk just to get this soil. It seems that the Foreman had talked the Boss into sending for it. I could not understand the reasoning for this, and asked why they could not find any kind of loam that was required on this large estate. They replied that this was the best loam in the country, and to mind my own business. Being the youngest of the crew, I thought maybe they were right in what they said and time would prove it.

I was also finding myself taking stock of other things around me; one seemed to be intermingling with the other. For instance, there had been constructed a maze in the pleasure grounds years before. I had never seen one before, and of course found it interesting. It had been planted with yew, and looked prolific. The underground icehouses and boathouses all added interest, as did the half-mile long herbaceous border. These and the different shapes of the lakes all meant deep study for a young man. The layout was really quite magnificent. On the side of the drive leading away from the mansion, behind a line of Linden trees, the deer park, containing varied species, added attraction to the place. With my natural interest in people and surrounding, I wondered about the local folks – what their duties were, where they learned and how. I had noticed several 'young' old men pottering around the hall, doing a few menial jobs, and was curious about them. A little private research gave me the answer. They were just 'beer soaks' and had lost any initiative that they may have originally had. The source of the trouble was the butler's pantry. There, in one spot, was always kept a copper jug of beer. Anyone who had work to do in the Hall, or could make a fair excuse for being there, had free access to that jug. If it was empty, a word to one of the footmen and there would be a refill at once. Like the others, I thought this was great as I had always had to pay my twopence a pint in a pub but now, seeing what was happening to these other young fellows, I decided there and then that it was not in the line that I was trying to follow. (I had already stopped smoking, having decided that it was no help to my singing.) The folks at the top were trying to be kind to their employees by supplying the free beer, but their generosity was abused and several of the help were destroying themselves because of the privilege.

In the summer, we had our own Cricket Club, where all was supplied bar your togs so that, all in all, if you did you duty, life could be pleasant in such surroundings. Unfortunately by this time, our foreman was making a beeline far too often for that copper jug of beer, which was impairing his judgement to the detriment of harmony amongst us. He was at least ten years older than the rest of us and was supposed to be the leader and set good example for us.

One crop that was considered at this time as a special necessity was the Autumn chrysanthemum and any estate, large or small, usually took

great pride in trying to produce outstanding blooms. There was a wide
range of varieties as regards size and shape: tall, short, large and small
blooms of every conceivable form. At this period, 1903, they had been
introduced in Europe probably less than 100 years before. They were still
highly prized both for exhibitions in the Autumn and for home decoration.
From the time that I had started gardening, I had taken quite a pride in
the cultivation of chrysanthemums, both at work and with Mother at
home. We had really worked hard with them and I had walked miles to
attend the Autumn shows. Now I was ordered to help prepare the mixture
for the final potting in nine to twelve-inch pots, of which there were
many hundreds. (The plants were presently in good shape in their six-inch
pots.) I may have been a little overly zealous on behalf of the plants.
When the mixture was complete and we were ordered to start potting,
I turned to the foreman and asked if he thought we would get a crop
out of such a mixture. He had used a large percentage of the 'imported'
loam and I felt impending doom. He wanted to know what in hell I
knew about it and told me also that if I knew what was good for me, I
had better carry on with my work, so I did. From then on, this crop
would be in the charge of the first journeyman, so for that season I had
no more to do with the growing of them.

I had my own section of the greenhouse plant – the orchard house,
for which I was responsible. In this orchard house, I had several hundred
six-inch pots of early strawberries. I was young, and anxious to produce
something special from these forced strawberries. This was my first experience with such plants and I wanted them to be the finest yet, so after
setting them, I began to feed them fertilizer. Not knowing what constituted
the mixtures in all the different fertilizers I chose clay fertilizer to feed
them, which was highly recommended at the time. The crop was wonderful, the finest you could hope to see! They hung around the pots in
large bunches – large, juicy berries and the pride of the grower. The
orchard house was absolutely scented with their perfume. While they
were at their best, His Lordship entertained Princess Beatrice of Battenberg
(Queen Victoria's daughter) and her daughter Princess Victoria Eugenie
(Ena), who was later to become the last Queen of Spain before the
Dictatorship. The prize strawberries were taken down to the Hall for the
special luncheon given in their honour. According to the information
given out later, when those attending the luncheon came to the strawberry
course, they felt something was amiss as the strawberries had a very peculiar
taste. It was unpleasant to the palate, and all refused to eat the berries.
His Lordship had sent for my boss, the head gardener, and told him of
the problem, wanting to know what I had been feeding the strawberry

plants. I showed my boss the fertilizer used, whereupon he told me that this particular mixture had been made from clay with combination of London sewage! This was the answer to the strange taste.

There was another lesson learned that was to last me all through life. I got by, with a slight reprimand as this was my first mistake. Of course, no more of that crop went to the Hall but the strawberries were not wasted. They still looked beautiful and so were cooked up for jam, etc. In cooking, the bad taste was lost and the incident was soon forgotten by everyone but me. Only a fool makes the same mistake twice and maybe the lesson was well learned, as the rest of the material in my charge did well that season, and I was commended for the results.

Alas, the chrysanthemums, from the time they were potted in the mixture to which I had objected, made practically no growth as the season progressed and were an eyesore and a disgrace to the establishment. Although I, personally, had no responsibility for them, I still felt disgusted. The Autumn shooting season was now here: a major event lasting a week at a time. We had the table decorations to attend to each night and the 'mums' were sadly missed. We received some dirty slurs on the side because of the loss, as the estate was employing so many gardeners.

The old Skipper's words returned to me often, for as times seemed charged and uncertain, the boys in the area were not looking forward to a very merry Christmas. I was considering going to Canada in the early Spring, and the Foreman wished to go with me. I was not being forced to consider moving on but I'm afraid *he* was, as the beer was affecting his work.

Yet again, as Robbie Burns put it, 'The best laid schemes o' mice and men gang aft agley.'(Quoted from *Burns Poetical Works* – Collins Publishers.) There were developments at home of which I had no knowledge. We managed to get by Christmas all right and, on New Year's Eve, were invited to the Head Gamekeeper's party. The Gamekeeper was Scottish, so for his family this was a very special Eve.

The next day, New Year's Day, I received bad news from home. It was that my Father was very ill. Shortly after receiving this message, a telegram came asking me to return home at once, as my Father was dying. My boss drove me to the station, five miles from the estate, in a cart drawn by a pony, which was our mode of conveyance at that time, and I was on my way to make the sad journey home. I still had the long walk to the house at the end of my train journey, so that it was quite late when I reached there. My Father had never been a strong, healthy man in his later years, and now was stricken with blood poisoning, apparently caused by the prick of a gooseberry bush he had pruned in the Autumn. My Mother and the rest of the family, some of whom were still young, were naturally very concerned and the worry was intensified by the fact that, if Father died, it would mean that they would have to find a new home. This one belonged to his employer and, although he had worked faithfully for over twenty years, the remaining family would have to move, as that was the rule, with no exceptions.

I was fortunate in returning in time to be with him on and off for many remembered hours, when we were able to discuss many things that would need attention after his death. One thing I had to promise was that I would not leave for Canada for at least two years. When he began to have visions of the far-away green fields, we suspected that the time was near. This came six days after my return home. As honoured and respected a man as ever was, he was buried in the churchyard that had been there since before Cromwell's time. All we had now were our revered memories of him.

I now had to forget my boyhood and take on manhood. My two older brothers were in the British Navy, or it would have been their duty to accept responsibility for the situation in which the family was left. However, both were out at sea, so it was up to me to resolve matters.

Before I could return to my job, I had to find new living quarters for the family, and move them there. When this was done, I finally went back to Norfolk but took with me the idea of leaving that job and moving back home to find work, so that I would be able to look after the family. Later, I talked this idea over with my boss, who told me that he wished me to stay where I was and gave me a promise of an advanced position, which included a good rise in pay. After receiving this offer, I decided to remain and carry on there. I realised then that, if there was going to be any future for me, I was the one who would have to make it. Now that Pa was gone, there was no one at home to help and advise me.

11. Harry in his British Navy uniform. He settled in Canada, moving from Toronto to British Columbia after retirement. He died there in 1958 at age 76. Three children, Harry Jr who lives in British Columbia, Ethel in Barrie, Ontario and Walter, deceased.

12. Ernest, taken in costume in China while on tour there with the British Navy.

I was really very interested in the work I was now doing and enjoyed it all the time, often working as others played, to make the most of every minute. I was first journeyman now in a different department, where there was lots of scope to show one's abilities. The foreman had gone. I had been promoted and another young man was in my previous place. Thus away we went for my second season there, and the change brought more pleasant company. Now things were going smoothly around me and it was a contented place in which to live and work. One aspect of this was that the new foreman was not a freeloader with the beer when down at the Hall. The greenhouse plant was rebuilt so much at a time each year, as the original one had been up for many years and was of far too heavy a construction, which reduced the light too much. The heating plant was also overhauled and brought up to date. With all this going on, I had an opportunity, by watching with my eyes and ears open, to learn the whys and wherefores of the construction of such buildings, from the foundation up. This season, the chrysanthemum crop was in my charge and I made sure from the start that, no matter whoever or whatever I had to fight, there would be no blunders or botches this time. This meant a few straight talks, with a lot of detail and overtime on my part all through the Summer and Autumn. When His Lordship came up to see the show of blooms, he told the boss that it was the best show he had ever seen in his conservatory. The boss passed on his comment to me, which made the whole effort seem worthwhile. To a young man it meant much and the world seemed brighter to me, buoying me up to start a new season. I'm afraid that showing appreciation for a job well done is one thing that is lacking in this world. I think that if more of this appreciation was given to good workers, we would be getting nearer to heaven on earth, with folks much happier, for a pat on the back means as much to a man as to a boy. I may say even now that the pat they gave me in Norfolk at that time was repaid many times over before I left their service. There were many things to attest to around the plant, with all the changes being made, and all were very interesting, giving a young man much to keep in his mind for future use.

Conditions continued to improve, with each worker trying to do his job as well as he could. This put things on an even keel with the new foreman who (unlike the previous one) stayed off the booze always. It was a very peaceful time.

A friend, one of my co-workers, and I made a trip to Sandringham Flower Show that summer, and had a tour of the King's greenhouses and grounds, which were very beautiful. It was quite a ride on our bike both ways, but that was the only means of transport available. On another

Sunday, we biked to Cambridge University to visit the grounds, lecture halls and other buildings. That was my only attendance at a real university – and completed in one day! Some people manage to go right along years after year, from school right up to university till maybe the age of twenty-five years or more, while the rest of us must obtain our education through the 'school of hard knocks'; learning by doing. I often wonder which side benefits the most out of this game of life, having lived with, and among, both sides for many years in my youth and early manhood, with many opportunities to observe. The rich ones certainly had more money to spend but they appeared harder to please, and I am sure that often they did not know themselves which way they wanted to go or just what they wanted out of life. Having personal acquaintance through my work with the 'top half', I never envied them their wealth. It seemed as though they never trusted anyone under them, and I don't think they often trusted each other, although now I am getting a little ahead of myself in this chronicle as, at Didlington Hall in my position, I had no reason for such thoughts. I was treated with all due respect and tried to give the same in return. My employer was in possession of this large estate and had more valuable holdings throughout the land, but I envied him not. With my regular work and my choir membership, I was kept fairly well occupied. Any spare time left over was spent studying my work. Even so, I was still looking ahead, wondering about my future. Reading the *Gardener's Chronicle* was no way to uplift your hopes for life ahead. Most of the ads in the 'Help Wanted' column of this paper in 1904 would be looking for a 'Gardener with no encumbrance' or 'Gardener with wife to help in the house' or 'Gardener-handyman with cows and poultry, wife to help in house'. This went on by the pageful, so that you knew your limit. Wages were not high enough to allow for savings with the idea of starting out on your own, should you have the ambition, and then again there was no land available for the ordinary working man, so there was no use dreaming.

Then back again would come the old Skipper's words: 'Timber, you will be out of England within the year.' Now, having reached the great age of twenty-one and having studied my situation carefully, I realised that, if I wished to progress, I had better make the move before my life became complicated in different ways. For instance, I now had a cat whom I had trained to near human intelligence and about whom I could write a book. I also had a young skylark that I had caught in the park, of whom I will write more later.

I did not see a future for me in my native land and I had fulfilled the promise made to my Dad to stay in England for two years after his death.

I had worked to make a home for Mother and the family, and now I made plans to move on. I felt that if I stayed around much longer I would probably add a wife, which would make the situation more complicated for departure. At the end of my third season, after deep consideration, I decided that Canada should be the site of my next effort. When I informed my Mother and family of my intentions, my younger brother, Bert, decided that he would like to go with me. After he made this desire known, final arrangements were begun.

Upon hearing of my intended departure, His Lordship sent for me. Meeting with him in his library, he commended me for going to the Colony of Canada. He approved of my choice of countries as, he told me, his ancestor, Colonel Amherst, had helped General Wolfe take that country for the Crown from the French. This I had heard previously. As he spoke, he pointed out the oil painting of Colonel Amerst on the library wall. He said he liked to see young people go to Canada to help colonize it and, with many other kind words, some commenting on my past good work, he handed me three sovereigns for good service and an extra sovereign because of my destination – Canada. He shook hands with me and we parted – God Bless him! His Lordship was one of Britain's finest noblemen of his period.

The old retainers and servants told me that I was foolish to leave, as in a few years time we would all benefit from His Lordship's pension plan and in due time from his Will. Some of them had been there as long as forty years while many more nearly equalled that time. I told them that I had never waited for 'dead man's shoes' and had no intention

13. Didlington Hall.

14. Didlington Hall Church, 1981.

of starting then. Little did any of us know, His Lordship included, what lay in store in the near future. We had sorrowful farewells as they were all real good everyday folks and I never expected to meet any better. They were mostly people whom only death could move, with sometimes three generations on the estate at one time. As such they found it hard to believe that I should feel inclined to move on to farther fields.

Before I left the estate, the housekeeper of the mansion, an elderly Scottish lady, sent for me and told me her story. She informed me that she had a brother living in Toronto, Canada – one whom she had never seen. After her birth in Scotland, her parents had emigrated to Canada, leaving her behind. Somehow she had never followed them, and her brother was born after her parents' arrival in Canada. She requested me

15. Didlington Hall Boat Houses, 1981.

to take a present to her brother from her when I went, which I promised
to do. I mention this as an example of how one thing in life seems to
weave into many others.

    In my preparations for departure, the cat had to be left behind, and
the skylark sent home to my Mother for the time being. I told the boys
I would not be back unless I could return a lot better off than I was then.

As planned, I first went to London before proceeding to Glasgow to board ship. There my brother-in-law Bob met me, with my younger brother, Bert. I handed over the skylark to Bob to take back to Upham and, after more farewells, we were on our way on the train up to Glasgow, and what a ride! It was the fastest train ride I had in my life. However, we arrived safely early the following morning. Off the train, we had a hearty breakfast, a quick look around Glasgow and then boarded the ship. The was the SS *Athenia* bound for St. John, New Brunswick, Canada, heading out in November 1905, to the country we had chosen although we knew little of it. The ship was used as a cattle boat to England and emigrants took the place of the cattle for the return trip, after the ship was scoured out. Deciding to make Toronto, Ontario, our temporary destination, the railway ticket was one pound, ten shillings, added to the cost of the passage fare of the ship, which was five pounds.

Our travel luck took a change for the worse after we boarded the ship. A heavy fog had enshrouded the whole of the British Isles so our ship moved out into the River Clyde where it anchored till the fog lifted, several days later, as it was too dangerous to embark while fogged in. One of the ships taking the Onion Sellers to the Channel Islands was lost in this fog, so it was a wise move to hold us back. However, in that old iron tub the *Athenia*, with no heat, I was never so cold in my life before or since, and it lasted four or five days. Our bunks were alongside the cold iron plate of the ship's side. As soon as the fog did lift, we were on our way. There were no luxuries on that trip and half the passengers were of extraction other than British. After recovering from the urge to die from sea sickness suffered the first two days, we made our own fun on board one way or another. As it was now the middle of November, the weather meant winter travelling so we were under deck most of the time. We had our own concerts and singsongs in the evenings which helped to pass the time. This helped to raise the morale of the crowd and there was some good talent amongst us. The old ship ploughed steadily along, taking seven days to reach port as she was not a racer. She finally took us to our destination, which we were happy to reach. It had not been exactly a pleasure cruise since we first boarded her. On arrival, it was hard to believe that we were standing on the dock amidst our baggage in the new land which we had looked forward to seeing so anxiously.

Snow was on the ground to assure us that we were in the intended country. A pleasant stranger appeared at my side and started a conversation. He asked how the trip had been, what work we did, where were we going and other small talk. He finally asked where our baggage was, and inquired of the contents. By now we knew that we were talking to a Customs Officer, though he was not in uniform. We were treated in a friendly manner and had no trouble for we were open and frank with him. Some of the passengers were not as lucky as us, although, unknown to us, there may have been good reason for their trouble with the Customs Officers.

Then it was on to the train as soon as possible, for our final journey to Toronto. The train was made up of Colonial Coaches with the pull-down sleeping quarters overhead. Again, as on the ship, no luxuries were provided.

The first part of the train journey was through the night so we saw very little of our new homeland till dawn. Morning saw us in Montreal, where we changed trains for Toronto. Snow covered all the landscape so, outside of the vastness, I saw very little else from which to form an opinion of our new land, though it did not look like the 'land of milk and honey'. Apparently that would have to wait for a while. On the evening of the second day of our train journey, we pulled into the old Union Station, Toronto. Here we were met by the great Tom Flanagan, a big tall Irishman who was well known in Toronto. He ran the Central Hotel at that time, and made it his business to meet all the immigrant trains. He was quite a 'broth of a boy' and well fitted for the niche that he had made for himself. I believe that he softened the arrival of many an immigrant with his Irish blarney.

The next day was a Sunday, so we decided to hunt up the housekeeper's brother and deliver to him the present that she had sent him. We thought that we had a good chance of finding him home as it was not a work day. We had no trouble locating him and found out that he was a master builder by trade, with a grown family. After enjoying the nice supper served us, he showed us to his den, where we spent the rest of the evening until late, as he wanted a lot of information. He asked numerous questions and, in turn, I asked him the same.

He now employed a group of men kept busy building some new homes for the employees of the proposed Casa Loma. This was to be built by a wealthy client, Sir Henry Pellatt, in the architectural style of an English

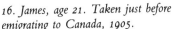

16. *James, age 21. Taken just before emigrating to Canada, 1905.*

17. *Bert, pictured before emigrating to Canada with James in 1905. He died in 1963. One son Edward lives in Toronto.*

castle. At the time of our arrival, our new found friend was building two houses for the gardeners at the north-east end of the courtyard. Before we left his home that night, he arranged to take me up to the estate with him the following day to check on the chances of obtaining work there myself. Monday morning found me out at his house bright and early, eager with anticipation. First he took me to the John Dunlop plant on Lansdowne Avenue, where there were about four acres of greenhouses. Unfortunately, I had no luck there as regards employment. After that visit, he took me to several different establishments to show me different jobs for which he had contracted. Finally, we reached the site of Casa Loma, where his workmen were busy on the two houses being built there. There was no Casa Loma there yet, just the cottage on the corner, and the greenhouse plant with the kitchen garden across the road. We looked around the greenhouse and then had a talk with the Superintendent, Mr McBittie. As a result of this conversation, I was hired to start work the following Monday, as they had no proper greenhouse man employed.

However, back at Tom Flanagan's that evening, after discussing this plan with my brother Bert, I felt that I should change my mind. I felt a responsibility for him as he was younger than I. It was mid-winter in a new land, and I could not leave him in the lap of the Gods. It was decided that, as we had always considered going west for the free crown land, it might be wiser to find out what farming meant in our new land first. Thus we made arrangements to work out on two adjoining farms, so that we could be together sometimes.

These farms were at Rosemount, near Alliston, about sixty miles northwest of Toronto. I was to be paid twelve dollars a month and board and Bert, being younger and with less experience, was to receive ten dollars a month and board. This was the going rate at this period. I thought that this would be the best plan until we had time to get our bearing and could strike out for the free homestead out west. We would have time to glean information from our new employers on the farms.

In the first week of December 1905, we left Toronto by train for the village of Rosemount and John Smith's farm. It took us from four in the afternoon until eleven the next morning as we had to stay overnight in Alliston and go on by Post Delivery Cart the next day. After an early breakfast in Alliston, we were ready for the last lap of the journey to the farm. When the postman arrived with his two ponies and the four-wheel light wagon, we piled on. It was a cold ride, being all open to the weather, but we made the best of his buffalo robe and, after a great deal of shivering, we landed at our destination – the farms.

Our luck held out. We found the folks there to be very kindly and sociable, so we soon fitted in well together. Of course, being winter we found that the work was quite different from what we had done previously. We did find, luckily, that we could stand the cold weather as well as the natives could. I pruned the farmer's apple orchard in ten below zero with no great discomfort. The big discomfort I did have, however, was that my bed was too short! On very cold nights, it was quite unpleasant but, being new there, I did not feel that I could complain. We had work in the bush, around the barn, some thrashing and clearing of the land. On our first Sunday, we attended local church services, where the minister asked me to help with the choir, upon hearing of my past history along this line in England. I complied and it gave me a new interest in the locality and its people.

We were working with good decent people who treated us well and fed us generously. Evenings after supper, the boss and I would sit by the kitchen stove and discuss the farming situation. He was a fairly intelligent man and gave me a great deal of information about the farming industry here and out west. Included in our conversations were systems, prices for the different produce, climate, growing seasons and many, many other things. On his own farm, he used quite a bit of ingenuity around his plant to bring it up to date. We had time for many talks in the evenings as then there were no other distractions such as TV, radio, etc. There was very little electricity available throughout the land at that period and straight horse power or steam power were used mostly. He explained to me the different prices he was able to obtain and what it was possible to clear under his methods in a year, on his 125-acre farm. The price of hogs that he took to market, after using a first class method of raising, was eight cents a pound. Beef was selling for eight to twelve cents per pound with other prices in accord. I had no reason to question his figures and began to wonder if, under these conditions, it would be wise for me to abandon my horticultural career, which I had worked so hard and long to learn.

The thought came to me that I had better take counsel with myself, as in the back of my mind I had hopes in the near future of making a home here for the family still in England. If I stayed in my present position until the end of the year and spent no money whatsoever, I would have the 144 dollars. This would hardly be enough to buy one horse and, the longer I stayed, the farther I would recede in my plans. After much consideration over two months, I decided that at present-day prices I would never be able to own a farm in my lifetime. It was time to return to horticulture as soon as possible, and build on that foundation obtained from my past experience.

With much trepidation on my part I approached the farmer and explained my dilemma. I had signed no papers so there was no hold on me but I wanted to depart fairly. It was not easy trying to explain my ideas to him but he was a just man and understood my plight. When it was finally decided that I should travel on, I accepted twelve dollars for the two months' work instead of the twenty-four due to me. Not heavy pay but we parted good friends, and I felt that I had made allowances to him for staying such a short time.

It was now the end of January and I thought that help would be needed in the different greenhouses I now knew about. So, at the end of January 1906, I made tracks back to Toronto and our new friend, Tom Flanagan, at the Grand Central Hotel. My brother was fine where he was for the present, so I was free to try fresh fields.

The first morning back in the city found me on my way to the housekeeper's brother, the builder, where I was due for more surprises. He was back in the 'old country' from where his parents had emigrated.

He had made up his mind in a hurry after meeting us, as he wished to meet his sister. From his home, I made my way up to the Casa Loma site where I was supposed to have started working before leaving for the farm. They were rather amazed to see me again as I had not turned up when I should have. In the meantime, they had engaged a grower from Scotland, Donald McIntyre, but he would not be arriving until the next month. After hearing my proper explanations, they decided that I could start later and in the meantime I could get work in one of the seedhouses. On reaching the seedhouse, I was informed that the Boss at Casa Loma wished me to return there at once. I did so and was informed that I could start on 4 February, two days hence. That settled, I then hunted for a room fairly close by. By the time I was settled in and to bed that night, I was a very tired but satisfied lad. I had travelled many miles mostly by foot, not being used to the ways of the streetcars and maybe a mite nervous. After a good night's sleep, I was ready for operations again, as I was to return to work in my own field.

However, here I stepped into a situation where both of my superiors knew little or nothing about greenhouse work, which made it very precarious for me. One would order me to undo what the other had ordered me to do and then redo it in his way. Until McIntyre arrived to take the full charge of it all, it was sure a touchy position for me to be in at my new job in my new land. He arrived in March from Scotland and, as he was very practical man, the work went forward from then on smoothly, which was better for all concerned. I was content once more. There was lots of work ahead for us, which left me no time for remorse, and I looked forward to the growing season outside coming up. Week followed week and still the weather was cold outside although it was well into April – so different from the English climate. I questioned the boys about winter holding out so long. How were the trees able to make their growth in such a short time? The middle of April brought an eighteen-inch snowstorm and I began to fear that all was lost. In came May and, before the end of the month, the papers were complaining of the drought! I wondered what had become of all the water from the snow and why conditions were as I found them, though over the years I found out.

Now I was living in the bothy on the estate, and could make my wages go farther on my eight dollars a week. Rooming and eating at a restaurant had not left much for the pocket or savings, so the change brought welcome relief.

Around us, things were beginning to shape up for construction of the proposed castle, stables and coach houses. Men had worked with hammer and wedges breaking off the frost top, which was about two feet deep earlier. They then carted the soil out by teams and wagons for the huge basements required. It was a mammoth undertaking upon which they had embarked! When the construction boys informed me what it was Sir Henry Pellatt intended to do, I said he was crazy to build such a bunch of buildings in the place and positions where they were to be constructed. I remarked that if he ever did get them up he would never have enough money to keep them maintained. The boys said that I was the crazy one, but I offered to bet them five dollars on my views as somehow I never had faith in his venture. I had just recently left one of the largest estates in Britain and had a fairly good idea of the cost of running such a place, but I was only twenty-one – to be seen and not heard!

Right at this same time, Spring 1906, events in another part of the world were developing which caused me much concern. One morning the mailman brought me a letter containing ill news referring to the estate where I had worked in England. It seemed that the first real indication of trouble came to light with the suicide of His Lordship's main agent in his London office. Investigation disclosed that the agent had been using His Lordship's ready cash, in stock and gambling ventures, to the point where he had practically ruined Lord Amherst financially. His Lordship, unfortunately, was now well advanced in years with no sons to help him with this burden. He had to meet this disaster head on, which was a terrible thing at his age, as throughtout his life he had given considerable thought to the welfare of the less fortunate of his fellow men in so many ways. The predicament in which he found himself resulted in sales here and there of his different assets. I read in our local paper in Toronto of a sale to the American millionaire Pierpoint Morgan of his hand-written Bible for 200,000 dollars, and finally the whole estate was sold. I'm afraid that the old retainers who had been waiting for 'dead man's shoes' must have found them empty in the end! I felt that I had been lucky making the move when I did but I was really sorry for them all under the circumstances. That estate had been running in top form for over 100 years, yet just a few months made such a difference. I was saddened by the news as His Lordship and his family were people worth looking up to as superiors compared to others for whom I had worked. The greed of one man had upset the lives and plans of probably hundreds. We little realize how the actions of each one of us going our way through life may affect the lives of so many of our fellow men. We mostly go blithely on our way if in good health and circumstances, giving little thought to those around us.

Life must go on, however, and around me then things were moving ahead rapidly, buildings going up all around the courtyard, dozens of

workmen of all trades busy at their jobs, and yet somehow the whole
concept did not seem real or sensible to me. Not the place, not the time
(1906), nor the idea of it all.

Electric power was beginning to take hold and electric streetcars were
in operation. Motor cars were coming into their own place and were
increasing in number. Sir Henry, who was having all this work done at
Casa Loma, had left England for Canada many years before and was one
of the most ardent pioneers of the advancement of the new power,
electricity. Yet here he was constructing, at great expense, stables and
coach houses and intending to build a castle. Everything here was in great
confusion with all the changes going on. All this on land that never should
have been considered in the first place. Somehow, along the line, he must
have been ill-advised. With my premonition that things were not right,
and being helpless to correct them, I again began quietly to consider other
fields.

Before I could make a move, more bad news reached me from my
homeland. In the space of six weeks, I was informed of the deaths of my
sister Rose, her husband Jack and their daughter Daisy. A young son,
thirteen years old, orphaned by their deaths, was then raised by my eldest
sister, Annie, and her husband, Robert Bible. He, like his father, was also
John Hitchcock, and upon reaching maturity made the Army his career
– a change from the Navy that others in the family had followed. He
rose to the rank of Brigadier-General: quite an accomplishment. My
brother-in-law Jack had been in the Naval Brigade with HMS *Powerful*
at the relief of Ladysmith in the Boer War. He served as a master painter,
and after the war was transferred to the King's yacht, the *Victoria and
Albert*. While serving in Africa, he suffered an illness from which he never
fully recovered. My sister, Rose, had worked hard in the Sailors' Rest in
Portsmouth throughout the War and became all run down in health and
probably half-starved, as they received very little wages in those days in
the Army or the Navy. This news, of course, had a very depressing effect
on me, being so far away from home, 'taking the wind from my sails'.
With so many disasters in such a short time I carried on very quietly for
a while.

A few weeks later, I was able to bring Bert back into the city from
the farm, as he wrote that he was very lonely. At least I had some company
of my own and knew where he was at all times. He looked after the
bothy, did the cooking, and replenished the supplies when needed, for
the seven of us who lived there, and worked outside in his spare time.
The boarders were all newcomers to the land and wished to save a few
dollars, so Bert's orders were to keep living expenses down to a minimum.

Provisions were moderate in price in 1906 compared to present-day prices, with butter at twenty-five cents per pound, eggs at twenty-five cents per dozen, three pounds of ground steak for twenty-five cents, and similar prices for other foods. As it was summer now, we were allowed some fresh vegetables which helped some, so that one week our 'caterer' managed to keep our board expenses down to ninety-seven cents each, but from then on, it had to go up a little. The reason for this rise was that, one evening at supper, we were sitting down to one egg each when in came Reuben, a big Yorkshire lad. On viewing the repast, he let out one big blast: 'What, only one bloody egg?' Some slight improvement was made after that, but slight it was. The boys by now were all running around with a wad of bills in their back pocket tied up with a bit of raffia and they wished it to grow bigger with each pay day. As yet, they would not trust the banks to hold their money, which was the first cash they had ever been able to save.

18. Rose, who married John Hitchcock, another British Navy man. They had a son, John Jr and a daughter, Daisy. After Rose, her husband and daughter died, John Jr was raised by sister Annie. He died in 1952. His son Raymond lives in Abbots Worthy, Hampshire, England, a few miles from Upham.

I spent my spare time searching farther afield to find out what was around the city in my line, as I felt that somehow I was in the wrong spot. In Toronto and the surrounding area at that time, there were very few private estates and these were small ones. The thought was still in my mind to bring out the rest of the family from the old country and make a home for them here but, on now nine dollars a week, I knew it would take too long. Toronto then was not an extremely large city so the streecar lines did not go great distances. As a result, if you were looking for a flower grower or market gardens in which you might be interested, you rode to the end of the car lines and then walked on. Brother Bert and I would go in different directions on a Sunday afternoon and drop into any garden places that we found. There, we would perhaps have a chat for a while, gathering what information we could regarding possibilities for ourselves.

In the middle of July, on one trip out of the east end of the city, I walked quite a way from the last car stop and, in the distance, I spotted greenhouses across some fields. I finally reached them and saw it was a plant for growing winter vegetables. Introducing myself to the owner who lived nearby, I found he also was from England. Soon I was in deep conversation with him about many things of the past and present. He had been here for several years and I felt able to speak freely to him about my prospects. When I left, I took with me the possibility of renting his plant for the coming season. He wished time to consider this as, after all, we were strangers to each other so I was to contact him in a few days to hear his decision.

In the following discussions, unexpected problems came to light. Apparently, his eldest daughter had worked with him for some time and he felt that she should still have some interest in the plant. He said that the only way he would consider making any changes was if I would agree to a partnership with her, with the understanding that he held the control. Looking desperately for a start, I agreed to this and on 1 September 1906, I took over with her, paying one dollar a day rent.

We had about 8,000 feet of glass and four acres of land plus a wagon for drawing coal and manure. When I examined the ground beds, I saw that they had never been worked deeper than about six inches. Knowing the value of intensive cultivation, I decided to trench the whole place through to a depth of thirty inches at least, packing in all the manure I could. My experience in growing winter vegetables was not extensive so I was learning again.

It was my first association of this kind and, as the daughter was not overly strong, it meant that I had to carry the heavy end of the load where hard work was concerned. The plant was very run down, which meant work for me day and night to get it under way as I wanted. I was young and ambitious and this was my first chance to be eventually independent. Being so eager for success, once again, while others played, I worked and did get the plant under way in my style. What work my partner was able to do, she did willingly and by pulling together time passed swiftly, one crop following another.

Along with growing the crops, I had the manure and fuel to haul with a small cob,[1] as well as firing the longest part of the night in the winter. At this period, in 1906, all sand and gravel was hauled by horses and in some stables in our locality there were perhaps as many as thirty teams.

---

[1] small pony

These stables were glad to have someone remove the manure for them so I drew hundreds of loads and turned it several times before digging it in. The neighbours thought I was crazy for putting so much work into the land until they saw the results. Drawing the manure and my winter's fuel in forty-bushel loads kept me busy for the cold months. After a few minor mistakes in the beginning, we were soon well under way. Room and board could be obtained for five dollars a week so I was able to keep expenses to a minimum. Outside of a monthly visit to a meeting of the Gardeners and Florists Association, which I had joined in the early Spring, I had nothing else of interest to take my time. My eagerness for success was still uppermost in my mind so I stayed closely to my work. We reaped forced rhubarb for New Year, and the other crops were coming along nicely then too. With so much to do, I continued to work all day, and most of the night.

In late Spring, when everything was coming along well, the owner informed me that he had sold the property to a developer for a housing development, and the greenhouses would have to come down at the end of the season. Again my stay was to be short. I did have the satisfaction of knowing that I had accomplished more than the owner ever had in one single season, though this was small comfort. Now again I faced the fact that I must make other plans for the future so I set my mind busy with that. I had put so much work into the plant, hoping to reap the results as the years went by, and one single season had hardly given me enough time to get my second wind. Now it as out of my control so I had to face it, and time was passing.

The owner then came back with another idea, suggesting that, as the plant had to come down, perhaps I would like to purchase it and rebuild it myself. He offered to sell me a lot on another part of his property, where he thought I could begin again. He was a good man and was trying to help me, so after much consideration this matter was settled. My partner, his daughter, had decided to marry and that ended our partnership, which had been congenial if maybe a little one-sided. Not having yet reached my twenty-third birthday, I realised that ahead of me was no small undertaking. My knowledge up to the present was more in the growing line than in building. I decided it might be wise to seek another partner and perhaps one a little older than myself would be advisable. I discussed this matter with my Casa Loma workmate, Donald McIntyre. We agreed on a partnership and, after the usual preliminaries, we were head over heels in the changeover. We made one big mistake, due to both being from the old land, in that we felt that we had to build to last forever and so we built really far better than necessary. We dug the basements ourselves

for the boiler and coal storage with pick, shovel and wheelbarrows, mixed
and poured the concrete by hand, carried bricks and mortar for the
fifty-foot stack. After many discussions, we made arrangements with the
King Construction Company to supply the materials with a deposit down
and a six months' note, as we thought it would mean a faster job. Of
course, it did not work out that way. Over the next months, we worked
our hearts out every hour of daylight and constructed the greenhouses.
By the time we had the soil fixed and the crops in, we were an exhausted
pair of men. The funds were nearly gone and the 300 dollar note was
coming due. Neither of us had much business experience and we were
scared to death of discussing our affairs with strangers. Now as I look
back in retrospect at that period of the following year, and for the benefit
of any young horticulturalists who may read this chronicle, I realise that
we began with two weaknesses. Although we were both good growers
and hard workers, our training in the horticultural field in both cases had
been on private estates. Our business education was practically nil, as was
our experience in the construction of a greenhouse.

We were working twenty-four hour shifts with two short sleeps, as
the next day we had to do a full day's work. We had also built a stable
and the potting shed ourselves. Afraid of the impending due date of the
note, we did not spend a nickel on ourselves. If we had only overcome
our feelings of being strangers in a new land and had sought advice, we
might have learned many things to our advantage. My partner McIntyre
even went without socks, as he would only draw his board expenses of
five dollars per week. My younger brother Bert and I lived in the loft
over the wagon shed. It was only tar-papered as yet, and the stove we
had bought was not a very good one so sometimes the kettle of water
left on the back of it would be partly frozen by morning, as the winters
then were so very cold. Going down to the St. Lawrence Market on a
Saturday morning, we would purchase a quarter of beef for five cents a
pound and a sack of potatoes for twenty-five or thirty-five cents. Upon
returning home with this, we would cut up the beef and pack it in a
barrel of snow outside: our fridge. Even with all these hardships, we came
through that winter without colds or any bad sicknesses. Time went by
and Spring arrived once more with the crops beginning to mature.

Somehow, though nearly starving and going without even bare essentials, we had saved the amount of money needed to pay off the note on
its due date. I made tracks down to the office of the King Construction
Company with the cash, feeling quite proud that we had been able to
meet our obligations. I met Mr King, the president of the Company, and
explained my intention. He nearly had a fit as he, in turn, explained that

he never expected us to meet the note and that we could have had it renewed. He said we still could, if we wished, only pay off part of it. 'Mr Trimbee,' he exclaimed 'you don't have to pay off all this money at once. I would be quite satisfied by a little and to renew the rest. I know what you chaps have gone through.'

'Mr King,' I replied, 'I don't think you will ever know!!!' I told him that, as I had it here, it might be better to pay the whole amount.

'As you wish,' he said, 'but if you should ever need, at any time, any other favours in my line, please don't hesitate to ask for them, as I appreciate very highly what you have done in this matter.'

I left his office 300 dollars lighter, but with my head held higher as now we owed to no one, although it left our cash balance very low. I think Mr King and I both understood each other far better for our little talk. He was a good man and I later heard that he had helped many others 'up the hill'.

In the meantime, progress had been made around us. The streetcar lines had been extended to go by us and the district was fast filling up with houses. One of the large banks, the Bank of Nova Scotia, had opened a branch office nearby, to accommodate the new residents of the area. We were surprised one day by a visit from the manager soliciting our business, and after a conversation with him, we were certainly wiser men. After his departure we had a lot to think and talk about. He had opened new doors, new possibilities, new visions, and had renewed our faith in ourselves. With neither of us partners having any business education, we were hesitant to plunge in further, being still nervous of losing what we had acquired. However, from the information that he had given us by word and inference, we were able to think and reason more clearly about the matters at hand. Already having a considerable amount of loose building materials on hand, we needed some cash for its erection so that it could become an income producer. I felt that we could work on this while the other crops were growing. We agreed that I should call on our new-found friend, the bank manager, and explain our problem to him, hoping that he would lend us 500 dollars to do the job. He heard me out and, after careful consideration on his part, decided to lend us 480 dollars as he would have to approach head office to allow us the 500 dollars. We now used no more starvation tactics but were still extremely cautious with the money. After all, it was not really ours but it sure took us over a bad period and floated us to calmer waters.

Our third summer brought us from home two of my younger sisters, Edith and Maude, and my youngest brother, Charles. My brother worked with us for a while and my sisters found domestic work. We lived close enough for weekend visits, which we all enjoyed. The plant was in full operation and we were all kept busy building up the business. The following summer, 1909, my Mother and another sister, Lottie, the youngest of the family, joined us and with them brought the skylark that I had sent home to Mother in Upham for safekeeping, when I left England. We then rented a house to start a new home here, as now there were seven of us together. It seemed to take Mother a while to accustom herself to the new home and country. The others soon settled into the new jobs they had secured and also into their new surroundings. McIntyre and I were still both working very hard and were within sight of being debt free.

The City of Toronto was developing at a rapid pace. Reports from Europe indicated trouble from Germany could be expected before many years elapsed and emigration to Toronto from Europe was heavy. With this influx, there were fewer houses now to rent.

Why I will never know, but it seems that from the beginning Toronto was always lax regarding its sewerage, large and spiralling though the City grew. The sewage was all directed straight into the bay at the foot of each main street, leading to the water. This resulted in open sewers along the front and connected to the drinking-water reservoir. From the time I learned of these conditions and saw them with my own eyes, I found it hard to understand how an intelligent, thinking group of people in great numbers here would allow an error of this magnitude to continue year after year. Then, at long last, things were to change. After a lengthy series of discussion, pro and con, it was decided to run a trunk line sewer across the full length of the City, pick up all the laterals and build a big disposal plant in the east end of the City. They would purify the matter there and release the liquids into the lake, after this process. A lot of people, including me, questioned this idea and the statements made pertaining to it but, regardless, the system was installed and finally finished at great cost. Was it efficient? No, and never will be! Two years after it began operation, the authorities had to extend the main-water-line intake one mile father out into the lake, as the effluent from the sewer plant was drifting across the water intake. So, after all the expenditure, all the authorities accomplished was to take the sewage from one part of the lake and dump it into another. From that time on, millions have been spent on the plant with little success. Time alone will tell whether the move was right or wrong.

We were all busy now with our own happenings. This year saw the arrival of my eldest brother, Ernest, his wife and son from the old land. He had served his twelve years in the British Navy and left with a first-class

19. Maude, the third youngest in the family. She came to Canada, Married James Walker and they had one daughter, Lottie. Moved to California with her sisters in early 1920s where she died in 1939. Daughter now lives in Texas.

20. Sisters Annie, left and Maude, right. Taken in England before Maude moved to Canada.

gunner's discharge. Had he received a little more human treatment from his superiors, he probably would have remained longer in the Navy. He had been placed in charge of the Canteen Committee and was inclined to fight too hard for the underdog, for which he was reprimanded and lost a rating. The Navy in turn lost a first-class gunner, badly needed before many months. In those days, one man counted for little, especially should he think too deeply or speak up too loudly. Happily for us, here

21. *Edith, who came to Canada with sister Maude and younger brother Charles in 1908. She married John Hooper, also from England and they moved to California where she died in 1974. No children.*

he was and the clan was growing in the new land. He also brought us the latest news from Europe. It was now thought that as the Germans had completed the Keil Canal, war was practically certain within the next five years. Now that Queen Victoria was dead, nothing would stop the Kaiser from making his plunge. Ernest was an intelligent man and brought us up to date on these and many other events. He was soon able to procure employment and, with our work and family gatherings, life was sliding along comfortably once more. Brother Harry had also joined us earlier.

The business was improving each year and we were developing a better, class stock, which made the outlook brighter. We were also attracting a higher-class trade. The bank balance, however, was not increasing fast enough for my partner, maybe because he was probably fifteen years my senior. I'm afraid that he thought time was on the wing and he was not yet married so thought we should be banking more. I tried to explain to him that we could not keep spending money on improvements which were necessary for the future of the business, and still bank all our profits. In any case, it was not a business whereby we could expect to pile up a lot of money in a short time, especially as we had started with so little with which to build up the company. No one should embark in the growing business without having natural love for all growing things as, whoever you may be, it takes a lot of patience, thought, care and time. If your only thought is for the money in it, don't enter it or you will probably die of a broken heart; but if you really love all living things, wanting to produce them for the satisfaction and interest you may get out of it all, there is no other interest you can take up that will give you so much satisfaction in life.

At our exhibit at the Canadian National Exhibition one year, a lady remarked to me, 'I know why you are able to produce such beautiful flowers. It is because you love them!' Who knows, that lady was probably right, otherwise I don't think that I could lavish the care and thought

required to produce them. There are few millionaires made from producing things from, and working with, nature. Other parties seize the
different materials after they have left the producer, and hand them along.
They are the ones who get the cream as that can be done in hours or
days at a profit, whereas with the producer, it all depends on what he is
producing. It may take him a few weeks, months or years before he is
able to put on the market the efforts of his production. It is the time
element that has the producer beaten before he starts. Then again, usually
he is not the person who sets the price on the produce, the result of his
work and time. You will see why I have taken the time to explain why
the actual producer seldom finishes up a millionaire.

My partner, although one of the best growers who ever came to this
country, had in his past life always worked on large private estates
as previously stated, with no experience in commercial establishments,
and could not quite comprehend the vast differences between the two.
He never had the chance to know just what the owners' circumstances
were, whether they made money or considered it all an outside interest
from their other circumstances. His trouble was expecting too much,
too soon.

One day, an old pal of McIntyre's from the old country appeared on
the scene. He told Mac that he had backing from his sister for 5,000
dollars if he wished to go into business on his own. Poor Mac began to
get excited and wondered if we were in a big enough way to make some
money with this added investment. From there on, over a period of
weeks, discussions continued regarding this possibility. Word reached us
of a company in Georgetown, a town not too distant from Toronto,
which wished to dispose of the plant they owned and it looked like a
good deal.

So, alas, in a roundabout way, we were talked into forming a company.
This involved buying the Georgetown Floral Company, which could be
acquired very reasonably. The Toronto Wholesale Floral House wished
to amalgamate with us and the combination of the three, including our
own plant, would form the company. The idea of the three together
looked very promising but here again ambition overruled commonsense
and reason. Before we could get a good toe hold of the new possession,
the other felt that it should be enlarged at the start in different ways. They
felt it necessary to build one more greenhouse right away at the acquired
plant to enable it to supply the wholesale house. This meant that we
would be forced to borrow 3,000 dollars for that purpose. Our credit
rating was number one so we had no trouble in securing the loan and
thus the company was duly formed and we were under way. It was

decided that the wholesale house would be carried on as usual with the same manager. My partner and the new man, his friend, were to take charge of the new plant and ship to the wholesale house. I would manage and operate our original plant and off we started with high hopes. However, as it turned out, 1911, was not a good year to begin such an undertaking. Of course we did not know it then, but it was too close to the Great War of 1914 and doubts and uncertainties were already spreading across the land. The unemployed that year were carrying a black flag down Yonge Street in protest.

That season I came out fine at our home plant, while the other two branches were in the red! Business conditions now were being tightened up all across the land. Our friend the banker was not allowed to be so friendly, probably because his superiors at head office knew what was ahead of us, and he was given orders to retrieve his loans. When the big corporations play, they play for keeps and the little fellow doesn't count for much, as they are on top. It is always easier to receive assistance when you do not need it than when you do. When you are doing fine, folks will go out of their way to offer you help if you should need it, but when that time comes, the answer will invariably be, 'Sorry, pal, but you got me at the wrong time', or some such excuse. If possible, the only way through life is to try to regulate your affairs so that you can remain independent without the need of outside help. Over the years and conditions created in life, not always personal, man cannot live alone but must mix and mingle with his fellow men. These conditions and affairs created by others may often affect an individual's life far beyond his abiliy to control them. Thus, as the banker found it necessary to call in his loan, we had to find a way to satisfy him. The value of the land that we had bought in the begining in the City had increased in value considerably. It was finally decided that we had better dispose of that and settle the note, which meant 'tearing up stumps' for me, as this was the plant that I was operating, the only one that was really going forward. So far, the other two plants had lost heavily, putting us in the red, but neither of them was disposable at that time so it was my loss personally in order to repay the bank. Because of that, I decided to pull out of the company with what I was able to salvage and try working alone, as the combination of partners had not worked out satisfactorily for me. I was now about twenty-eight years old.

CHAPTER 7

The plant I had operated had to be removed as the land was sold for housing development, so it was decided that I should remove the plant and be allowed 2,000 dollars for relocation and forefeit all interest in the Company. It was a bitter pill to swallow but I felt that it might be for the best. Now began a period of much uncertainly, as every good fellow knew of a better place to locate than the other fellow. Toronto was a good city for a florist but much exploration needed to be done before deciding on a new location, which entailed quite a lot of travelling time. Locating a greenhouse plant in 1913 was not easy. We were still in the horse and buggy days. Very few businesses then had truck deliveries, therefore it was not only the growing of the materials but also their disposal that had to be kept in mind, as well as procuring water and fuel to run the plant. After travelling literally hundreds of miles on many scouting expeditions, I decided to locate near the city of our first choice, Toronto, and chose land in the swamp of Mount Dennis in York Township. This would provide the reasonable soil needed and availability for workers needed also for extra help. With all this in mind, it had not been easy to find just the right location on which to build a greenhouse plant. Land that we would have preferred for relocation was very expensive now so this swamp land was the only acceptable spot we could afford. This was virgin land that had never been touched so far to bring it into production. There were five acres of muck land, full of logs and stumps but, once cleared and fixed up, it would be good growing soil. This to start with, though, was quite a chore and, because of underlogs, all had to be hand dug at first to remove the wood. Every foot had to be cleared by hand as it was waterlogged. I first had to dig an open ditch around the whole plot to release the water and then blast out dozens of pine stumps. When I finally tried to plough on a likely part, it cost me sixteen dollars to repair a broken plough as it caught under a log ten feet long just under the surface of the land, so I returned to doing it by hand. I then had to concentrate on the chosen spot for the greenhouse, boiler plant and work sheds, forgetting for the time the balance of the land. The

22. Brothers Bert, Charles and James, 1910. Charles settled in California where he died in 1977. No children.

construction work was to keep me busy for the next five months. Certain phases of this called for some ingenuity because we had a 100 horse-powered boiler and eighty-foot stack with a running sand and swamp foundation. I took no chances and came through successfully with the structures. One good thing was that we had the finest water, and plenty of it. The drawback was that someone before us had spoiled our outlet on the roadway, which in time we were to find inconvenient.

November found us with the land drained and construction on the greenhouse plant well along. Then the first bad slam caught up with us in the form of a very bad accident to my youngest brother, Charles. As he was at loose ends at the time, he had kindly offered to assist me for a while before deciding on his own vocation in life, and he was a great help to me in many ways. I had previously bought in the City a quantity of four-inch drain tiles but in the rush of construction work had been unable to bring them home, and now we were being hounded to take delivery of them. Charles offered to take the team and market wagon to fetch them. As the weather was now getting cold for driving on an open wagon, I suggested that he wear an old coon coat of mine for protection. He was young, about seventeen, and did not relish the idea of being seen in an old coon coat, but I insisted, and away he went in it. Between 1.00 and 2.00 p.m. I had a call from the City Police, informing us that he was in Toronto General Hospital, and requesting that we send a man down for the team and wagon. Mother and I went immediately, full of trepidation and worry over Charles. Mother and the family had moved out to Mount Dennis also, when I relocated the plant. The investigation revealed that Charles had inadvertently packed the tiles too high up under the seat on the wagon and the jar of the wagon dropping off the curb on to the roadbed had caused the seat to roll, throwing him off in front of the wheels of the load. The team, still in motion, pulled the load over his body with a three-to four-ton weight. When Mother and I were allowed to see him at the hospital, he was in terrible shape. Even the doctors in attendance were at a loss as to the proper approach in treating him, for a young lady admitted the same day, after being run over by a pony cart, had already died. Everyone surmised that my brother must have been protected by the old coon coat which acted as a cushion. Otherwise the weight of the load could have cut him nearly in two. Yet here he was in agonizing pain. The doctors' decision was that nothing be done for the present, and they just let him lie there suffering. Everytime we visited him, he would ask us to bring in something to end it all and he begged the doctors to finish him off. He was given nothing, and his lips cracked for moisture. He was left in this state for many days and then the doctors told him that he could have anything in the way of food and drink of his desire. The result of this was that, over several days, his stomach swelled up abnormally. I was sent for and the doctors explained that an operation was now necessary but they needed my signature for approval before proceeding. During the operation they found and removed a large cyst that had formed as soon as he had been allowed to eat and drink. After the operation, he lay with a syphon in his body sucking out all the corrupt matter as it formed. Weeks went by in this manner with steady visits by us all to the hospital until late March of the following year. Finally, the syphon was removed and, while visiting him one afternoon, he informed me that he was going home with me. I could not believe this, but he said he could stay in the hospital no longer and thought he would be better off at home. I said that if he was determined about this I would go and get a taxi for the ride home. He refused that offer, saying that he would go home with me on the streetcar. He asked for his clothes and we were on our way and on the streetcar, not by taxi! This was the only hospital case in all my long life experience with illness for which, from the admittance to the discharge, we were never asked a penny. It seems that the case was so rare that one doctor paid the charges, asking only that my brother appear at different medical conventions and seminars, where his case was discussed in detail. He did this for years afterwards to repay the hospital for care. Had the hospital charged us for all the treatment and care he received, I'm sure that we would still be in debt to them. We are still thankful to them for all the kindness and care given him. He took things quietly for the following summer and, being young, gradually recovered but was of no use for heavy work for years afterwards. He found his vocation in the world of horse racing and is now over seventy years of age and one of the foremost racing secretaries in the USA. That was a trying period because, as we waited and watched during his recovery period, our business had to carry on.

My sisters were working at Naismiths, a large establishment in Toronto, and through them I met a co-worker, Jean Turnbull. Although I was still working extremely hard and with long hours, I did take time out for courting Jean as I knew this was the girl I wanted for my wife. Our wedding was planned for 28 September 1914, at St David's Anglican Church, Toronto. I was then twenty-nine years of age.

We were not into production as yet and money was becoming scarcer; 1914 was developing into a tough year for most businesses, which added to my worries. February brought one of the coldest periods we had ever had in this part of the country. Even after installing the heat, it seemed to make no impression on the soil, so that after waiting a few days and seeing little results, we had to blast the soil in all parts of the houses to loosen it up, before the heat was able to penetrate to take out the frost. We had no mishaps with the blasting, having approached the job with extreme caution. Once the place was thawed out, we soon had the crops in and spring was near, bringing more sunshine. In the new black soil, we sowed sweet peas and the result was the finest, heaviest crop of them in the country by May 1914. Alas, we were about a month late with them, due to the late start because of the necessary thawing of the soil. We had Toronto and Montreal loaded with them, but as conditions were bad all over our returns were disappointing.

One experience I had at this time I have never forgotten or forgiven. As I had all the flower shops here full with the crop, I then approached a big department store on Yonge Street. After some haggling over prices, they agreed to take a few hundred but at a lower price than I was receiving for them on the road. Having thousands still back home, I, now think foolishly, agreed. What angered me was that they did not pay me then but in a few days sent me a cheque less ten per cent for cash. I wanted to go to the store then and there to fight it out as I had made no such an agreement, but my family did not think it worthwhile to try to fight such a large company. It is easily understood how such a concern was able to spread across the land, if they were able to save at least ten to twenty per cent on the buying, and then subtract another ten per cent when paying the suppliers for the purchase. Operating like this, three or four more corporations the same as the above mentioned can own all the land, and all therein, within 100 years if not controlled differently. Personally, I made an effort never to do business with that company again in either selling or buying. I felt that was a bitter lesson and one never to be forgotten. The report published a few weeks ago showed the owners, a family concern, to be worth 400 million dollars, which is incredible. It may have been of more value to the country had it been spread out through 100 hundred families instead of one whose power becomes increasingly greater. Time alone will tell and thank the Lord that all the people with whom I dealt were not so greedy.

Spring passed and Summer arrived with all of its uncertainties. War rumours were becoming more insistent daily and everyone was on edge. The rumours had been around for years, even way back when we were children. Then the little German bands were all through every village in the British Isles. Stories went around that they were spies and this could easily be believed, as they never collected enough money to pay for their shoe leather because the people had no money to give them had they so desired. Now all the talk was of the coming war, of how it would start and who would start it. It was a very worrisome time and everyone was fearful.

Then came the fateful news of the assassination of Archduke Ferdinand. Hardly had we time to digest the full impact of that when our country was in the War also. This was just the beginning, and only the Lord in Heaven knew as to what length and depth it would develop. There would be so much suffering spread around the world, with many lives sacrificed and for what and whose benefit? All over the world for many years the different nations had been busy educating their people in how to live more sensibly, how to make life more interesting, how to live in peace with each other, and how to get the most out of life by better and improved methods. We had been introduced to steam and electric power to help us greatly. Our lands were full of religions of every variety. We had now reached a stage where it was possible to make Heaven on Earth, with all these newly-found advantages. Somehow, though, it was not to be.

Greed again stepped in to make the nations want many things that their neighbours possessed. They used their built-up power for force,

24. Jean, wife of James, 1914. Died 16 December, 1948.

23. James, 1912.

forgot the Golden Rules, their religion, their humanity. Everything was to be sacrificed to the God of lust and power, considering no one, not any one thing. They felt that their place was at the top and that they would let nothing deter them until they achieved their goal. When you consider to what depth of misery and sorrow a few persons, not worthy of the name of Man, have been able to plunge the rest of their fellow beings, it is simply beyond the comprehension of any sane thinking man. Had it affected their own people only, it would have been a different matter, but the whole world had to suffer for the greed of just a few. It would have been far better for all, had those few been shot, somehow, at the start and sadly we are not learning any lessons from this. We go through life and some, worse when in power, do not learn or consider commonsense.

Before you had time to think, brothers, cousins, brothers-in-law and some other relatives were in uniform preparing for overseas service. The news coming from the Front was bad, bringing reports of terrible battles and many deaths. I worked day and night to hold on to the business, hoping for the end of the War. From the beginning of the War prices were very low and I had a hard time selling. We had a young baby now and I had to seek other employment to keep going. This was Autumn 1915.

Friends and acquaintances as well as relatives had offered their all, so it was hard to keep your reason and balance but I was in a difficult position. I carried responsibilities that were not easy to release at a moment's notice, as I could not find anyone to carry on for me if I signed up. Though I yearned to join my relatives in the service, I was forced to delay this. I had just completed building a range of glass and, if I left it for any length of time, it would be destroyed. So, after a lot of thought, I decided to turn the plant into a vegetable-growing plant as people still must eat. This was considered another way of serving the country's needs. Now I entered two and a half years of torment, working day and night with help uncertain when needed to most. Prices were very low for, if possible, people were turning their flower gardens into vegetable plots.

So I stayed at home, carrying on under very difficult conditions, working and hoping for the best, month by month. The casualty list noting who and how lost kept coming in, getting longer by the week. Then came the notice of my wife's brother Bob's death in the battle of the Somme 1916. A few months after that my brother Earnest was lost at sea. One other brother-in-law was shell-shocked and, though he returned home, was never in good health again, dying at an early age.

Everything and everybody's life disrupted, millions killed, millions maimed, homeless, misplaced, uncertain and hopeless over most of the earth before that War was through, and for what? To satisfy the pomp and conceit, arrogance and verbosity of Kaiser Wilhelm and a handful of his conceited hirelings, all seeking world power. A few in the business of war materials such as munitions, etc., made millions in blood money from the miseries of their fellow men. Many, many valuables were transferred to the USA to pay for the implements of war, food and other materials needed to help gain victory. This put that country in the top position in the world for the first time at the expense of the life blood of many other nations. So much for the 'fortunes of war'!

Personally, I had been working day and night for the duration, often not seeing my bed for a week at a time. I would doze on the boiler top to keep warm, jumping down every so often to tend the boiler, depending on the weather, and then, at dawn, get down to work or off to market. Labour was hard to find to help me out and prices for our produce were low. Then, finally, after four years of slavery, on the false Armistice night I was awakened by shouts telling me that the plant was going up in smoke! It was partly burned out – boiler house, sheds, and part of the greenhouse. the fire apparently started as a result of folks setting off fireworks, falsely assuming that the war was over, but no blame could be attached specifically to any one person, so I was the loser.

I found out then that I had not been carrying the proper kind of insurance protection so I could not receive the benefits from the insurance company that I expected. The adjuster came out and informed me that it was too bad but I had been carrying joint insurance and was responsible for the larger part of the claim! This was my first lesson with fire insurance and a hard one it was. Again, it was too late to benefit

25. Ernest in his British Naval uniform. He left the Navy and moved with his family to Canada. In World War I he rejoined the Navy and was "lost at sea" in 1916. Was awarded a medal for bravery posthumously. Two sons, Walter and Harry, both deceased.

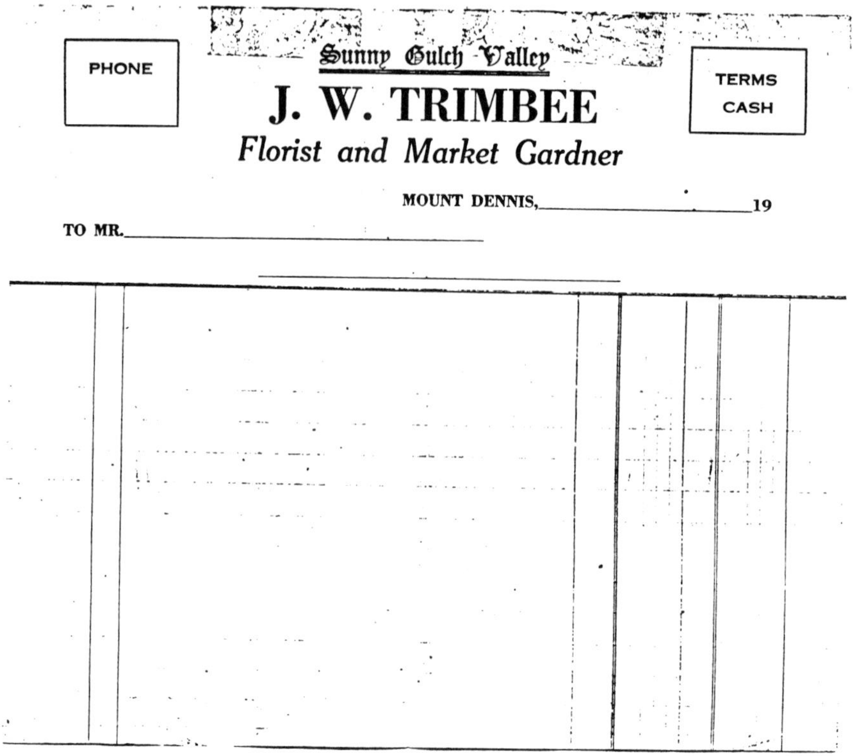

PHONE

Sunny Gulch Valley

J. W. TRIMBEE

Florist and Market Gardner

TERMS

CASH

MOUNT DENNIS,_____·_____19

TO MR._____

from the lesson learned. Along with the loss of the buildings, I had lost the winter crops that were in the greenhouse.

Now, just when I had thanked God that the War's end was near, I was back in a fight for survival. I had lost a brother and brother-in-law in the War and now had two sons, who added to my responsibilities, so could ill afford the latest misfortune. Winter was on us and the crops in the greenhouses were totally lost but we were still alive with a young family and other obligations to consider.

The War was over and prospects ahead should be more promising if we could once more get underway, but like thousands of others we were beginning to question if all this extra effort was really worthwhile. Here I was, after twelve years of hard slogging, going without everything possible, obeying the rules of the game honourably, able to look all men in the eye. A war on the one hand, a fire – the result of folks celebrating the end of it – on the other hand, resulted in us being down and out at the beginning of winter. If mankind in general cannot live

and control such things as war after years of education, remain unable
to reason and settle their differences peacefully, amicably, with faith in
their fellow man, giving all faith in the future, then frustration takes
over hope. Without faith, we have absolutely nothing and under these
conditions what sense is there for us to forge ahead, raise a family, if
it's only to provide cannon fodder in the end; after we have struggled
to raise, feed and educate them for twenty to twenty-five years, just to
be put up for slaughter at the whim of a few in high power? Somehow
such terrifying power should be denied. When an ordinary individual
has no control over these circumstances, is it any wonder that so few
try to improve their positions from birth, and just float with the tide?
Seeing just how fast it is possible to be brought down to the bottom,
through no fault of your own, it makes you wonder if the effort is
worth it. This was the position in which I found myself at the end of
the War, but after much soul searching and reviewing the past, I decided
to make the supreme effort and rebuild, trying once more to get under
way. The insurance company was as fair as possible, but it was far from
covering the loss because of the type of insurance I had bought, thinking
it suitable.

Because of the small settlement I received, I soon found myself in
financial straits. In the past, a few of my acquaintances had told me that,
if I needed a little help at any time, to see them, but now when I did
have the need, it was a different story. I'm afraid that the War had
changed mankind considerably. Before the War, people would go out
of their way to help each other in so many ways but now it was 'what
is there in it for me?' and unfortunately it had remained that sad way.
The only way out now was to take out a second mortgage for 2,000
dollars. Unfortunately for me, the man from whom I sought the mortgage
was much sharper than I. Then, on second thought, maybe I had been
taking such a beating over the past three years that I was not as sharp
as I should have been. Anyway, I had to agree to so many of his ideas
in order to obtain the mortgage that it gave him the whip hand. Now
that the War was over, the government was trying to re-establish the
veterans. I had lost relatives in the fray and felt that I should have gone
as well so I tried to help that was myself by just employing veterans.
Some of them just returning did not yet feel like getting down to hard
work, so for me that was another bad and sad investment, as I put me
further in the red. However, I felt that it was the least I could do and
I don't regret it. But before many months I was again short of capital.
Notes and accounts that were owing me, from before the War even,
were impossible to collect, so I decided to close the plant for the winter

and obtain outside employment for that time. With a young family to support, I had no other choice.

I decided that I should open up again in the Spring and go on from there but my Second Mortgage Master changed my plans. While busy getting underway in the Spring, I received a special letter in early May from his solicitor informing me that his client had bought the first mortgage, which was now due, and that the land and business would be put up for auction in a few days, without any other notice. Disaster had struck again and me with a small family and another child expected the following month, no money in the bank, and living on the site. Unbelievably, I was back where I had started out fifteen years ago. I had worked day and night, cut out all pleasure, wasted no money, played the game of life honestly and now must suffer for another man's greed, getting no further chance at my business. This man would not show any compassion for me in my unfortunate position, giving me a lift when so desperately needed. Here it was Spring, with all its promises, but out life's foundation had been taken from me.

Again, it meant serious examination of our position and problems as now, with a family, I had more obligations than ever before. I had no intention of going into bankrupcy for, other than the property, I had no outside debts. Personally, I still wanted to fight it through for the sake of my young sons, as I was still a comparatively young man with a fair hold on life. I had surmounted great odds before, but this time was different. The welfare of a young family was at stake so that a new approach was needed. Here I was having to decide on one more obstacle in life's path so many family conferences were held. My good wife stated that, due to her close confinement date, she would not stay on the premises to be ordered out, which was quite understandable. She also stated that her view was that, if a man could not get to the top, after seeing and knowing all that I had endured, then life was not worth the struggle and the sons, when old enough, would have to do as we had done – find their own way. Then I gave the matter much thought on my own. When I had taken on the job of rebuilding on our present location, I knew that it would be a struggle, yet I still had faith in my fellow men; but now I found that the man from whom I needed help showed me less consideration than would be shown a dog. He had put a rope around my neck in preparation for the hanging, with no opportunity for adjustment. This was Spring of 1920, and I was thirty-five years of age.

After much deliberation, I finally came to the decision that, even if adjustments were made for me to carry on, it would mean at least another five years of slavery for all, and after fifteen years of that and now knowing a little more of life's way, was it worth it all? In my mind I knew that the man holding the mortgage thought himself superior to me so I would give him the opportunity to prove this. I knew that, in the move he proposed to take, he would burn his fingers badly as I was sure that he would be unable to find anyone who would be able to run the business. In his hands he held not only the mortgage but a hot poker along with it. I intended to make a new start with less responsibility.

With all this in mind, I called up his solicitor and made an appointment for discussion. After acknowledging receipt of his letter, I asked him whether, if I vacated the property and left everything as it was, I would be liable in any other way regarding the matter. He said not, whereupon I told him to tell his client he could take it and go plump straight to Hell with it, and then walked out. The auction was held as advertised but not one bid was offered. He tried different ways to run it and get others to run it for him, but with no success. At last it was dismantled and sold piece by piece. Before finally disposed of it, he had learned a lesson in life, too. Had he been willing to negotiate with me, giving me a chance to rebuild the business, he would have eventually received his money without all the headaches he had to endure himself.

Now, having been stripped bare, I had to find a new home and a new position to support my family. By this time I was well known around the City by horticultural groups, and soon found employment as superintendent of a first-class golf course. This was the first time they had made such an appointment, so they also formed a two-man committee to oversee and supervise me. Thus, I was no longer a free agent but under a certain amount of supervision. I was not worried by this, as I knew my work and believed that time would prove my worth and bring confidence, as we were all obligated to each other and fear would be replaced by faith. As yet, still feeling the impact of the recent upheaval, I worked quietly, not wishing to voice too many opinions.

A few months later, a friend of long standing dropped in to see how things were going for me there. I told him fine and that I was just going along quietly. 'That's the trouble, Jimmy,' he replied, 'you are going too damn quietly!'

'Thanks, Fred,' I answered, for then he had given me a new line of thought which turned a humdrum job into a respected position, as from then on I gradually opened up. I realised that, with my knowledge, I could be a leader and not the led and this put me back into a better frame of mind, with my outlook on life taking on a new meaning. The rich gentlemen members of the club sure had much more money than I but

26. James, Jean and children, James Jr, William and Eileen, 1923.

27. *Postcard to James from his mother living in California, showing her continued interest in flowers.*

were often glad to have me around for advice, and we were good friends. By living carefully, we were able to live comfortably and look forward with hope to the future once more. My young family was growing up and, as the Club wished me to live near the golf course, they renovated an old cottage for us to live in, which had the Humber River bordering the bottom of the garden. To us, it seemed a good home with lots of room in which to raise a family. It was on a good road and there was a school within walking distance. The family had grown to four children now, with the birth of Jean, another daughter, in that home. Circumstances had improved for us and looked even more promising. With a five-year contract with the Club, my employment was secure. Yes, Lambton Golf Club offered contentment at last.

One of my superiors at the Club had handed over his dahlia stock to me and I began exhibiting at the Canadian National Exhibition. Once more adversity struck! One of my overseers, a Mr Wallace, was intensely interested in the horticultural world and, working together, we had formed quite an attachment one to the other, and were planning maybe a business future together. We had reached the point of absolute trust in each other, not always easily acquired between men but, once formed, invaluable. One day the shocking news came that he had broken his neck in a fall from a tree. This was right at a time when I was busy preparing for him a bed in which he would grow show peonies. He lingered for a few days before the end came. Attachments such as this take a long time to overcome, for he was a man well worth knowing, and my friendship with him has never been forgotten.

Before I had recovered from the loss of my great friend, adversity plagued us yet again, this time in my own family. Living on the banks of the Humber River, the children were in the habit of playing around in the water in the Summertime. The river at our location was only about fifteen inches to two feet deep, just a fine depth for small children, and in appearance looked quite clear. They spent a lot of time playing around in the water, having a lot of fun enjoying themselves. Then the elder girl Eileen, four years old at the time, developed ear trouble, the source of which was finally traced to polluted water in the river; and this was back in 1924. Here was a little girl who would have hearing trouble for the rest of her life and I wonder how many others are suffering similar trouble for the same source. There I was, passing through life admiring all God's creations, appreciating all Nature, still trying to have faith in my fellow man. Many times I had taken a drink of water from that river, never suspecting that farther up the river someone was using this steam as a sewer and, on investigation, I learned that the tributary, Black Creek, was as bad. This was proved one morning, when we saw all the little Chub floating on their backs, showing the pollution's results. I received orders to find the source of the pollution and did so, but at that time those responsible were considered too mighty to fight, so nothing was done. Had the authorities remedied this cause, then, it would have saved untold misfortunes.

At that time, when the ice went out from the river, our basement was flooded for probably two weeks or more. Those were long winters with lots of snow and thick ice formed on the river. The chunks of ice came up close enough to push the pump sideways and fill the well with river water. For the welfare of the children, because of the spring run-off, the Doctor advised us to move to higher ground. Through working long hours and careful manipulation with our money, we had managed to save some, which we used as a down payment on an old house we found after a long search in a higher location up in Lambton Mills. We did some repairs on this house and then it was quite comfortable, though still missing some of the better conveniences which we hoped to install in due time.

Again we were hopeful for the future but, alas, Old Man Adversity had not yet finished with us. We had only been living in the house for a few months when, upon returning home from work one evening, I found the good wife lying on the couch. She had suffered the misfortune of falling down the stairs, when taking the youngest child up for an afternoon nap. Somehow, upon reaching the top of the staircase, she had lost her balance and tumbled down to the bottom. This was a long, hard fall and affected her greatly. First it was the hospital for many weeks, then extra help in the house for another six months, followed by further treatments and finally an operation. Times were tough again for the family with the mental and financial strain. The outlay was more than the income, so I was working night and day to keep a balance and the going was hard with the children still so young, and needing care. Gradually my wife recovered to some extent and we struggled to catch up again. I was now doing my daily work at the golf course and running a little independent dahlia business on the side. We did quite well at the Canadian National Exhibition, which we used as a showplace to take orders. I also did extra landscape work on my own time for some of the Club members, Spring and Fall. During this period I created a new variety of dahlia which was quite a success on the market. I named it the 'Jean Trimbee', after my younger daughter. But now, as the time went by, all this extra work finally caught up with my health. I was laid low with a bad case of inflammatory rheumatism in the Spring and, when suffering from this, you are well aware of the illness. I struggled to accomplish my work until

28. *Jean with the "Jean Trimbee Dahlia", 1929.*

I could carry on no longer. Two doctors attended me for three or four weeks, with no easing up of the illness.

Finally, one Saturday morning my wife came into the bedroom to inform me that two doctors were coming at four o'clock in the afternoon that day to take out my teeth and my tonsils, thinking them as perhaps one source of my illness. I told her that I would not allow it as it was all I could do to bear that present suffering. I told her that when Dr Scott, my own physician, saw me, there would be a difference of opinion as I had great faith in that gentleman. She wondered how I could argue with the specialists's diagnosis and we awaited the doctors' arrival. When they came, Dr Scott looked down at me, then turned to the other doctor and said, 'Herman, we can't touch this chap, he has more than he can handle now.' He then questioned as to what treatment I had been given and if he had tried some certain drug. Receiving a negative reply, Dr Scott made out a prescription immediately and ordered it sent for right away. The instructions were for me to take it every two hours until it made me vomit. Following his orders, I found that every dose became more repulsive to take but by midnight I began to feel an improvement in my condition and, by daylight, I felt better than I had for weeks. I had not vomited but the medicine had literally pushed the poison through my body; the bedroom smelled evil but I was a new man. Dr Scott's prescription had done more for me in eighteen hours than the other two doctors had done in five weeks. That was a good lesson in obtaining more than one person's opinion in such matters. I have never forgotten Dr Scott for that, and for all he did for me and mine over the next few years. The following week, I had my tonsils removed and was instructed to have my teeth attended to when I felt stronger, which I did. Before long, I was back in the thick of things as in those days I was always overloaded with work but, with good health back again, I enjoyed it.

29. (30 & 31) Some of Father's CNE displays.

30.

31. Another CNE display.

The children were growing quickly but my wife, Jean, often had her bad turns, which kept us from becoming exuberant so that we had to live rather quietly. Our different interests kept us all very busy, with little time for any regrets or self-pity. The years rolled by and, as one human being passing through life, this was one of the better periods of my journey on this earth. I now had the strength once again, the ability to acknowledge my love of life, and the gift to observe and appreciate the glories and beauty of Creation. I thanked God daily for the privilege of allowing me to pass through but, alas, as He opened my eyes to wonders, He also opened my eyes to the ways in which mankind was using the resources placed here on earth for our benefit.

I was appalled when I realised what was happening to these resources, as in the beginning God had created and built up the Earth in such a simple way that nothing would be lost but forever it would grow, die and decay to replace and replenish all life for all time. It could not overgrow and smother all life because he had created the balance – so much growing, so much decaying, and to take care of this wonderful balance, He also created the by-product of bacteria. This army, when required, can increase to the desired strength for any operation, large or small, so that today there is no more in the world than there was thousands of years ago. This replenishment may be in different locations all the time to what it was then but still prevalent. Today, though, instead of following the Creator's plan and passing the waste back to the land as our Creator intended, we build incinerators that cost the tax payers millions of hard-earned dollars which pollute the sweet air given us in the beginning of time. I also find all of our beautiful streams, rivers and lakes are being turned into open sewers from one end of the land to the other. We dump our sewage back into our drinking water reservoirs after so-called treatments. Can you imagine just for a moment how appalling and repugnant this is to me, when I know that those three elements are the mainstay of life itself? How, after all these years of higher education, have we allowed these things to happen? With

LAMBTON MILLS DAHLIA GARDENS

GOLD MEDAL DAHLIAS

4214 Dundas St., West   Lambton Mills, Ont.

Dear Sir:—

   We have on file under your name, order for Dahlias

taken at..192...., amounting to $ ....

   The above order is now in perfect condition to be
shipped to you. Would you prefer to forward a Cheque, P.O.
or M.O. if convenient, or if you wish we will send same C.O.D.
through the mail. (If sent C.O.D. an additional 15¢ will be
added to cover this charge).

   Again wishing you a very successful year with your
garden.

        Yours very truly,
         J. W. Trimbee.

P.S. If we do not have a reply to this letter we will send
same C.O.D. and same will arrive in good time for planting.

Our Annual Offer

   The specials listed below are four gorgeous Dahlias and we ensure you that
this is the greatest offer yet made, and would advise all to take advantage of this
wonderful offer. Note the Price, (Limited Number). Orders for this Special Offer will
be filled in rotation. Order at once.

AMBASSSADOR ELINORE VANDEVEER TRENTONIAN YELLOW JEWEL

This Collection $3.00.

Montbretias — Owing to an oversight these were omitted from
our Catalog of 1929 issue, so we take the opportunity of bringing this wonderful Flower to your notice. The culture of this
flower is so simple and should be more fully grown as it is one
of the best flowers for decorative purposes coming in all the
Autumn shades of Salmon — Reds— and Orange—4 choice varieties
to choose from — caused great admiration at C.N.E.—Bulbs like
all Gladioli $3.00 per 100.

LAMBTON MILLS
DAHLIA GARDENS

Dahlias   Iris

Gladioli   Trollius

1926

JAMES W. TRIMBEE

4214 Dundas Street W.   Lambton Mills, Ont.

all the different inventions now known to man, electricity and the internal combustion engine, for example, many undertakings are possible, so why have we used our God-given elements, as a drunken sailor, without thought for the future of mankind? This all saddens me and I vow, in whatever time I have left in my life, to persuade those in power to correct these mistakes before destruction overtakes us. Each one of us should make our own individual efforts on this behalf.

The family was growing up and, as part of life, the grocer, the butcher, the doctor, taxes, and many other things had to be provided for as we went along life's way, so that our cup was rather full. The year was 1929.

32. The Family, 1928.

BOOK II

Sadly, my Father died before completing his life story, and unfortunately because the rest of his life was far from uneventful. That is what influenced my decision to finish his story, bringing an appropriate conclusion to his eighty-seven years of fulfilment. It is impossible to write of his thoughts as he did himself, but time, places and events are recorded. I am his youngest child, Jean, and with knowledge gleaned from the family, my personal memories and some research the story continues on from 1929, where it stopped in Book I.

CHAPTER I

During the year of 1929 Father was employed at the Lambton Golf Club. One of the members offered him a job as Superintendent of the large estate he owned, called Glenalton, Ridley Park, in the Armour Heights area just outside the northern limits of Toronto. The offer was made by Albert Leroy Ellsworth, generally known in the business world as A. L. Ellsworth, a self-made millionaire who had accumulated his great wealth through financial wizardry. He had the foresight, in earlier days, to see the future of the automobile and its related products and formed the British-American Oil Company, commonly called BA Oil, which was sold many years later in 1968 to the Gulf Oil Company.

With the great success of this company, further fields were opened to him and he formed or acquired other companies, including British-American Oil Refineries Ltd., Toronto, British-American Oil Producing Company, Tulsa, Oklahoma, The Toronto Pipe Line, The Toronto Iron Works Ltd., Fess Oil Burners, Clear Vision Pump Company, Service Station Equipment Company and United Utilities and Service Corporation. He held directorships in such companies as Amulet Mines Ltd., Noranda Mines Ltd., Bank or Nova Scotia, Securities Holding Corporation, Canandian Copper Refineries Ltd., and Charted Trust and Executor Company. Also he was a Freemason and belonged to many clubs – York, National, Empire, Canadian, Granite, Carlton, Lambton Golf, Rosedale Golf, Ontario Jockey, Toronto Skating, Eglinton Hunt and Canadian (New York).[1]

There is the outline of the financially and socially powerful man who offered Father the position and at a fairly good salary for those days, as shown in the following letter outlining his duties and obligations.

[1] *The Canadian Who's Who*, Vol. II. Published in Toronto, Murray Printing Co., 1936.

ALBERT L. ELLSWORTH
ROYAL BANK BUILDING
TORONTO CANADA

January Third, 1930
Mr. J. W. Trimbee.

Dear Mr. Trimbee:-

This will confirm the terms of your employment and your services thereunder, effective December 14th, 1929.

Salary was to be Two Hundred and Eight Dollars and Thirty-three Cents ($208.33) per month, payable half-monthly, unless you prefer otherwise; I to furnish you with living quarters; the heating of the house, the supplying of water to be at my expense; you to pay for electricity used for the purposes of cooking and lighting. Since current consumption at the two cottages, the apartment above the garage, the garage and the stable, is registered on one meter I propose that the charge for current be divided monthly into five parts, you, on account of your larger family, paying two parts, Jamieson one part, Sketchley one part, and the garage and the stable one part. If this is satisfactory I shall have my Secretary compute the proportionate charge monthly and shall advise each interested party.

Your duties will be –

The general supervision of my property;

Full charge of all the services thereon outside of the house itself.

This means, somewhat in detail, that you will be responsible for the employment and discharge of all workers in the greenhouses and on the grounds. I shall personally employ the Chauffeur, the Groom, and the Houseman, but it will be your duty to supervise the work of the first two and of the Houseman during such time as the household may not have use for him. The supervision of the Chauffeur will consist of your having regard to his time of starting work, of the cleanliness of the cars, and the tidiness of the garage. Of course, his driving orders will come from the household. The same supervision will apply to the Groom and stables.

With regard to material of any kind required on the premises, I have supplied order forms. It is my desire that when I am present that I sign all orders and I shall be available for this purpose at the breakfast hour each morning. In case of emergency in my absence these order forms may be signed by you as Head Gardner or Superintendent. Should it happen that you can purchase various things more cheaply than I can, please, as we have agreed, order this material in your name, submitting the bill to me and I shall make payment to you therefor. I desire, however, in the event of you placing orders in your own name, that you enter in the order book your own name as the seller, this that I may have a record of all orders. The order book is in triplicate, one copy for the seller, one for my personal files, and one to remain in the order book for your own information and for the purpose of checking the goods when received. I shall instruct Miss Waghorne to check invoices with the copy of order in my personal files, then to give the invoice to you that you may approve for goods received. The invoice should then be returned to Miss Waghorne for payment.

I have also the following suggestions to make –

I has been our practice to have the Houseman assist the Chauffeur each morning in washing, polishing, and other preparation of the cars. Such assistance should not be required by the Chauffeur during the good weather but should be furnished when, in your opinion, and that of the Chauffeur, it is necessary.

You will delegate the Houseman, the Chauffeur, or some other employee, to keep the garage court free of snow in the Winter weather and swept clean during other periods.

As you have been informed, it is necessary to drive the maids to and from the stop, and this work should be divided between the men on the premises, youself, the Chauffeur and the Houseman (and the Second Gardener, should the one we will later obtain, live on the premises).

With reference to the Second Gardener, provided we do not keep Saunders, should the Houseman and his wife occupy the premises above the garage, then it would be preferable to obtain a single Gardener as Second man and he board with either the Chauffeur or the Houseman. Such an arrangement would give the services of a fourth man for the purposes of taking his turn in driving the maids and for any other service, such as watering, etc., which might be required of him after hours.

The Houseman will spend a part of his time in the house, generally only until 12 o'clock each day, after which he will be subject to your disposition. At the present time the Houseman takes care of the dogs. I recommend that this practice be continued and that as soon as possible during the cold weather the three dogs be quartered in the kennel East of the potting shed.

Please report to me each morning during my breakfast hour that I may discuss with you and you with me any matters that may occur to either of us and also for the purpose of my signing orders for any material that you may require.

Yours very truly,
A LE/LM.

Mr Ellsworth and his wife were parents of four children – Eric, Betty, Elaine and Marion, all attractive and involved in the kind of life that wealth affords. Those were the days of 'high society' and the Ellsworths lived it to the full, which meant much entertaining with extensive use of the house and gardens. Glenalton surely was a grand showplace for all the various social events held there.

There would be a considerable amount of work and planning involved for Father in new layouts for gardens and maintaining those present, encompassing his knowledge in growing the many flowers that would be needed for show and entertaining. Cut-flower arrangements were required for the house every day. These requisites, plus the supervision of the outside staff as listed in the letter of employment, comprised a challenge to Father and, with a growing family of his own, the extra money in wages could be well put to use. Therefore, in December 1929, we had made the move to Glenalton, after Father had disposed of his dahlia business.

Many years later, this grand estate would be sold by Mr Ellsworth to the Royal Canadian Air Force, to be established as a Staff College. I quote in part from the *History of the College*, with a few comments of my own in brackets.

Sometime before 1837, Lot 11 came into the hands of John Armour. With the exception of the east quarter of the lot, the part which is down in the Don Valley and fronts on Yonge Street, which was sold about the middle of the century to the Hogg Brothers [the area is still know as Hogg's Hollow], the property remained in the hands of the Armour family. It was this family which gave its name to the Armour Heights district.

The promoter who started the chain of events which changed the farmland of the Armours and their neighbours into the fine residential area it is to-day was Colonel F. B. Robins, honourary colonel of the Toronto Scottish Regiment, a flamboyant figure who became a legend in his time. It was to be his misfortune that he was twenty-five years ahead of his time and few of the projects he planned were realized while he was still in the position to profit from them. One thing he did accomplish during the period when he was a power in real estate circles in Toronto was to build the country estate which he called Strathrobyn and which one day was to be the Officers' Mess of the Canadian Forces College.

Strathrobyn was built in 1914, a fine stone house of eighteen bedrooms which was set in beautifully landscaped grounds. The previous year a plan for the subdivision of the Armour Heights area had been filed by a company called City Estates of Canada whose president was listed as Henry M. Pellatt. [This was the man who later became Sir Henry Pellatt, the builder of Casa Loma where Father obtained his first employment upon his arrival in Canada, as told earlier.]

The outbreak of World War I kept the planned development from being realized and postponed the test of whether people were willing to buy lots six miles north of the settled part of Toronto.

Early in 1917, when it had become apparent that power in the air was going to be an increasingly important part of the battle, The Royal Flying corps established in Canada a World War I version of the Commonwealth Training Scheme. A headquarters was set up in Toronto, six major airfields were built and one of those airfields built was at Armour Heights on land made available by Colonel Robins, and which was the western portion of old Lot 11 and part of Lot 12.

Early in 1918, a 'School of Special Flying' was opened at Armour Heights and the forerunner of to-day's Central Flying School had a brief summer of glory. A number of men who later became prominent in Canadian aviation took instructors courses here, including a former Chief of the Air Staff, Air Marshal Curtis.

The Officers' Mess for the old Armour Heights airfield was somewhere along the edge of the ravine towards Colonel Robins' big house and he extended his hospitality to these men, including many famous personalities. It is said that a dance was held at Strathrobyn for the Prince of Wales and another frequent visitor was Vernon Castle, the famous dancer who served with the R.C.A.F. before his untimely death in a flying accident in Texas. One of the most noted guests was Earl Haig, a leading military figure in World War I and for whom North York's first high school was named in 1930. [This is the high school my brother Jim, sister Eileen and I attended while living at Glenalton.]

After the War Colonel Robins embarked on another plan for the development of the Armour Heights area. Time, however, was still not ripe for the development of the area and Strathrobyn continued to sit in rather lonely splendour amidst pasture and a few houseless boulevards.

In 1926, Strathrobyn was sold to Mr A. L. Ellsworth, of BA Oil for $175,000. Mr Ellsworth also bought land from Colonel Robins to the west of the main property and the last of colonel Robins' interests in the area was closed out. Mr Ellsworth renamed the property Glenalton and used it as his residence until shortly before the R.C.A.F. rented it from him in 1942 for a War Staff College.

He was reputed to have spent $100,000 in improvements on the building and grounds. In the fall of 1945 the government bought Glenalton to be the permanent home of the R.C.A.F. Staff College from Mr Ellsworth for $103,500.

In 1964 unification and integration of the Armed Forces became law and in 1966 the College was re-designated Candian Forces College.[1] [This is continuing in operation as such today.]

I do not know whether Father was completely aware of the history of Glenalton; the family was not until a short time ago when, into research

---

[1] Permission for use granted by Dr W. T Traynor, Education Adviser to the Commandant, Canadian Forces Staff College.

for this story, I had the opportunity to visit the estate once again, bringing back many memories. It was then that I was given the article, part of which has been quoted. With the history of the estate outlined, I shall return to our days spent there.

The layout and mansion architecture of Glenalton reminded Father of some of the large land holdings on which he had worked in England. It was of course on a smaller scale, but still of a considerable size for like estates around Toronto. There was an admirable Tudor-style home said to contain forty-four rooms, including eighteen bedrooms and nine bathrooms, with a great hall as a core, set in twenty-two and a half landscaped acres surrounded by a high wrought-iron fence with gates at three entrances. Inside the west gate was a house called the 'West Cottage', not occupied during our stay there.

Attached to the west side of the mansion was the conservatory, leading off from the billiard room, and this was a showplace for exotic plants. The conservatory also contained a small waterfall dropping into a pool, on which water lilies floated. A series of switches on the wall controlled the waterfall and coloured lights, which turned the conservatory at night into a picturesque setting for the lovely flowers and plants. Leading out from there were the greenhouses with the potting shed at the back. On the east side of the house, there was a large stone terrace with a cement balustrade all around it. Steps from this led down on to the formal garden in which Father grew lovely, rare flowers. At the end of this there was a raised arbour, running across the width of the garden, which was covered with trailing foliage. Below the steps on the far side of the arbour lay the rose garden, a magnificent showplace for many, many varieties. In the summer it was a scented sight to behold.

Inside the east gate was a square-shaped enclosure comprising two semi-detached, three-bedroom homes – one of which we occupied – that formed the west side of the square; the stables were on the east side and both joined at the ends by the long garage on the south. This garage held five or six cars and had an apartment over it, topped off by a huge clock tower that could be seen from quite a distance. The north side of the square was walled with a gate in the middle, usually kept open. This was all around a cement courtyard. Backing on to the garage for the full length was an unused chicken coop. This was divided into small rooms which Father used for storage but there was always available space in which I could play 'house'. Under the garage was a full cellar, which could also be entered from our basement. This cellar held a huge furnace, and I believe this was one of the first oil burners installed, influenced by the fact that Mr Ellsworth owned Fess Oil Burners and BA Oil companies.

33. Canadian Forces Command and Staff College. (Photo courtesy of Dr W. T. Traynor, Education Adviser to the Commandant.)

Behind all this was the kitchen garden where Father grew enough vegetables to supply all living on the estate. This was before the days of freezers, so there was also a root cellar in which to keep turnips and like vegetables for use in the winter.

The back of the stables and tack room, where the riding supplies were kept, led out to the riding ring. I spent many a time watching the groom train the horses and the Ellsworth children practise their riding. The horses were called 'Watch Me', 'Follow Me' and other similar names. These horses and riders participated in the big horse shows, such as those held at the Canadian National Exhibition and the Royal Winter Fair.

Father had become quite well known for his ability with flowers and was often a judge at flower shows such as those held at the 'Ex' and the 'Royal'. So, with the use of his passes to those places, we often had the opportunity to watch the Ellsworths compete in the horse shows there. Sometimes extra passes were given to Father by Mr Ellsworth and they were put to full use by the family.

All these things intertwined into a fairyland for one my age, as I was only five years old when we moved there. From all the descriptions, one can see that Father had taken on quite a responsibility to keep things running smoothly on such a large scale.

The staff for the 'Big House', as we termed the mansion, was large, to fulfil all the needs for the upkeep and high-scale entertaining. There were upstairs maids, downstairs maids, kitchen maid, chef, butler, house-man, laundress, French governess, and extras, when needed, all supervised by a housekeeper. As Father mentions in his story, life has a queer way of intertwining one with another, as will be shown later in this story.

Father had a good group of men working for him, each with his specific duties and, under his supervision, all worked in harmony. Extra men were employed in the summer because of the extensive lawn cutting required but again Mr Ellsworth was ahead of the game and Glenalton's lawns were cut by some of the first gas-powered lawn motors.

My older brother, Bill, had finished school and was working, his transportation a walk away, while the car provided took us pupils to school, and from, if necessary, in bad weather. There were no other children around with whom to form friendships, though we did have chums we enjoyed at school. Soon, though, the second gardener, Ernie Trewin, with his wife and daughter, Marion, moved into the house beside ours. Then I had a playmate and my Mother had a companion, who became a close friend. Marion and I spent many a happy time with our dolls, playing 'house' together in the old chicken coop.

They were busy days for my Father but he was accustomed to hard work, having started at the age of twelve. This job was no exception and he gained great satisfaction from seeing all the new floral gardens take shape and the greenhouses full of beautiful flowers.

One highlight of the summer of 1932 was a visit by my Father's mother, his three sisters and their families, who drove up all the way from California where they lived. From their stories, it had been quite a trip as one can imagine, remembering the old models of cars used then. They came in two cars and took turns staying with us, and Father's brothers, who lived in Toronto. As Father tells in his story, he had always enjoyed a very close relationship with his dear Mother, relishing every moment spent with her. As he probably knew in his mind, it would be his last visit with her. This came true, for she died later that year, on 7 November. Grandma was eighty when she made that trip, which meant crossing mountains and desert to see her 'boys' once again. She had always loved flowers, and so took great delight in viewing all the floral spendours of Glenalton, proudly shown her by her son. There were many family get-togethers while the

relatives were here and much reminiscing about the 'old' days back in
Upham, where the family grew up. Sad was the day of their departure
for California.

1932 was a big year for Father in his work at Glenalton. The Ellsworths
announced the engagement of their eldest daughter, Betty, with the
wedding date set for 17 September. The estate was to be put to full use,
with the wedding ceremony in the arbour which ran between the formal
and rose gardens. The reception would also be held on the grounds of
the estate. This entailed much planning for Father, in order to have the
flower beds at the height of their seasonal glory with flowers whose colours
would co-ordinate with the bridal party's colours.

To best describe the grandeur of the occasion, I quote in part from
the write-up of the wedding which appeared on the social page of one
of the newspapers that day.

The gardens of 'Glenalton', the beautiful estate of Mr and Mrs Albert L.
Ellsworth, were brilliant with autumnal glory on Saturday, the seventeenth
day of September, when, at half-past three, the marriage of Mr and Mrs
Ellsworth's daughter, Betty, to Mr J. Beverley Balmer, son of Mr and Mrs
J. L. Balmer, was solemnized.

The wedding ceremony took place in the formal garden with its beautiful
flower beds, planted for the occasion with predominating shades of pink
and blue. Myriads of pale pink roses with misty blue ageratum formed a
floral cascade, the beautiful background for the wedding service, while tall
silvery urns of roses and ageratum appeared at intervals on either side.

From the moment when the clear boy-voices of St Paul's Church
choristers floated through the gardens, singing 'The Voice That Breathed
O'er Eden' to the final flurry of farewells, the wedding was a fairy-like
pageant. Surely the grounds must have been landscaped with just such an
occasion in mind.

The lovely pageant began when down the winding path came the singing
white-robed choristers. As they took up their position by the floral bower,
the strains of the 'Lohengrin' wedding march was heard from behind
flowers and shrubbery where an orchestra, under the direction of Mr J.
Stanley St. John, was concealed. As the music filled the air the wedding
procession, advancing from the great hall, passed slowly across the terrace
to the formal garden, down blue-carpeted paths, around the fountain to
the bridal bower banked with blue and pink blossoms, colours which
repeated those of the glorious flower beds planted with ageratum and
slender stalks of pink gladioli.

The blue and pink of this formal garden sounded the entrancing notes
of colour to which the whole perfect bridal picture was tuned. The eight
bridesmaids who followed the ushers down the path were as lovely in gowns
of chiffon in graduated shades of delphinium blue, a perfect complement

of colour to the picture that followed as the bride appeared with her father. The bride was gowned in shell pink peau d'ange lace, an exquisite dress by Norman Hartnell of London.

A detailed description of all the gowns was given followed by:

After the Ceremony, while the choristers sang the wedding anthem, 'O Perfect Love', the bride and groom with their attendants descended to the terraced rose garden for the formality of signing the register, where they were joined by Mr and Mrs Ellsworth and Mr and Mrs Balmer. Then at the first notes of the Mendelssohn Wedding March, they returned to pass down the aisles of assembled guests, and proceeded to the broad eastern lawn, where the wedding reception was held. There, with multi-coloured flower beds as a setting, the bridal party received the guests.

The wedding breakfast was served in a marquee on the upper lawn, where large bowls of brilliant zinias adorned the tables. The bride's table on the stone terrace was the object of much admiration, so striking was the beauty of the floral arrangement, consisting of lovely lalique bowls of pink roses, blue delphinium and pink larkspur. To add to the picture, the bridesmaids placed their flowers along the front of the table.

After the bride and groom departed from 'Glenalton', the younger set remained to dance under the large marquee to the lilting strains of the large dance orchestra, while others strolled through the glorious gardens.[1]

The description of the flowers and gardens certainly received their deserved prominence in the above article. Obviously, this write-up was prepared ahead of time because, during the morning when Father and his crew of helpers were ferverishly working with hundreds of pink roses and other flowers to decorate the gardens where the wedding was to take place, rain began to fall! Immediately, alternate plans were activated. We heard that Bell Telephone operators were instructed to phone all 600 guests informing them that the wedding was moved to St Pauls's Anglican Church on Bloor Street. Father and the crew removed the flowers already in place, packed them and the rest not yet placed, and swiftly headed for the church to decorate it instead. Time was of the essence as the wedding was scheduld for three-thirty and, with literally seconds to spare, the last flower was set in place as the first guests arrived at the church. The men had started at the back of the church, worked their way up to the altar from where they had to move quickly into an adjoining room to escape detection. They made their exit through a side door to return to Glenalton for further duties.

[1] Reprinted by permission of *The Toronto Star Syndicate.*

My Mother, sister and I attended the wedding, which went well in its splendid setting. Upon returning home, we watched from our windows as the guests' cars poured into the estate for the reception. As I remember, the gates were closed and only those showing invitations were admitted. The workers, including my brother Bill, parked cars in the surrounding area and the party went on long after my bedtime.

Because of the absence of freezers in those days, we were the happy recipients the next day of some of the left-over delicacies. I shall never forget one huge treat in the form of a flower basket made entirely of shortbread decorated with spun sugar in many colours.

Father enjoyed much pleasure and satisfaction from all the attention and compliments given the landscaping, for which he was fully responsible. His months of hard work and planning had a great climax and, though it had rained for the wedding, the weather cleared later, enabling the guests to view the results of his labours.

One year, the 'Hunt' was held nearby, and riders assembled at Glenalton, going out from there to the surrounding fields to 'chase the fox'. I do clearly recall looking out our back door into the courtyard, which seemed to be filled with barking hounds jumping around waiting for the Hunt to begin. Surely a sight not everyone is able to see in a lifetime! Another memory that remains from Father's tenure at Glenalton.

The fields around the estate offered diversion. We would hunt for wild strawberries and, under Father's close supervision, mushrooms, which Mother put to good use at the dinner table. We walked across these same fields going to and from school, taking time out for a slide down a haystack in early Fall or to watch the cricketers in their white outfits competing at the nearby Toronto Cricket Club. The fields have been replaced by residential areas, though the Cricket Club remains.

Mother had bouts of ill health while we lived at Glenalton and I remember one period when I went over daily to the kitchen of the 'big house' to bring home the special food that the Chef had been instructed to prepare for her. More than once, as I walked across the grounds to the back door and home again with my basket of food, I felt like 'Little Red Riding Hood'!

At this time, Father became an Executive, and later President, of the Gardeners and Florists Association of Ontario, and we enjoyed some social life from that connection. There were picnics in the summer and concerts in the winter, in which the whole family could partake. Also, there were social evenings for my parents, as well as the many meetings Father attended. He continued his active life in judging different flower shows and garden competitions, putting his floral knowledge to full use.

Sunday was his day off work and he was given one week's holiday a year which, if possible, was spent on a family fishing trip. Father did love his fishing and always kept those trips jocular. I remember hearing of one such trip, when the men went away on their own: Father, my brothers and uncles. On their last day out, they were left with only angel cake and green onions to eat but, according to reports, Father convinced them they were having a 'banquet' and, with songs added for entertainment, no-one complained as hilarity took over.

Father continued to work as hard as ever running the estate to keep it in top form – never a lawn showed need of cutting, never a hedge showed need of trimming, nor did the flowers ever lack attention.

34. Glenalton, 1932

35. Rose Garden.

36. The Tea-House.

37. Father in conservatory.

38. The Conservatory Pool.

The Ellsworths extended their lifestyle in purchasing a summer home, Robinson Crusoe Island, in Lake Muskoka. There was a large house, though not nearly as big as the one at Glenalton. Close by the island, in fact nearly adjoining it, was another small one called 'Friday', also part of the property bought by Mr Ellsworth. This increased Father's workload, as he went up every spring with some of his helpers to plant and clean up the grounds to make this into a summer showplace. A local man was hired to maintain the grounds during the Summer and then, in the Fall, Father would go up again with his crew to close the place up for the Winter. This entailed removing the annual plants, bedding the grounds against the cold weather ahead, as well as closing up the house and putting up the boats.

One Fall, he had an experience which bothered him for quite a while. The steamer which ran supplies around the lake was caught in a violent storm, which came up suddenly. Word came around later for all to go out in the boats for 'search and rescue'. Father was the one to find the drowned Captain and he and his companions hauled the body into their boat for removal to shore. That was one of Muskoka's Fall storms that had horrendous aftermaths. A minister who had been aboard was also drowned, trapped in his cabin.

There were many happy times for us while living at Glenalton: Christmas and New Year being two of them. It was the ritual to exchange visits on these days with my Mother's sister and family, one year Christmas at our home and New Year's at my Aunt and Uncle's, the Flacks. The other sister, Aunt Cathie and her husband, Uncle Sam, who had no children, would join us. We always looked forward to these gatherings as the families enjoyed each other's company and music played a big part of the visits. Part of the ritual was that, after enjoying a big turkey dinner, the men washed up the dishes. I was always amazed that Father could put his hands in extremely hot water without feeling pain, owing to the fact that his type of work had toughened up the skin on the hands.

39. *Robinson Crusoe Island, Muskoka.*

40. *Father at wheel of boat in Muskoka.*

After the cleaning up was finished, our family concerts would begin. Brother Jim was taking violin lessons and Eileen piano lessons, so each had to contribute to the evening's entertainment, usually much against their wishes — especially Jim, who was very shy. Brother Bill gave more freely of his talent as a singer of popular songs. Mother had a lovely singing voice and had sung in different choirs in Toronto when younger, so her songs were received with much appreciation. It was always her wish and thought that I had inherited her singing talent so I was constantly coaxed to contribute, but shyness prevented me from performing to the utmost and I would take refuge behind a door for my forced singing! Cousin Doris also played the piano, though a jazzier type of music, and Lorraine and Shirley took tap-dancing lessons, so they were called upon to demonstrate their ability that way. Then the evening would end with a sing-song in which we all joined. Dad could still sing well, he too having sung in choirs when younger, as mentioned in his story. He could also whistle a fine tune. My Mother and her sisters were of Scottish descent and the Fathers of English, so there was always a good mixture of the songs of both. Happy days, happy times!

When the Gardeners and Florists Association held their concerts, home-grown talent was in great demand so into the evening's agenda went Jim and Eileen, much against their wishes again, and of course cousins Lorraine and Shirley with their fancy costumes, setting off their tap-dancing! One year, in response to my Mother's forceful coaxing, Eileen did some reciting of poems, called 'Elocution' on the programme. She always felt the audience was more interested in the dancing than her reciting, so refused all further requests! Thankfully, I was young enough to be kept out of this but enjoyed it all as an onlooker.[1]

At the Association's picnics, the men, most of whom had been trained in their trade on English estates, would organize a cricket game and Father eagerly looked forward to partaking in this. British traditions upheld!

Another outing we could enjoy now and then was the hockey game at Maple Leaf Gardens with the home team, the Toronto Maple Leafs – everyone's heroes. This was made possible through Mr Ellsworth's con-nection as one of the directors of the Club, and his generosity in giving Father tickets. Saturday night was hockey night and the evening's enter-tainment on the radio, so it was with great delight that we took turns in using the tickets with Father, when available.

My Father's brothers, Bert and Harry, often visited us with their families, and we in turn visited their homes. These were not the musical kinds of visits that we spent with my Mother's side of the family, but still enjoyable in their own way. When the brothers got together, talk was often about their own years in Upham, and the hard times they endured while there. Much of what was said was difficult for us younger ones to believe, but Father's story changed my thinking. Current events of the day were discussed freely and usually led on to politics. This always seemed to develop into great arguments, as each man voiced his opinion, but they just considered it part of the visit and always the evenings ended on friendly terms. Any outsiders would have been appalled at the heat of the

---

[1] We always thought that Mother, being the wife of one of the Association's executives, was determined to get her own 'in on the act'!

arguments, but it was just a 'friendly discussion' as far as the brothers were concerned. Father was always greatly interested in the politics of the era, an interest that remained with him all his life.

There were also two cousins, Bert and Will Trimbee, brothers, who lived in the west end of Toronto who, with their families, also traded visits. They were quieter men than my Father and his brothers, so those visits were placid. Two of the other families whose friendships were enjoyed were the Kirbys and the Doveys. Mr Kirby worked at Lambton Golf club, and he and his wife were my Godparents. Mr Dovey worked at a small estate near Glenalton, and he and his wife were Eileen's Godparents. The Kirbys' daughter, Bea, eventually married Tom Cooper, one of the groundsmen, who boarded with the Trewins, next door to us. Dear Mother was the matchmaker in that case and the Coopers visited us often throughout the years.

Another groundsman was a tall Welshman, Hugh Hollingsworth – an amiable fellow who spent many a night visiting us and who also remained a friend long after the days of Glenalton. Mother and Father made friends easily, and even the breadman, whose call brought him to our house near noon, was often invited in to have his lunch with us. He and his wife exchanged visits with my parents, even enjoying a game of euchre together. Liquor was never a part of these evenings, though Father was not one to promote temperance, thinking rather that each one made his own decision that way. He smoked a pipe and enjoyed a cigar once in a while, until ill health later in life forced him to relinquish those pleasures.

As Father told earlier, his younger brother Charles had made it to the top in the sport of horse-racing and he came to Toronto occasionally for the racing meets held here. These were visits for which we prepared well in advance, almost as if royalty were coming! The meal was planned meticulously, with Mother putting an extra effort in her cooking. Eileen and I gave great thought to our choice of dresses to wear for the 'big event', so that we would look our best for Uncle Charles and his wife, Aunt Margaret. Sometimes we were given clothes by her, and were very appreciative of them. She kept up with the latest styles and, even though we knew they were hand-me-down, they were much better clothes than we would have had otherwise. Aunt Margaret was a sweet lady and Uncle Charles a handsome, soft-spoken gentleman, full of exciting stories for us, including action-packed adventures in the racing world, which took them all around the United States and even to Cuba, in their younger days. One was about them being chased in their car by bandits down in Key West, Florida. No wonder we all looked forward to their visits. Father took all this in his stride, never becoming overly excited like the rest of us but questioning Uncle Charles extensively on his very different life-style. It was obvious that these men had a close feeling for each other dating back many years. As recounted earlier, their Father had died when Uncle Charles was very young, and Charles had then looked upon his brother as a father image as the two older brothers were away in the British Navy. On their trips to Toronto, Uncle Charles and Aunt Margaret also visited her Mother who lived here.

These were the depression days of the thirties and it was impressed upon us that we were lucky our Father was employed, as there were so many men without jobs. It was obvious to us, knowing of schoolmates whose fathers were unemployed suffering through the great depression more than we did. I can remember more than once a man coming to our door, asking for food − never refused. These were men travelling around the country, seeking work.

Unhappily though, Father did not escape the toll of the depression completely. When we moved from Lambton Mills to Glenalton, he rented his house to friends, hoping that the rent would carry his mortgage payments for him and he would have an investment. However, the depression caused the tenant to lose his job, he was unable to find another and, finally, was uanble to pay his rent. Father felt sorry for him, would not evict him for new tenants, so eventually, unable to meet the mortgage payments, taxes and upkeep, the house was repossessed. This was the effect of the great depression on him, with his investment lost.

Brother Bill also became unemployed and could not find work in Toronto, although he searched day after day. Finally, through Mr Ellsworth, he obtained a job in the mines up in Noranda, Quebec − a long, long way from home. That summer of 1935, Father decided that we would spend his week's vacation taking a trip up there to visit Bill. It was a trip to remember, riding in his old Ford, camping gear and food packed on the running-board, suitcases and five of us in the car. We had tyre blow-outs and car trouble, went over unbelievably rough roads but through it all, Father, in his own cheery way, made it a happy, adventurous outing. Tenting-out up there was fine in the daytime but we nearly froze at night sleeping on camp cots. Being a parent myself now, I realize how much they wanted to see their son again and so put up with the discomforts of the trip for that satisfaction. The following winter, Bill returned home, having had enough of mine work, and he found other employment in Toronto.

Our next-door neighbours, the Trewins, decided to return to Cornwall, England, as Mrs Trewin was homesick for family and homeland. After many tears from the females in both families, they departed on 31 October 1935 when I lost my Pal, and Mother her dear companion. However, the lines of communication were never broken. Letters went back and forth and their family's name will appear again later. The newly-married chauffeur and his wife replaced the Trewins as occupants of the house next door.

Jim won a prize for poetry in the Spring of 1936. It was published in the year book, during his last year of high school at Earl Haig Collegiate. Not knowing then that he would someday follow his father's footsteps, making horticulture his life's work, it seems a coincidence that Nature was the theme of his poem, as shown.

> Let's wander down a valley,
> Let's follow a rip'ling brook,
> Let's explore the far horizon,
> Please come with me and look,
> You'll see a little squirrel,
> A fish in the mirrored blue,
> A Blue-Jay chatting noisily,
> And they are all for you.
>
> You'll pick some gay wild flowers,
> Then for a while you'll dream,
> Should from the ground a snake pop up
> Then indeed you'll scream!
> But as the sun falls lower,
> And we make our homeward way,
> You'll softly whisper to yourself,
> 'It's been a perfect day.'

Those thoughts are similar to Father's back in Upham, as he had made his way to and from work when a young boy, observing the sights. Certainly, both showed great appreciation of Nature's glories, all out there waiting to be discovered if one would only take the time to look.

Time passed, with Father always busy supervising the estate and Summer home property. Every Spring and Fall he was away for a few weeks up north, and the hot summers called for continuous watering of the extensive, well-kept lawns and gardens. His was not a nine-to-five job! Often he would be back at night to attend to something in the greenhouses, seeing to the watering hoses, taking his turn driving the maids to and from the car stop at the city limits on their nights off, and even rounding-up the dogs, when they went missing. We had a two-way phone in the house connecting us to the 'big house' and it was put to good use. Summer blended into Fall, Winter would be upon us and then Spring, with all its heavy gardening load, and the hot Summer would return once again.

Jim and Eileen finished high school and I entered it the year after their departure. Then the two brothers and my sister were working in Toronto. Eileen and I would walk to the city limits together every morning, she to take the T.T.C.[1] downtown and I to take the old radial car up to Willowdale, to high school.

Gradually it became apparent that conditions on the job were deteriorating for Father. Mrs Ellsworth really wanted Father to be a dressed-up supervisor but he was a worker. Sometimes she would want flowers cut when he knew that they had not reached their full potential, and thus he would dispute her decision. Little differences developed into big ones and, even though I was too young to be included into all the discussions at home, I was old enough to know that Father was unhappy with all the circumstances surrounding these differences. It all ended when Father gave in his resignation and, in December 1937, we left. Our days at Glenalton were over but the connnections with the Ellsworths were not completely severed for all time, as will be seen later.

[1] Toronto Transportation Commission.

We moved to a house on Roslin Avenue, a few blocks south of the city limits and Father went into private landscaping. He did not lack for work once the word spread among the gardening people of the city that he was on his own. The early ambition of owning his own greenhouses returned and he was on constant watch for such an opportunity. This came in the following Summer, 1938, when he purchased greenhouses on Spadina Road, just north of Eglinton Avenue West. Mother found a house on Latimer Avenue, two streets east of the greenhouses – so another move for us!

These greenhouses were run-down, not having been worked for a while, so Father was back to his early beginnings in Toronto! He worked day and night, seven days a week. Bill was married by this time, out on his own of course, and the rest of us settled into our new home. Jim was working in the office of the General Electirc Company, on King Street, and, bless him, worked nights and weekends with Father, giving much needed help. Mother also went over to help bunch flowers, as the crops came in, to be made ready for market.

One eventful evening during our stay on Latimer Avenue will always be remembered by the family, and I was held responsible for it. It was a Sunday night and Father and Jim were over working in the greenhouses, readying the flowers for the next day's market, Mother had washed her hair and Eileen was putting up the rollers for her, as I sat in the living room listening to the radio. Suddenly the announcer broke in to say that Martians had landed in New Jersy. I went rushing out to the kitchen to break the news to Mother and Eileen. Yes, it was the Orson Welles' famous play being acted out, but I was convinced, and also convinced Mother and Eileen. Pandemonium broke loose as Mother phoned her sisters to come up so we could be together when the Martians arrived this far north! Eileen and I rushed out to bring Father and Jim home but not before we nearly broke down the door of the house next to ours, shoved Mother in, crying that we wanted her to stay with them while we brought Father and Jim home so that we could all die together! Not listening to the radio, they knew nothing of what was going on but, seeing the agonised looks on our faces, did not attempt to reason with us. Their startled looks were really something to behold!

Eileen and I ran all the way to the greenhouses, each taking her turn leading while the other watched the sky for signs of the impending invaders. We implored Father and Jim to come home right away, and again they could see it was useless to argue. Back we went to the house, this time each girl being led, hanging on to a man's hand and still watching the sky. We arrived home just in time to be reassured that it had been only a play. Father and Jim had no words of retribution, just shook their heads and returned to their work. Mother was terribly embarrassed having been caught with her hair half in the rollers, half still hanging wet. Oh me! Of course, the next day, when the newspapers' stories proved that I was not the only one taken in, I was very relieved – and forgiven. It was a long time before I lived that one down though, and sometimes, even to this day, my cousins will laugh about it at family get-togethers.

Cousin Jim Flack, though only a small child at the time, recalls that episode as 'the time of the great world-ending catastrophe', with the hysteria I caused the whole family to endure. He remembers 'that I was supposed to be frightened but wasn't sure of what.' When the Flack family did visit in those days, Jim and his Dad, my Uncle Charlie, would walk around to see the greenhouses. Jim says now: 'While at the house, Uncle Jim would never be able to sit for too long, as there was always something he had to do back at work. Early in life, I decided that I was never going to be a gardener!'

Father took landscape-consulting jobs on occasion, to help meet expenses involved in building up the business. One of these jobs was for James Franceschini, a wealthy contractor who lived on an estate in Mimico, overlooking Lake Ontario. The estate was not as large as Glenalton, though still very extensive, with conservatory and greenhouses adjoining the house. This man was another self-made millionaire who had arrived in Canada from Italy penniless, and with little use of the English language. However, through hard work, he made money, only to lose it to a partner because of contract disputes. He began again and, with more hard work, after conquering the language and contract knowledge, he amassed a fortune in the road-paving business. Owning the Dufferin Paving Company, he then branched out with the Dufferin Shipbuilding Company and other interests. Pleased with the landscaping that Father produced for him, Mr Franceschini offered a full-time job.

Even though by then Father had the greenhouses coming along in a productive way, the offer made was too good to pass up and we were on the move again. Mother surely must have had her fill of packing so often!

In August 1939 we moved to Mimico, just before the beginning of World War II. One thing that might have influenced Father's acceptance was the fact that young Jim, with General Electric, was in line for a move to Windsor and possibly into the Service because of the imminent war. All that would mean that Father would lose his hard-working helper.

Shortly after our move, a letter from California brought the sad news of the death of Father's sister, Maude. This was the first death in that generation since World War I, when Uncle Ernie was lost at sea. Maude had moved to California with her sisters and their husbands in the early 1920s, the move taking her and her daughter Lottie away from an unhappy broken marriage in Toronto. She had eventually re-married in California many years later, finding happiness which was, unfortunately, cut short by her death.

Mr Franceschini made things very comfortable for us, providing us with a large house, adjoining the chauffeur's, situated on the road that ran down the east side of the estate, almost to the lake. The street-cars ran along Lakeshore Road with a car stop at the top of our street, so Mother could get out to shop and visit on her own. Jim and Eileen had close transportation to work, and high school for me was a short walk away. There we were in an area completely new to all of us, but with the benefits it provided, and it was not long before we felt quite 'settled in'. It did not have the isolation of Glenalton and also, was closer to Mother's sisters. The chauffeur and his wife were Scottish – an added bonus for Mother.

It was a beautiful estate called 'Myrtle Villa', named for his daughter Myrtle, who was also beautiful and – although I saw her infrequently – she was always friendly. One coincidence to mention is that a close girl friend of hers was one with whom I had attended public school, when living at Glenalton. The results of our stay at the Ellsworths' kept showing up throughout my life.

Mr Franceschini's hobby was hackney horses and ponies. Before we lived there, he built, on the west side of the estate, one of the largest private horse stables and enclosed training rings in Canada at the time. There were more houses on that side of the estate for the horse trainer and help. As at Glenalton, I often sat on the fence watching the horses train on the outside track that was also there.

Again, we went to the Royal Winter Fair and the Canadian National Exhibition, where Father was still judging flowers, and would see Mr Franceschini's horses in competition. He won many prizes and trophies, which were displayed in the elegant tackroom. Times were happier again for Father as he busied himself with new challenges.

The main house was close to Lakeshore Road with a stone wall running along the front of the property. The formal gardens and the lawns, with their beautiful flower beds, ran back from the house to the lake. The conservatory which backed on to the house included a beautifully tiled swimming pool in the centre, surrounded by tropical plants. Father had all sorts of unusual plants in the conservatory, including a lemon tree and a night-blooming Cereus, a rare plant which, as the name implies, only bloomed at night and then not very often. Father would know when that event was to happen, and it would be a treat to be called out to see it blossom forth.

Frequent visitors to our home then were the Flacks, most times the whole family, although sometimes Uncle Charlie would drive out by himself to have a chat with Father. Those two men had a common bond, being married to sisters, but more than that, they enjoyed each other's company at all times. Cousin Jim recounted to me some of his own personal recollections of Father.

My earliest memory of Uncle Jim is that he always called me 'Jamie', a name which was to continue in later life. I remember the trips out to Mimico from our home in Parkdale. I looked forward to Christmas because we had two Christmases, one in the morning at home and then, alternate years, for the dinner, one at our home with the Aunts and families, and the other year at the Trimbees. It was always a double Christmas for me and great fun. Going out to Mimico, I remember how vividly I was impressed with the estate and Uncle Jim would take me out every time – after I bugged him continuously to which he always relented – and show me the wagons they had for use with the show horses. It was quite a collection as I recall and as much as I would want to stand on them or sit in them, I knew better than to do so. There was also an inside training

41. Jean. Indoor training track and horse trainer's home in background.

42. Back of House, showing ballroom, conservatory, swimming pool and formal gardens.

43. Conservatory and swimming pool.

ring and I couldn't understand why it had to be inside and why horses couldn't be trained outside only. I also remember standing beside an inside swimming pool, the like of which I had never seen before and wanting desperately to have a swim but of course that wouldn't be allowed either.

Uncle Jim used to wax eloquently – always had an opinion on any subject. It seemed, during the visits, I would be sitting around with the others listening to the deep discussions between he and my Dad. One of these times, I was lying on the couch, very tired, wanting to go home while Uncle Jim was telling a story. When he paused for a moment, I said 'go on' from the couch. Well, it struck him so funny, maybe coming from a child, that he started to laugh and he couldn't stop and that got all of us laughing. He and I had to leave the room and I thought I was going to be sick, I laughed so hard. The tears were streaming down his face from laughing. He would recover, come back into the room, start to talk and then break into laughter again and I laughed along with him. That was typical though as any time we were together, laughter would come and I can recall him laughing till he had to remove his glasses, wipe the tears from his eyes and clean his glasses. A serious man with a great sense of humour, he was always lecturing me as elders are wont to do, but it was meant for my benefit, I'm sure. There was never any change in his appearance from the time I remember him – always seemed like an older man. I don't know if it was the big moustache or the way he moved, but he looked the same from the time I was five or six as long as he lived.

I was not a vegetable fan and he was a great vegetable man and every time we ate at the Trimbees, I would be given what I thought was an enormous amount of vegetables and very unfair. Uncle Jim would chomp away and reprimand me about not eating and then tell me the same story each time according to the vegetable given that day. One time he had been the champion asparagus eater of seven counties or the champion carrot eater of five counties which didn't mean a thing to me and I wasn't too impressed. If he was the champion, I thought, he could eat my asparagus 'cause I sure didn't like it! Now I see the humour in it all. Another story that he told me about asparagus was a kind of lesson in philosophy. When he was employed in earlier years at the Lambton Golf Club as gardener, he was also to grow vegetables for use in their dining-room. He thought that he should grow asparagus but the man in charge thought it a waste of time because it would be five years before the plant would bear the vegetable. Uncle Jim's reply had been that if you never plant it, you'll *never* get any asparagus! I have remembered that over the years – if you never do anything, nothing will ever happen! I quote that philosophy often and always give him credit for it.

Uncle Jim was a great tease and one of his victims was Uncle Sam, Aunt Cathie's husband. I was always aware of when this was happening by the glint in Uncle Jim's eye and, of course, my Father was not much better, so between them they had their fun that way. It was never harmful though and any get-togethers always ended on a friendly basis.

One of Uncle Jim's favourite expressions was 'I'll tell you lads just what's going to happen' and often he would stand up, hitch up his pants, and proceed with this paraphrase and then tell how the world was going to unfold. Probably that was one term used when the aforementioned hard laughter came after I said 'go on'.

Mr Franceschini often entertained people high up in business and political life and, many a night, Eileen and I, as we had done for the Ellsworth wedding, watched from our bedroom window to see these socialites enjoy their festivities in the gardens. There were coloured lights hidden in the bushes and flower beds and, when lit at nightime, they truly turned the place into a fairyland again for us. Charitable events were often held in the gardens of the estate.

This storybook era was not to last, however. War had been declared against Germany in September 1939 and in June 1940 Italy declared war against the allies. A few days later, Father broke the news to us that Mr Franceschini had been taken into custody in the round-up of Italian-born people. It was reported in the papers that in 1934 Mr Franceschini had sent a horse to Mussolini and rumours abounded. He was very well known in the province, through his business and horses, and made the news again with his detention. Even though he had become a Canadian citizen in 1913 and married a Canadian lady, he was taken into an internment camp.

Father was instructed by the authorities to carry on with his duties and life continued as usual, at least for us. An appeal was expected in Mr Franceschini's case and his business carried on, so Father received his pay without difficulty. Of course, living on the estate, we were expected by all our friends and relatives to know exactly what was going on with the case, but this was not so.

Jim had been transferred to Windsor, where he met his future wife, Wilma, who also worked in the General Electric office there. I continued in school, and many of the schoolmates that I met there have remained close friend through the years. The move to Mimico was one of the best made by Father, for me personally. By the next year I had finished school and was also working in Toronto, as did Eileen. I remember one night, coming home late after working overtime, seeing a man lurking in the garden, who I was later told was a member of the RCMP[1] on watch duty.

Thus, the flowers still bloomed, the gardens showed their beauty as ever, but no more entertaining was done. Because of this, we more or

[1] Royal Canadian Mounted Police.

less had the run of the place and took the liberty often to show our friends around. A little to the south of our house was a doll's house that had been built for Myrtle, in her younger days. It was in complete scale, furniture and all, which made it quite a showplace on its own.

In June 1941, Mr Franceschini was freed from the internment camp on compassionate grounds, as he had been taken ill, but it was not until much later that he was completely absolved by the government of any wrong doing. After his release, he built a country home at Mount Tremblant, Quebec, but he still retained the Mimico estate.

Again, a resemblance to Father's life at Glenalton arose. He had to make the trip to Mount Tremblant to supervise the landscaping of the place there. This, of course, was a longer trip than his earlier ones up to Muskoka. He did not relish this added burden so far away from home, totally unexpected when he took on the job in 1939, but the War changed many things for many people. Our own family was included in these changes as Jim was now in the Air Force, Bill in then out of the Army, released because of poor eyesight. Father listened to the latest War news on the radio and read the newspaper accounts of it avidly. He was appalled that another war was upon us, and it reached home again this time, with cousins and my brother in the Service.

In the summer of 1941 cousin Doris Flack was married, – a happy occasion we all attended, but it was tempered by the fact that her Father, Uncle Charlie, was ill. He had never been in perfect health since being wounded in World War I and, sadly, the end came for him in September of that same year. Not only did we lose a member of the family in his death, but Father lost a good companion, and felt his loss very keenly. Our days of the happy musical family get-togethers were over, cousins grown and some moved away because of the War. My Aunt and the younger cousins, Shirly and Jim, continued their visits, but Uncle Charlie was sorely missed. From then on Father adopted a fatherly attitude towards the young boy as shown in more of Jim's recollections which follow.

44. Eileen at front door of Doll House.

I recall Uncle Jim coming in to our house in Parkdale in the late Spring of 1942, to get the back lawn in order. After he had planted the flowers and trimmed the grass, I watered it all. This was with a hand-held hose, as we had no sprinkler and after I thought it was finished, Uncle Jim stood there and said, 'It had to be wet an inch down.' In my young years I thought, 'Who's going to measure it?' He came in one other night in the summer and I had cut the grass the night before, because I knew that he would reprimand me if I hadn't. After he weeded and cultivated the flowers, the garden looked good. Then he turned to me and said, 'OK, now cut the grass!' I replied, 'What do you mean? I cut the grass last night.' He said some unforgotten sharp words and then, 'Cut the grass, it needs it again', and I cut the grass again though I wasn't too pleased to do it. He seems to have instilled in me some love of gardening because I do enjoy it now and do quite a bit at my own home, and I do remember many of the things he taught me.

Mr Franceschini was in and out of hospital due to his illness, and most of the times in between was spent up at Mount Tremblant. Father's work periods up there became more frequent as the property was developed. I remember one time when Father was up there, that a deer skin was delivered to our house much to my Mother's surprise. We knew that Father with his love for animals would never have been the one to have shot the animal, and the reassurance of this surmise was given when Father returned home, telling that the skin had been given to him by a hunter.

Jim and Wilma were married in July 1943 in Windsor with the reception held at her home in Detroit, to where she and her family had moved. This happy occasion was the cause of another reunion for Father and his brother Charles, who had ceased coming to Toronto for the race meetings a few years earlier. The man who gave Charles his start in racing had died and Uncle no longer felt obliged to work in Toronto, keeping his activities confined to the United States. Now he was spending his summers working as Racing Secretary at the Detroit Race Track and, though he could not attend the wedding because of his work, he showed up at the reception. He came alone as Aunt Margaret, who he said was not in good health, had stayed in California. Our family was all present and enjoyed the wedding and the reunion with Uncle Charles.

Shortly after we returned home from the wedding, more changes took place. Mr Franceschini, his health deteriorating, decided to live permanently at his Mount tremblant home and wanted Father to move up also to take care of the grounds. This was not a change Father favoured, and Mother was against it also, so we moved again in early October 1943.

We went back into Toronto, to a house on Bathurst Street, just south of Dupont and Father went into 'War Work' in a nearby factory. This was the first time in his life, other than when at sea, that he worked away from 'nature', and an unhappy time it was for him. Jim went overseas at the end of October, parting from Wilma at her home in Detroit. After a sad farewell at the Union Station in Toronto from Father, Eileen and I, he was on his way. Mother could not bring herself to go to the Station, and gave her goodbye and blessing to Jim at home.

The house we moved to was large enough to enable Mother to take in two roomers to help out financially while she and Father built up their savings so that he could strike out on his own again. Life seemed full of adversity for him at that time of his life. He had worked so hard but, somehow, obstacles always prevented his headway.

Word came later from overseas in a letter from Jim that he had fulfilled two requests made by my parents when he left for England. On leave he went over to the Isle of Wight to visit Father's oldest sister, Annie, the only one of the family who remained in England. She was then in her seventies and still living in her own home alone, having been widowed many years earlier. Father was very happy about his son's visit to her, not having been able to go back himself since he came to Canada in 1905. Jim had answered many questions as she wanted to hear about the whole Trimbee family in Toronto. Her letter came soon also, telling us how much she had enjoyed his visit with her. On another leave he visited our former neighbours from Glenalton, the Trewins, in their home in Cornwall. Another quiz from them — questions and answers flew back and forth — as he reported in his letter home later. Then followed a letter from the Trewins, telling of their pleasure in seeing him again.

Later, when Eileen's fiancé, Alan Steel, went overseas, Jim and he managed to obtain leave at the same time and together they tried to reach Upham, Father's birthplace. Unfortunately, by the time they found their way near there, the problems in lack of transportation and leave-time running out overtook their efforts, and they were forced to return to their bases without reaching the tiny village. At least they tried and it was unfortunate that they did not have the opportunity to try again.

In June 1944 a girl friend and I signed on as 'Government Girls' in the employment of the British Army stationed in Detroit. This was in connection with the mobile supplies built there in the car factories for the Allied Services. It was my first move away from home and I remember dear Father taking me aside before I left and telling me that 'no matter what happened' I still had a home to come home to though he did not elaborate on what 'what' was. I did have a close link with the family in Detroit as Jim's wife Wilma was living there, while he was overseas.

While I was away, Father found another greenhouse plant, this time in Weston, and he took possession of it in late Summer 1944. Jim had written Wilma from overseas that he really did not want to go back to an office job, even though his employment with General Electric in Windsor was guaranteed at the War's end. His only other working experience had been assisting Father in greenhouses and at gardening jobs during the summers, while still in high school. He had written to Father asking him if they could go into business together upon his return from War service. Eileen believed that some of Jim's desire for the partnership was to help Father out in a time of need.

Thus, the partnership idea came first, ahead of the purchase of the greenhouses. Wilma, with her great understanding and devotion, went along with Jim's plan and sent her 'nest egg': money saved from her 'wife's allowance', to Father to help finance the project. It must have been hard on her, living then in the big city of Detroit, to wonder of her future ahead in a stronge locale, but through her faith in Jim's desire, and many years of hard work, the decision proved to be profitable for all parties concerned.

This was a far cry from Wilma's first impression upon seeing the newly purchased greenhouses on a trip from Detroit to Weston in 1944. She recalled, 'Then you couldn't honestly call them greenhouses – just framework – with all the glass broken and because of idleness, with no good soil in the beds, weeds grew up six feet tall! They had not been in operation for years and were a real mess. I could not believe that anyone could make anything out of it all and was slightly sick at heart that I had put Jim's savings into the project.'

It was a repeat performance for Father, who again, as in years earlier, worked day and night to build it up. He soon had one house in operation so that he could grow a small number of flowers whilst continuing to repair another, and in time the operable size increased. Having been abandoned, probably children had broken the glass over the empty years.

It doesn't take long for a greenhouse to go down without constant care. Insurance was never carried on the greenhouses, the premiums being too costly due to the wood and glass construction.

There was a very small house attached to the back of the greenhouses and Father, Mother and Eileen made it habitable for themselves. Mother knew that she would have to be close to take proper care of Father who, if on his own, would have neglected his own well being for the constant care the greenhouses demanded. She had been through this before and was surely adaptable, which enabled her to make the house a home. I can remember going home for weekends and holidays, lying in bed at night listening to the pipes crackling when the heating boilers were in operation.

After my arrival in Detroit, I phoned Uncle Charles at the Race Track to inform him of my residence and job there. He invited me up to see him and, on the scheduled day, I made my presence known at his office. After inquiring about the family he then, much to my surprise, took me into his confidence, telling me that he and Aunt Margaret had been divorced a few years ealier and that he had remarried: thus the truthful explanation as to why Aunt Margaret was absent when he attended Jim and Wilma's wedding reception the previous year, 1943. The reason for this deception, he told me, was that Aunt Margaret's elderly mother was still alive and living in Toronto. She was a devout Catholic and, because of her religion, would have been greatly distressed had she known of the divorce. Uncle Charles and Aunt Margaret had agreed to keep the news of this from the family, thinking it best for her Mother's sake, as long as she lived. However, as Uncle Charles theorized, he had decided to tell me only because I was then living in Detroit and he would want to see me frequently, and have me meet his new wife, June, who worked with him at the Race Track. Then began for me a happy and enjoyable relationship with the two of them, seeing them often that Summer until they returned home to their ranch in California for the Winter. As Uncle Charles had hoped, June and I developed a great friendship which was to continue into our later years. They were very kind to me on my visits with them, seating me in their private railside box for the races, followed by dinner out with them and usually some of their friends. I did feel guilt when I came home for the weekends to Weston, when I was questioned about my visits with Uncle Charles, but I had given my word to him that I would honour his confidence in me, and so I did. June was more my age than Uncle's but their marriage was a happy one that lasted until their deaths many years later.

Eileen found transportation from Weston to her office in downtown Toronto very inconvenient and time consuming but perservered, knowing that her help was needed when time permitted. She gave up her spare time to help around the greenhouses with the heating, bunching flowers and so on, as it was obvious Father could use all the help available. I think back now and appreciate the fact that she never showed me any resentment in that I was away enjoying my work and my life, while she unstintedly gave her time and effort to help out at home.

Father's great knowledge of growing flowers was put to full use and all the crops developed well. He arranged with another grower in the Weston area to pick up the Trimbee flowers ready for market and sell them for him. There was no time for him to do this himself, and he did not have the means of transporting them if time had permitted. The care of the greenhouses was a full-time job. The arrangement made, of course, cut into the profits, as the other florist had to have a commission for doing the selling, but Father had no alternative if he was to get the flowers out to market.

The winter of 1944–45 was the date of the record-breaking snowfall in the Toronto area. Schools were closed, transportation was halted and at home my parents and Eileen were snowbound. There was absolutely no way Eileen could get out to work as, even if she had made it to the train station, the trains were not running! The flowers kept growing though, as the heat from the greenhouses melted any accumulation of snow on the glass roof, letting in the light. Fortunately, Father did not cut for the regular take-out until the roads were cleared, so no flowers were wasted.

One day in the following Spring, cousin Jim was out to give a helping hand, even though still quite young. He vividly recalls the episode of the chimney repair done by Father.

Uncle Jim was not one to call a repairman when he could do the job himself. Finances then would make this a necessity. I think he would have had some experience at this work as he had operated greenhouses before and though I don't know if he had any cement or brick-laying skills, I do know that the lack of them would not deter him. I watched him as he went up the ladder cautiously because I think he was nervous of heights. His method was to climb up very carefully with one brick on his head and his hat on top of the brick to hold it in place. He would lay the brick, make his way back down the ladder to get another brick and repeat his perfomance. I know he didn't do it that was for show but he sure got a lot of people's attention!

Cousin Jim had more recollections of visiting Weston.

Often my Mother and I would go out to Weston for a visit with Uncle Jim and Aunt Jean, and it seemed there was a multitude of street-car changes ending with, what I thought then, a long, long walk to the house. When we entered the greenhouses, we were met with the marvellous perfume of the growing flowers. After my Dad passed away, I was taught the game of euchre so that I could replace him at the card table. Uncle Jim enjoyed that game and it was usually he and Mother against Aunty Jean and I. Whenever he would 'euchre' me, he would slam those cards down hard and say, 'Aha, Jamie, I caught you with your pants down again', whereupon my Aunty Jean would be horrified and reprimand him for using that kind of language in front of a young lad!

In the Summer of 1945, Uncle Charles returned to Detroit for the new racing season, but this time alone. June had been forced to remain at the ranch in California to supervise the care of the race horses then boarded there. Her interest in horses was as keen as Uncle's and her knowledge of the care needed enabled her to take charge. I missed her companionship but Uncle Charles and I enjoyed our visits and dinners together as we had in the previous Summer. Again, on trips home, I was questioned about Uncle Charles but June's absence did make the answers a little easier. Then in a few years, Aunt Margaret's Mother died and word was quietly circulated in the family of Uncle Charles' changed marital status, which was accepted without any great concern.

Finally World War II ended and we all looked forward to the return of 'our boys' from overseas. Alan was the first to reach home, and he and

Eileen were married in September 1945. It was unknown when Jim would return as some of the servicemen were to remain overseas for the Occupation Forces but, happily, he came back at the end of October. After the family celebration of his return was over, he and Wilma spent a few days away on their own, following which he immediately began his task of helping Father build up the business. When Jim came back, he was twenty-seven years old but Father would not trust him to get up on the roof of the greenhouses. Father was sixty-one and was sure that he would be right up there, but didn't want Jim up in case he fell! He thought experience counted more than youth!

I was home from my government job, which was terminated in the Fall of 1945 due to War's end. Brother

45. Charles, 1944.

Bill, now the father of two, was living and working in Toronto. Accommodation was very hard to find, naturally, due to the return of the servicemen but Mother heard of a place for Jim and Wilma, one room on the third floor of a house only two streets away from the greenhouse. This they quickly rented and soon took over all the third floor, staying there for four years. After years apart, the family was re-assembled and, needless to say, that Christmas of 1945 was a happy reunion for all.

Father's friend and former worker from Glenalton, Hugh Hollingsworth, had been sent overseas when we lived in Mimico. He had been living on his own, not being married, and knowing how trustworthy his friend, Father, was, had left some personal belongings with him for safekeeping while he was away. Upon his return home Hugh arrived to tell of his experiences overseas and to claim his possessions, which had made the two moves with Father since Hugh's departure. He told, then, of valuable bonds which formed part of the things stored with my parents. I can remember Mother and Father being so amazed that he would have left them just packed in his suitcase there, to which Hugh replied that he knew that, if they were aware of the bonds when he left, it might have caused them worry for their safekeeping, so he had said nothing, knowing his things would be well taken care of by them. It shows the kind of trust he had in them.

Hugh approached Father and Jim with the idea of making the partnership into a three-way deal including him. They decided on a trial basis for a year, Hugh having growing experience which could certainly be well used in the greenhouses. At the end of the year it was decided that the profits made then were not enough to be split three ways until some time in the future, so, after being recompensed for his time, Hugh left to make his own way elsewhere. This was on very friendly terms and he stayed a friend of Father's throughout their lives. He later did marry and he and his wife visited frequently.

When Father and Mother first moved to Weston, the greenhouses were in a fairly open area. I can remember going down Church Street a short way to buy fresh cream from neighbours who kept a cow out back in the field, where there was also a barn. It was not long before the area was built up and the cow and the barn were gone.

In 1946, a truck was purchased for flower delivery. This was a sedan delivery type which was also the family's means of transportation for some time. Then Jim took the flowers out to the florists' shops regularly twice a week, working up a steady clientele. Jim had the business acumen and Father certainly had the growing knowledge – an excellent combination.

Father had ceased driving, so usually visits to his brothers' homes included Jim and Wilma. Father and his brothers still enjoyed voicing their opinions about politics and other matters of discussion. These arguments were 'old hat' to the families but Wilma, raised in a family of women, was horrified upon her initiation into one of those evenings and thought for sure the men were on the edge of fisticuffs. When she later expressed her dismay to Jim, he just laughed and explained that they were having the time of their lives enjoying it all!

Time passed by, with the flower business growing slowly. The family also grew when, in 1946, Eileen and Alan became the parents of a girl, Linda, and Jim and Wilma welcomed their first-born boy, Bruce. Mother was in her element with babies around, so our family get-togethers were highlighted by their attendance. Sadly, Mother's health deteriorated as her heart trouble recurred. She had given up helping with the flower now that more help was in the greenhouse with Father, but she still kept house as well as ever, though it took more effort than before.

I married in 1948 and it was a happy event with all the family participating, but it was Mother's last enjoyable event as her health worsened. It was a grim Fall as we watched her weaken, resulting in her death on 16 December 1948, at the age of sixty-one, with all the family sadly gathered around. She had been a good wife and a good mother, giving of her love and devotion to the family. There had been all kinds of misfortunes to weather with Father as outlined earlier, and she was always ready to pull up stakes and start again with him, but probably the years of hard work and worry finally caught up with her and she was past any more fight. Mother always had a happy disposition, with a friendly smile that encourage friendship, so her loss was felt by many. The lovely voice that gave us so many times of musical enjoyment was stilled forever. It was a bitterly cold, snowy day when we buried her and returned to the home that would never again be graced by her presence. Our lives would never be the same without her.

46. Mother and Bruce, 1947.

CHAPTER 5

L ife had to go on, though, and Father spent every waking moment working in the greenhouses except for time out to eat and his once-a-month meeting of the Gardeners and Florists Association. He stayed on in the little house and Wilma tended to his needs as much as possible, shopping for him, taking over meals to him and doing his laundry and cleaning. An independent man, he would ask no favours, although grateful for any received. Wilma was a very thoughtful daughter-in-law and I'm sure Father's health and well being would have suffered without the care she gave him. His care fell on her as I was expecting my first child then, and Eileen and Bill were living out-of-town. Of course Jim worked with him daily so he was not completely on his own.

One day in the greenhouse, Wilma noticed that Father was wearing worn-out shoes and remarked that he needed to get new ones. He agreed with her and requested that she buy him some. Wilma told him that she couldn't get shoes for him as he would have to try them on. No way was he taking time out to go to the shoe store so Wilma took his size, bought the shoes and he wore them without difficulty. Mother had always shopped for his clothes and shoes so Wilma continued to do so, amazed that she could do so with success.

In January 1950 Jim and Wilma bought their first house which was on Church Street just a few doors away from the greenhouses, well located for easy access. Upon moving in, they fixed up a room for Father and fully expected him to join them but he politely refused, thinking it not right because they should have a chance to be on their own. He said to them, 'No, I shouldn't live with you – I'm quite all right here', meaning the little house where he had lived since Mother died. The time had passed quietly for him, the most notable events being the arrival of our two daughters, Marilyn and Kerry, giving him two more grandchildren to brighten our visits to Weston.

He had agreed to have his meals with Jim and Wilma once they moved into their home close by his, but would never sit around for long afterwards, thinking they needed their home to themselves. One evening

Wilma went over to the greenhouse to call him to the 'phone and found
him sewing a button on a coat. She said, 'Oh, Pop, I would have done
that for you', but he had not asked, not wanting to bother her. Of course
he went to bed early, as he was up and working at break of day or before
in the short days of Winter. His brothers came out to visit him in the
greenhouse but the visits that he and Mother made to relatives and friends
were past. It was a lonely life for him but his life was soon to change for
the better.

Those changes began in 1950 in early Spring, when the flowers were
blooming in the greenhouses, being made ready for the peak days of
Easter and Mother's Day. Word came from Wilma that Father was taking
a night out more frequently, then regularly once a week. Did he have a
lady friend we wondered? Not our Father, we agreed. It must be some
political or horticultural group he had joined, we thought. It all came to
light about Easter time when there was a great show of flowers in the
greenhouse, geared up for the day. One day, during the previous week,
he was on his way out the door going back to work after lunch when
he stopped, turned to Wilma and said, 'Oh, could we have company for
dinner on Sunday?' Wilma replied affirmatively and he was out the door
like a shot, before Wilma could find out just who was coming for dinner!
The next day he told Wilma that he had made arrangements and could
she meet this lady where she got off the streetcar? Wilma said, 'Well, you
know, you just have to stop right now and tell me what this lady's name
is. I can't meet someone and not know who she is.' Wilma and Bruce,
then three years old, met her and, from the moment they saw her standing
on the corner waiting for them, Wilma says she knew from her appearance
that this lady would be good for Father. Getting to know her verified
that impression.

This was Emily Butler, who had worked at Glenalton and was still
employed by Mr Ellsworth at his home, now in Forest Hill Village,
Glenalton having been sold a few years previously. Father apparently had
decided that he did not want to spend whatever time in life he had left
living alone. He thought of the eligible ladies he knew, and Emily topped
the list. Again, 'Glenalton' returned to our life. The nights when Father
went out without telling Jim and Wilma where, he was courting Emily.
He had been very secretive about this and it was only discovered accidentally when someone called one day to leave a message for him 'not
to come and visit Emily that night as she was ill.'

Mother's Day was the time of another great floral display in the
greenhouses and Father again requested Wilma to have Emily for a dinner
guest. He was proud of the results of his growing ability and, quite

understandably, wanted to show them off to her. From then on, Jim and Wilma saw more of her. One day when I was alerted ahead of time of her impending visit, my husband Merv and I, with our two daughters, 'dropped in' and so met her. I did remember her from Glenalton once I saw her again and a dear person she was. We all agreed that Father had used great judgement in renewing his acquaintance with her, knowing what a lonely life he had been leading since Mother died.

In the summer of 1950 Humber Memorial Hospital was built next door to the greenhouse property. What progress from five years earlier, when the cow was kept down the street! Jim Flack's memories of the beginning follow.

> I was out visiting Uncle Jim one day and noted the first sign of construction which appeared when some trucks pulled up on the hospital property. From them out came a large number of men who worked diligently all day and when they were finished at day's end their accomplishment was a three-seater outhouse! All at the greenhouses were impressed with the fact that if this was the start of building a hospital, it was really going to be in good hands! I don't remember his words but Uncle Jim had some very astute remarks to say about that.

The completion of the hospital was of course a boon to the business as many visitors going to the hospital would first go into the greenhouse to buy fresh flowers to take to patients. At that time, there was no street entrance into the greenhouses from Church Street other than going down the lane between two houses which was the only entry. Father and Jim realized that the time had come to build something that would resemble a store front but access to a street must be obtained first. In the meantime, the customers were increasing the retail trade in the greenhouses, all quite happy to make the trek down the laneway knowing they were buying fresh flowers, cut to order.

In November, on his way out again, Father asked Wilma to go shopping with him. This was unheard of from him so with great surprise Wilma agreed, asking for what they were shopping? He replied, 'A wedding ring', and disappeared! Father had never mentioned Emily's name to the rest of the family so it was quite a shock to us when we heard that he was planning to be married. One day, shortly after his shopping trip, Wilma and I were going down to Bowmanville, where Eileen and Alan lived, to have lunch with her. Father gave Wilma a letter to take down to be read there when we three were all together. When it was opened, Eileen read aloud the first page and passed it to me. I read some and passed it on to Wilma and very shortly we were all in tears! It was a most beautiful letter, in which Father tried to explain to us that no one would ever replace our Mother but he needed someone with whom to spend the rest of his life. This fact was easy to accept as he had worded his letter with such grace – and Emily was the right one for him. We all loved her and respected her as a member of the family in a short time. Emily wistfully told me, a few years after Father's death, of the tender proposal Father had made. One night in the Summer, she had walked with him to the car stop after he had visited her and, as they turned the corner of the street, they could see a beautiful sunset in the sky. Taking her hand, he had asked her, 'Would you consider walking into the sunset of our lives together?' She had been overwhelmed by his choice of words but still answered that she had to think about it. Her heart obviously overruled her caution as before long they planned their marriage. This took place on 24 November 1950, on a blowy, cold day, at the Weston Presbyterian Church with just Jim, Wilma and Bruce with them as they wanted no fuss. They did go to the home of a friend of Emily's afterwards in Mount Dennis to mark the occasion. Wilma remembers that Betty Ellsworth sent a bottle of apricot liqueur to toast the bride!

Father and Emily planned to live in the upstairs flat at Jim's house but, just prior to the wedding, the furnace in the house malfunctioned and, because of the delay in obtaining parts needed for the repair, there was no heat for about four weeks. This postponed Father and Emily moving in because the only heat in the house was a quebec heater brought over from the greenhouse and a portable electric heater. Emily returned to the Ellsworth's to live until the furnace was fixed and it was nearly Christmas when they finally made their abode at 170 Church Street. Hardly an auspicious beginning to a new marriage but, like Mother, Emily took it all in her stride. Even their first Christmas together was spoiled as there was trouble with the boilers at the greenhouses, which occupied the men most of Christmas Day. Emily soon learned, like Wilma, that a crisis in the greenhouses came ahead of a celebration at home.

Father and Emily were both sixty-six years old when they were married. Emily had been engaged shortly after coming to live in Canada many years earlier, but her fiancé had died suddenly. Since then, she had spent her time in the employ of the Ellsworths, until her marriage to Father. Mr Ellsworth died ten days after Emily's wedding and she once commented with a wry smile that maybe it was the shock of her finally getting married that finished him! She also remarked at the same time that she would have delayed the wedding had she known that he was so close to his end. A faithful employee for sure! Mr Ellsworth acknowledged her years of service with a bequest in his will. Even though she had left to make her own life at last, the Ellsworth family never forgot her and always acknowledged her birthday and Christmas with lovely gifts, and visited her regularly.

Early in the new year of 1951, Wilma held a small reception for Father and Emily with all the Trimbees, to meet Emily, and she was warmly welcomed into the family.

The following Spring there was a fire at the greenhouses, which was blamed on the fact that neighbours had burned trash during the day and probably sparks had flown into the big old garage located at the end of the lane close to the entrance to the greenhouses. The garage contained tar paper and, once it caught, the fire was quite large and smoky. This happened in the evening after Jim and Wilma were out visiting at the home of one of the men who worked in the greenhouses. Father and Emily were at home entertaining Father's cousin, Uncle Willy, and his wife, Aunt Daisy. There was a pathway between the garage and the first greenhouse and, once it became a roaring fire, the side of the greenhouse was completely burned with all the glass broken. Jim and Wilma were visiting just a few miles from the greenhouses and they were there only a short time before another invited couple arrived. Upon their arrival, the couple, unfamiliar with the Weston area, and Jim and Wilma, remarked that on their way they had just seen a terrible fire with flames leaping into the air. Not long after they had made those remarks, Wilma looked up to see another greenhouse employee at the door. Without being told, she sensed immediately that he was there to tell them that the fire was at the greenhouses. Jim and Wilma left immediately and, by the time they arrived on the scene, the garage was completely gone, as was the wood on one side of the greenhouse.

Of course, by then Father was inside with his hoses helping the firemen on the outside to control the fire as much as possible. A real mess resulted from the fire but Father, well used to setbacks, blessed the fact that it could have been a lot worse. Two of the neighbours, who were very good carpenters, gave a helping hand quickly, repairing the damage and it was soon back in good shape. Another calamity overcome!

Christmas 1951 was doubly celebrated as Jim and Wilma's daughter, Martha, was born in the hospital next door. I remember our family going to Weston to celebrate Christmas as planned with Jim, Wilma, Bruce, Father and Emily. We enjoyed our Christmas dinner cooked by Emily and then went over to the hospital to see Wilma and the baby, taking Wilma's Christmas presents to her. Quite a day!

In the summer of 1952, news came of an impending visit by Uncle Jack and Aunt Ede, Father's sister, who lived in California. Upon their arrival they were joined by Cousin Lottie, her husband Fred and their two children, Ken and Myrna, who came up from New Jersey to where they had moved from California a few years earlier. Uncle Jack had retired by then and brought Aunt Ede up, knowing how much she wanted to see her brothers again. This was the first of many trips they made up here in the following years. Uncle Jack was a quiet man but Aunt Ede made up for him, regaling us with stories of the relatives in California. I was so young when they had made their previous trip in 1932 that it was like meeting them for the first time but, enjoying all the talk of 'family', it wasn't long before we were fast friends, not just relatives. They took turns staying with Uncle Harry, Uncle Bert and their families and some great stories of the 'old days' were brought forth once again. Shortly thereafter, upon his retirement, Uncle Harry and his wife, aunt Mary, moved to British Columbia where their son Harry lived. Soon after that, Aunt Ede and Uncle Jack made a trip from California to visit them there. Family ties are hard to sever.

Time passed and the business grew. Wilma took an active part, doing the book-keeping, putting her past working experience to full use. This she did in their house, using the dining room table as a desk – the only available space. By now, they were employing more help at the green-houses so with payroll, book work, phone orders and raising two children, she was kept very busy.

The Trimbee family was growing too. Our third daughter, Janis, was born in November 1953. Jim and Wilma's son Robert James arrived the following March and in time, son David completed their family. Also, in time, Eileen and Alan's family increased with Andrew, Christopher, Mark and Caroline. Bill and his wife Elsie had Joan and Brian. Thus, eventually, Father had fourteen grandchildren.

On one of her visits with the Ellsworths, Emily mentioned that I was expecting my third child and received the kind offer from Betty Ellsworth of her bassinet and crib for me, her son having outgrown them many years before. This offer, I accepted gratefully and my new daughter came home to sleep in very stylish furnishings. These are still put to good use by my grandchildren, the crib standing now in a bedroom for their use on visits to me.

In May 1954, finally a legal partnership was drawn up between Father and Jim who until then operated on only a verbal agreement made years earlier when the greenhouses were purchased. Father was approaching seventy years of age and, even though he had not even considered retirement, the legality of the partnership had to be protected.

By now, the house was getting crowded. Jim and Wilma had made a bedroom for themselves in their basement out of necessity and all but

Father knew that other living arrangements would have to be made. Father was quite content, never having been one to want for more than the necessities of life, but Emily thought otherwise, realizing how cramped Jim and Wilma were in their accommodation. Emily knew that the time had arrived for she and Father to find a little place of their own and allow Jim and Wilma and family to occupy their whole house. Therefore, she and Wilma walked around the district looking for houses showing a 'for sale' sign and, before long, they found one at 231 Church Street which would suit them perfectly. It was a nice little two-bedroom bungalow down the street from the greenhouses, so that it was not too far for Father to walk up to work, and they moved into it in July 1954.

That Fall, Hurricane Hazel hit Toronto and surrounding areas, creating a lot of damage and causing many deaths near the Humber River, which wends its way south through Weston. Thankfully, the greenhouses were not affected but the storm caused much concern with the high winds which, it was feared, would blow out glass and possibly topple the high chimney over the boiler room. Many homes, including Jim and Wilma's, had flooding in the basements. I remember that the phone lines were out, the bridges over the Humber River impassable and we, at home in Long Branch, which was also badly hurt by the storm, had no way of communicating with Weston, worried as we were about the fate of the greenhouses, and everything. In time, all was repaired and thankfully, we learned the greenhouses had withstood the storm.

There was quite a mixture of employees at the greenhouses by then, including two young Englishmen who, for a short time, boarded with Jim and Wilma, increasing her workload; also two young Irishmen, one of whom loved to goad Father for being a loyal Englishman by birth. Father resented this as he was proud of his birthright and the monarchy. Later these two Irishmen left but soon wanted to return to work in the greenhouses. Jim thought it prudent not to have Father upset and only the more 'subdued' one was rehired. Another employee was Borg, a Dane who fit into the work pattern well and became a personal friend, as did many of Father's co-workers. Long after Borg returned to live in his native Denmark, he kept in touch by letter. The radical Irishman was the only man who raised Father's ire by not respecting the loyalty he felt for his birthplace. Father even had a fairly large Union Jack which he proudly flew on days of celebration.

Father was a great one to joke with the children whom he fondly called 'the young-uns'. He had nicknames for them all, such as 'nip 'n tuck' and 'Gaffer'. One of this favourite tricks, and one which I remember from my own childhood, was to ask the children if they would like something to eat. Invariably the answer was in the affirmative, whereupon he would offer them a choice – bread or bread and pullet? The latter sounded like more so that was usually their choice, whereupon he would produce a piece of bread and tell them to 'pull it'! It never failed to work, much to his amusement and, eventually, theirs.

Jim's children, living in close proximity to the greenhouses, saw much more of Father than did the other grandchildren, so naturally have more memories of him. They loved to play in and around the greenhouses but often Father had to chase them out, for fear of them breaking the fragile flowers. Through necessity, Father was quite strict with them about the greenhouses – he didn't particularly like the way Bruce pulled all the lables off his seedlings one year, resulting in a long wait to see what grew up! It was forbidden for them to bring a crowd of childhood friends in and go racing through the greenhouses, as they liked doing. He loved to have them go in and look and admire the flowers but wouldn't have them running around in rough play, which might cause damage. They loved to get down behind the big boilers but their Grandpa told them of elves hiding there to keep the children away, in fear of them getting burned by the hot pipes in the cooler weather. Father always kept watch over the children when they were around, to avoid trouble. Bruce remembers the 'Summer greenhouses' out the back which were beds of plants with plastic covers in which the Fall chrysanthemums were started, and where he and his buddies like to play, leaving all kinds of junk there. His Grandpa soon put them out of there! There were plum and pear trees out the back and the boys would sit up in them eating the plums before they had a chance to ripen. Again, Father chased them out from there, fearful of them falling out of the trees and hurting themselves. He had raised two boys of this own and knew what to expect of youngsters. Boys will be boys and, though Father expected obedience, he was never harsh or cruel and there was always a loving relationship between him and his grandchildren.

By this time, Bruce was old enough to be put to work for which he was suited. In the Summer he would have to crawl into the boilers to clean them, which entailed crawling in the back through a little trap door to clean out the soot. Only children could go in, as adults were too big for the opening. He would go into the crawl space, open the door, and, digging himself into the soot, pass it out by bucketful to someone waiting outside the door. A dirty job but a necessary one.

As noted earlier, Father had a great way with animals and birds. One year, there was a vicious German shepherd dog who had made his home by the little house at the back of the greenhouses. He had tunnelled under the house which, by now, was only used for storing and packing the flowers. The dog was a danger to anyone but Father who, with his own unique manner, was the only one allowed to approach. When the dog-catcher had to be called in to remove the animal from property, Father was the one to coax it out from its tunnel.

Alas, 1956 was not a good year for Father and Emily. First, Emily was admitted to hospital to have a very large tumour removed from her stomach. She was seventy-two years old at the time and naturally quite fearful of having an operation. The operation was a success. Thankfully, the tumour was benign and Emily recovered well. The day she was to return home from the hospital, Father did not go to work and phoned Wilma, asking her to come down to his house as he was not feeling well. Wilma stayed with him for a couple of hours and then he seemed to be resting quite comfortably. Just before preparing to leave, Wilma took a cup of tea into him in the bedroom where he was lying in bed, and found him to be unconscious, breathing very heavily, perspiring profusely and very red in the face. He was seventy-one at the time, being six months younger than Emily. Suddenly he shuddered from head to foot and, with a great deep breath, he regained consciousness. Wilma left him just long enough to phone the doctor, who came immediately. After he examined Father, the doctor announced that he would stay with him a while for observation. The doctor said that, from Wilma's description, he thought Father had suffered a slight stroke and if so, there was the possibility that another one could occur very quickly. Fortunately, however, this did not occur. I arrived on the scene with Emily and, because of her convalescence, we did not tell her of the doctor's diagnosis, not wanting to alarm her. Surprisingly, he was back at work in a few days and as good as ever!

That same year, in the late Summer, my husband and I drove to Florida and from there crossed to Cuba to attend a convention connected with his work. After returning from our drive home, I went out to tell Father all about the trip in which he had shown great interest. I had brought to him a cotton boll, picked by the side of the road to show him, and also a container of the red soil of Georgia, thinking they would be something he had never seen before. To my amazement and, I must admit, some chagrin, he recognized them immediately! He had seen both these things fifty-five years earlier when, in the British Merchant Navy, his ship had landed in Georgia. He had also then witnessed, as we had, natives diving down into the water to retrieve coins thrown overboard to them. Although nothing had been new to him, he did appreciate my efforts to please him.

Father still attended the monthly meeting of the Gardeners and Florists Association and enjoyed the visits with his fellow florists. He was a charter member of that organisation and by this time was an Honorary Life Member. Old friends, such as Hugh Hollingsworth and Tom Cooper, kept up their friendship and often came out to see him. I think all of these men really relished their visits and thought they gained a lot from the time spent with him. They were also members of the aforementioned association, and met each other at the meetings.

Of course, as soon as Father and Emily moved into their own home, his showmanship showed in his garden. He had an excellent vegetable garden at the back of the yard behind the house which was always very productive. Nothing of their garbage could be put out for collection if it was usable for the compost heap, which, in turn, would be put back into the soil. Emily was quite soon aware of 'the difference and co-operated fully. The results of 'Nature-to-Nature' was very apparent. The flower gardens were always beautiful front and back, attracting many favourable comments from the neighbours. In a sheltered spot at the front was a rhododendron bush which was quite large, not often seen in this part of the country due to the climate with its cold winters. He was very proud of this and it did quite well, increasing in size year after year. Many people would stop and photograph it when it was at the height of its beauty. The back flower beds were typical of an English country garden, with flowers *en masse*, colourful all season. The fence which surrounded these border flower beds on three sides of the yard was covered with grape vines. Those vines produced grapes that hung in huge bunches everywhere on the vine. We all enjoyed grape juice and jelly made from this delicious fruit. He did not necessarily want the grapes, but just needed to prove that he could grow them well. Yes, everything he grew was better than anyone else's around, no doubt about it. Growing up the back of the house were runner beans which, by the end of the season, had reached the roof and started up the television tower which stood to one side.

In June 1957 I received a surprise phone call from Uncle Charles who, with his wife June, was in Toronto for a short weekend stay. They visited the local race track, of course, and then came to our home for dinner when they met my family for the first time. The next day I joined them to go to Father and Emily's home for dinner and it was the first meeting of the two brothers with both the new wives. Father proudly took them on a tour of the greenhouses and, with June showing her great interest in flowers, she made a big hit. Uncle Charles, aware of all the setbacks Father had encountered in his life, was pleased to see that the business was going so well at last. Jim and Wilma joined us for the evening and, though the visit was short, it was a happy one for all.

That year the town of Weston wanted part of the property at the west side of the greenhouses for the extension of Pine Street to Woodward Avenue where more houses were to be built. This would divide the property but it would also give it frontage on a street. When the extension was completed, one end of a greenhouse was immediately changed into a small store with a basement to be used as a working area – designing, etc. From then on more of the flowers grown were used for their own retail use and the balance sold to other flower shops. As time went by the amount of flowers used in the store increased, thus the amount sold wholesale decreased, until all the flowers grown were absorbed in the retail use completely. Father did not usually enter into the retail business, spending his time with the growing in the greenhouses. He loved every plant that grew and one thing that upset him very much was the fact that his son would decide that a certain unpaying crop must be torn out. Father would be sick at heart to see his flowers destroyed. Jim had to keep track of the business end of it so that they could survive, and Father just loved to grow his plants and see them come into full bloom. He was drawn into the retail side of things to a certain degree when they sold the annual plants in the Spring. The steady customers who returned year after year sought him out for advice on plants, and he would whet their interest enough to have them grow plants that they had never grown before! He had quite a following of people who came to him for advice on growing plants and trees. If he walked straight home from the greenhouses, it would take him about five minutes, but it usually took him about an hour in the growing season, because so many people who lived on the street would watch for him and come out of their houses to ask advice on plants.

47. Father's rhododendron bush with 80 blooms.

Father became a grandfather again in April 1958 with the birth of David, son of Jim and Wilma. The girth of the Trimbees was contained somewhat in the death of Uncle Harry in September 1958, in British Columbia. He and Father were the two most eloquent in the political discussions of years gone by during family visits. I know Father missed Uncle Harry when he made the move to BC and the news of his death caused him sadness.

Father's birthday, 1 November, was a day when the family gathered to celebrate. His house was rather small but the crowd of us would squeeze in for dinner, to which all the girls contributed and which was always topped off by a delicious birthday cake, baked and decorated beautifully by Eileen.

The business kept expanding and, at long last, Father could see his hard work and dedication paying off. He never slowed his pace, even though he was well over seventy, an age when most men had retired. His anxiety grew as he thought of pollution increasing in the country. He began to write his views on the subject and sent letters to government authorities, urging them to take the matter under study, hoping for preventive action to follow. Wilma and I were often asked to type his letters and papers on the subject, to make them more presentable in his appeal, but,

48. Father and Uncle Charles, 1957.

unfortunately, no one would take him seriously and frustration set in. Now, at this time of writing, pollution problems have certainly aroused the public, but then the only replies he received in return to his letter were ones of appeasement, with promises to look into the matter; promises never kept. However, he never gave up his battle and continued on with his writings, hoping that some day one of his letters would be received by a man also concerned with pollution.

June 1959 saw Father suffer a serious bout of illness, when he was diagnosed as having an ulcer and was hospitalized for the first time in his life, in Humber Memorial Hospital, next door to his beloved greenhouses. The doctors attempted to cure him with a milk-drip treatment – very uncomfortable – but this was not successful and finally he underwent surgery for removal of the ulcer. He came through the operation well but was surprised that he could be in such rough shape post-operatively, and survive. While in hospital he was, of course, examined thoroughly and the doctors at one point commented to Wilma on what 'terrifically good feet' he had for a man his age. She then thought back to the fact that he had never had shoes fitted at a store and it seemed to her that he could wear anything on his feet without trouble.

Once he was feeling better, he enjoyed entertaining his visitors with his newly-gained knowledge of hospital life. During one visit I made to him, Martha came in shortly afterwards telling Father that the man who lived across the street from the hospital had been turned back in the lobby as only two visitors were allowed in at one time. When I was leaving he asked me to go across to tell this man, who I did not know, to come over then as I had finished my visit. With his sense of humour returned, he muttered some crazy word to me as the friend's name. I crossed the street, knocked at the door and said, 'Mr Wooslybang?' or some such ridiculous name, repeating Father's instructions, whereupon the man denied that he was that person. Smartening up fast, I looked around up to my Father's window which faced the street, to see him looking down at us laughing uproariously, aware of the predicament into which he had put me. After explaining the situation, I was assured that I was at the right house, he was the right man, and obviously enjoyed the joke also. Then I really knew for sure that Father was feeling better and back in form.

After his post-operative recovery he was discharged but was advised to cease pipe-smoking. He set his mind to it, and began sucking a small pebble, which he kept in his mouth, replacing his pipe. This substitute intrigued all, though Emily thought it silly, but, with his usual determination, he overcame the urge to smoke. The pebble was discarded months later and he never did return to his pipe. For his recuperation period at home, Emily bought a comfortable 'chaise longue' on which he could relax in the garden. Father led the role of a 'country gentleman' for the first time in his life and, when visitors came, Emily would serve tea, English style, outdoors. She certainly gave him her full attention, hovering around to fulfil his every need and aid in his complete recovery.

To help alleviate the boredom she thought Father would feel, having to take life easy for awhile, Emily purchased a budgerigar which Father named Joe. This was the first pet bird Father had owned since the skylark he tells of in his story, and he did enjoy teaching it tricks. If the bird could have spoken, it would have had some great conversations with Father, who talked to it all the time. One trick he taught the bird was to sit on the edge of a glass of water and, when Father told him to have a drink, the bird would lean forward and take a sip. Gradually Father would lower the level of the water until, when the bird leaned in, he would fall into the glass! The bird was never hurt and obviously didn't mind as he repeated his performance time after time. Another trick was to have an ashtray with dimes in it – never nickles as they were too heavy – and Father would say to the bird, 'Come on, Joe, go and spend all your money', whereupon the bird would sit on the edge of the ashtray, pick up a dime with its beak and fling it across the room.

Having relaxed for the rest of the summer and, by then, feeling well, Father resumed his daily workload at the greenhouses. By now, Bruce was helping out in his off-time from school and remembers when Father and Jim were changing the gutters on the roof of the greenhouses, to give more headroom. Father had his own proven method and, in his waste-not style, instructed that the used nails be hammered out, to straighten them for re-use. He taught them to lick the rusty nails when re-using them, to avoid splitting the wood! The amazing thing was that no one suffered any ill effects from this.

Martha also at an early age began her chores in the greenhouses. At ten, she was given the job of making-up the boxes to be used in flower delivery. As she grew older, her workload gradually increased until she also spent her off-time from school working in the store, or at office work. When Rob and David were old enough, they joined their brother and sister in the business, as time permitted.

Father's knowledge was put to task in many ways. Martha recalls one day when, after playing in the back field picking wild flowers or weeds, she came home with a big brown splotch on her white blouse. Wilma immediately sent her over to Father with one of the flowers to show him, knowing that he would know what to advise for removal of the stain. he surely was an expert in Nature!

Time passed by quietly with no upsets until one night in February 1962. There was always an alarm bell in Jim's house, set during the winter to ring a warning if the temperature became dangerously low in the greenhouses. On the night in question, the weather was very, very cold with high north winds – the worst kind. The alarm was tested about 7.00 p.m. and proved to be working correctly. Jim had been up half the previous night tending the fires, and spent that day working continuously doing extra funeral orders. He decided to have a short sleep. Wilma went out for a brief time, and was to call Jim upon her return. This she did, and he assured her that he had been over to check the fires while she was out. The alarm did not ring but in the early hours of the morning, when Jim went over to check the fires at the greenhouses, he found half the place frozen out. Father was on the scene shortly afterwards, always taking the early shift for firetending in the winter. It was another unfortunate occurrence in his life to be overcome, so he and Jim tackled the job of cleaning out the beds and went on from there. Why the alarm bell stayed silent was never discovered, and no insurance covered the loss of the crops, which were mostly chrysanthemums and snapdragons. All had been going well but their luck ran out that night.

The main crops grown were chrysanthemums, carnations, snapdragons, stock with ferns and other greenery, for accent, and of course at Christmas, poinsettias; at Easter, lilies and azaleas. In the early days they grew sweet peas, which proved non-paying and thus were excluded from future crops. It certainly wasn't an easy life as they worked from morning until night, seven days a week, but Father loved his work – it was his life, thus he never complained. There was always concern in the cold weather over the chance of flowers freezing, so they had to be constantly on guard, splitting the hours through the night, before they installed an oil furnace. Coal was used for heating for years and the oil iron fireman was not put in use until much later. Jim's children took on more jobs as they grew older. They did a lot of watering, tying the beds – tying string across two ways over the beds so that the flowers would grow up straight. In the summers, Rob took his turn with Bruce, cleaning out the boilers. The boys also cleaned the glass and whitewashed it, to ward off the hot sun in Summertime.

October 1962 brought more sad news when we learned of Aunt Annie's death in England. Father had not seen her since he left England in 1905 but they had always kept in touch by letter. Her sisters in California had been over to see her early in the 1930s; Uncle Bert and his wife Emmy

49. Father viewing the flowers.

50. Ethel and Aunt Annie, England, 1962.

visited her later; Jim had met her during his time overseas in World War II, and cousin Ethel visited her just a few months before, so the whole family had kept in contact. She had lived on the Isle of Wight most of her life, alone in her house since being widowed many years earlier. The eldest in the family, she lived to be ninety-one.

In 1963, Jim and Wilma moved into a bigger house at 180 Church Street. It backed on to the greenhouse property, making it very convenient to the store, which was located at the back of their yard. Many of the family get-togethers were held there, making good use of the larger premises. We always had birthday parties for Father and Emily, never neglecting one as they were getting older. At 180 Church Street, many of these were held as it was larger than Father's house yet close by.

JAMES TRIMBEE FLORIST

•

Bedding Plants List — Spring 1961

Alyssum	- Carpet of Snow—white - Royal Carpet—violet-purple - Rosie O'Day—lavender-rose	**Petunia**	- Comanche—scarlet red - Pink Magic—best bright pink - Ruffled White Magic—dwarf - Blue Magic—finest blue grandiflora
Ageratum	- Blue Mink—powder blue		- Crusader—striped red and white
Aster	- Royal Mixture - Ball White Early - Royal Shell Pink - Royal Azure Blue		- Coral Satin—coral rose, dwarf - Maytime—salmon pink - Sugar Plum, dwarf—bright orchid with wine-red veins
Carnation	- Chabaud Formula Mixture, 15" to 20"		- Glitters—scarlet crimson and white—medium height
Celosia	- Fiery Feather, dwarf 12"—red - Golden Feather, dwarf 12"— yellow	**Phlox** **Portulaca** **Salvia**	- Globe Mixture, dwarf - Double Mixture - St. John's Fire, dwarf 12"
	- Toreador, 18" to 20"—bright red		- America, 20"
Cleome	- (Spider Plant) Pink Queen — rosy pink—4' tall, 3 to 4' across	**Snapdragon** **Verbena** **Zinnia**	- Hit Parade Mixture, 1½' to 2' - Ideal Florist Strain, dwarf - Lilliput Mixture, 18"
Coleus	- Ball Formula Mixture		- Dahlia-flowered Gold Medal Mix-
Lobelia	- Crystal Palace—deep blue		ture, 2' to 3'
Marigold	- Spry, dwarf 10"—yellow and mahogany		- Dahlia-flowered Canary Bird—can- ary yellow, 2' to 3'
	- Lemon Drop, dwarf 9"—yellow - Petite Mix, dwarf 6" to 10"— orange and yellow		- Dahlia-flowered Scarlet Flame, 2' to 3' - Dahlia-flowered Exquisite — light
	- Sunkist, dwarf 9"—orange - Ball Giant Orange—cut flower		rose with deep cerise center, 2' to 3'
	- All-Double Lemon—cut flower - Crackerjack Mixture—cut flower	**Tomato**	- Crimson Cushion or Beefsteak - Stokesdale—75 days
Nicotiana	- Crimson Bedder, 15" - White Bedder, 15"		- Ball Extra Early Fl. Hybrid—55 days
		Sweet Pepper	- California Wonder—72 days

Price: 40c per box or $4.50 per doz. boxes   —   — · —   All in clean plastic plant boxes

POT PLANT VARIETIES

Geraniums - 4" Pots
Red Irene - Salmon Irene, etc.
Price - 50c ea. or $6.00 per dozen.

Tested Outdoor Cut Flower Mums
Yellow, Salmon, Cream, Bronze, Pink.
4" Pots, 40c; 2½" Pots, 20c.

Dahlias - Unwin's Dwarf Mixture Hybrid, 3" Pots, 20c.

Impatiens - Dwarf Mixture, 3" Pots, 25c.

Petunias - Ball All-Double Mixture, 4" Pots, 25c.

Thunbergia - Alata (Black-eyed Susan), 2½" Pots, 15c.

Tomato - Ball Extra-Early Fl.-Hybrid, 3" Pots, 20c.

MINIMUM LOCAL DELIVERY VALUE - $2.00

TELEPHONE - CH. 1-6951   OPEN MAY 21st

GREENHOUSES - CHURCH and PINE STREETS
(Next to Humber Memorial Hospital)

Brother Bill was employed with the Toronto Parks Board, first at Allen
Gardens and then transferred to High Park, where he worked until
retirement in later years. Naturally, when he visited Father, the main topic
of conversation was horticulture. Alan, Eileen and family were still living
in Bowmanville but made the trip up to see Father and Emily quite often.
Merv and I, with our daughters, had moved to Mississauga, a short distance
from Weston, so the whole family was no great distance from each other.

Bruce was working then at a car dealership in Weston, apprenticing
for his mechanic's papers, having decided that greenhouse work was not
the vocation for him. Rob, still in school, showed more interest in the
business; an interest that was to develop through the years.

In September 1963, Father lost another brother in the death of Uncle
Bert. This ended another long companionship, as Uncle Bert had come
to Canada with Father and they had worked together for a while, until
Uncle Bert started his own business. Their visits back and forth had
spanned the years and after Uncle Bert's wife, Aunt Emmy, died, he
would drive out by himself to the greenhouses to chat with his brother.
Father, then, was the only one of his generation of the family alive here
in Toronto area: his two sisters Ede and Lottie, in California. His remaining
brother, Charles, made his home on a ranch in the northern part of the
same state where he lived when not working elsewhere at a race track.

In the Summer of 1964, Father finally thought of taking life a little
easier. It was certainly about time. He was heading for his eightieth
birthday, the business was flourishing, and it could well be left in Jim's
capable control. His years of hard work had resulted in success and so the
legal partnership was dissolved, for business reasons, and the four lots they
still owned on the west side of the property were sold to a builder. This
did not mean that Father was retiring completely but he would work
part-time, until he chose to give up permanently.

Uncle Jack and Aunt Ede returned that summer for another visit from
California. Much to our surprise, they somehow persuaded Father and
Emily to make the return trip with them. Father had always wanted to
see the different horticulture there would be in California's climate and
thought 'now or never'. The plan was to drive to Uncle Jack and Aunt
Ede's home in Ventura, north of Los Angeles, sightseeing along the way.
There they would stay for a few days and then the four of them would
drive north to Alameda, near San Francisco, for a reunion with Father's
youngest sister, Lottie, who lived there. After a visit with her, they would
continue north again to Uncle Charles' ranch at Laytonville. Uncle Charles
and June, unfortunately, would not be there, as they were still in Vermont
working at a race track for the season, unable to return to the ranch until

51. Emily, Uncle Jack, Aunt Ede and Father, Weston, 1964.

the end of October. However, as we had learned from Aunt Ede years
before, Aunt Margaret would be there to greet them. Yes, Uncle Charles'
first wife was still considered part of the family, even though she and
Charles were divorced many years earlier. Apparently, she and June had
a great regard for each other and, as Aunt Margaret was still supported
by Uncle Charles, the situation worked out to the benefit of all three.
Aunt Margaret had her own apartment at the ranch, though she spent
part of her time with old friends in San Francisco, and when Charles and
June were away from Spring to Fall at a track, she would supervise the
maintenance of their property.

Uncle Charles knew we had the knowledge of this arrangement and,
by now, his Christmas cards to Father and myself were signed with all
three names! Because of this he planned, when hearing of the proposed
trip, to have Aunt Margaret fill in as hostess for Father and Emily, while
they stayed at the ranch. According to Aunt Ede, Aunt Margaret and June
had almost a mother and daughter relationship, with such a difference in
ages, and showed great respect for each other.

Uncle Jack and Aunt Ede were staying at my home for their visit here
and so, very early on the appointed morning, Wilma drove Father and

Emily out to join them for their departure on the long journey. Wilma and I waved farewell as the four of them rode off and I had thoughts of my own that they would never complete the journey which lay ahead. Uncle Jack and Aunt Ede both seventy-eight, Emily past her eightieth birthday and Father nearing his. Thankfully I was wrong, and the reports later showed the trip to be quite an adventure which they completed! I had given Father a trip book in which he could record what he saw and, as shown, it was the 'nature' of the trip that impressed him more than anything else. With the book now in my possession, happily these can be related in his own words.

15 September 1964   Well, here we are on the first night of our departure at South Bend, Indiana. It seems to be a wonderful state—well-clothed in bush and protected with wind breaks. Far ahead of Ontario and with far less dead and decayed timber. Most of the crops seen were corn—were good and the general appearance was healthy all through the state. Michigan was good and Indiana was better—a nice state. We left Ontario early this morning and it was dull and dreary weather most of the day. Crops were fair but saw few ponds and lacked bush or wind breaks.

16 September   Tonight we are staying at Tama, Iowa and are well through the state. Corn by the thousands of acres, also large crops of soybeans and sorgum. We passed by Chicago which is quite a place and several other large cities that were interesting. Good farming country mostly but no fruit trees and little vegetables were noticed. So far the bush and trees seem to be in a healthier condition than in Ontario.

17 September   *Ogallala, Nebraska.* We have been passing through Nebraska most of the day and are still in that state. We went through a lot of lovely country where the crops of at least half the state were corn and beans. Corn crops look good and ready for harvest in most cases. The wind breaks are far better than in Ontario. Very little fruit or vegetables seen growing. The west side is changing with more and more land unfit for cultivation and crops changing also with alfalfa growing on thousands and thousands of acres. They are cutting the late crops now and drying it for special feed in dozens of large plants along the roadside. This end of the state seems to have fall wheat and cattle. I'm told that rainfall here is only about seventeen inches for the season. Lots of cattle showing up now. The weather so far has been very cool and dull with not much sunshine.

18 September   *Rock Springs, Wyoming.* We arrived here after going through some of the most desolate parts of America, the latter part of the day especially. Hard to describe hundreds of miles of useless land with no water and no grass. We stopped at Medicine Bow after which we stopped for gas at Laramie—not much like on TV! Quite a few folks live there but the stage coach did not come in while we were stopped!

19 September   *Filmore, Utah.* We woke up to frost this morning and had to
scrape it off the windshield before we could get under way. Stopped
at 'Little America' for breakfast. This is a million-dollar outfit in the
middle of nowhere with everything including fifty-five gas pumps! We
saw it advertised from 900 miles away. By noon we had reached Salt
Lake City. Some city—right up against the Rockies and spread out for
miles, south, north and east. Stayed to hear the organ recital at the
temple. Some square, some buildings, some organ! Hard to believe such
a place could exist so close to the Rockies. A surprise after travelling
through the hundreds of miles of desolation before reaching it. After
leaving there we travelled down a valley for the rest of the day, where
the terrain was much better than that which we traversed yesterday.
We are now south south-west. This Filmore is in a valley of the Rockies.

20 September   Las Vegas, Nevada. Reached here 4.00 p.m. after going through
another different climate. Have been travelling all day down through
the Rockies. There are a few spots where folks are able to live but,
on the whole, the country is made up of thousands of miles of mountains
and useless space of every conceivable shape and formation, with a little
juniper and sage. Now we have reached cactus country after passing
through a corner of Arizona. Saw pampas grass growing in one small
town near the Rockies. This Las Vegas is hard to describe. It's away
out in the desert, the night life goes on all night long with the gambling
places too numerous to count. Some place! We visited a few of the
places to see what they were like but were back to our own 'shack'
by 10.00 p.m. All are well.

21 September   Ventura, California. Left Las Vegas early this morning after
having a terrible wind storm through the night. Stopped at the Hoover
Dam which is about forty miles from Las Vegas and not much out of
our way. After going through some terrible cuts in the mountains, we
reached there in time for the first tour of the day. This dam is sure
quite a feat being 700 feet high but like other places around us, they
are not getting nearly the amount of water to justify the dam's height
because the high water mark shows the dam need not have any more
than 300 feet or, at the most, 400 feet high. According to the guide,
regarding holding water, there is not much chance of adding to the
water supply without a cloudburst in the mountains. We could learn
from it. I could have stayed and studied the dam all day but we had
to be on our way. Oh, by the way, on account of low water, the dam
is only working at about thirty per cent of its potential. From there
we went on our way to Ventura, going through valleys with the
mountains all around. There were miles of useless space with the
occasional little town or village where a little water has shown up. They
have done wonders where possible. This type of terrain carried on until
we reached the outskirts of Ventura where we entered areas of orange,

lemon and walnut groves for several miles down a valley. This took us into Ventura about 6.00 p.m.

22 September   Ventura, California. Here we are in Ventura, a nice town between the mountains and the Pacific Ocean which we have viewed. Today we went up into the mountains for spring water—about forty miles north of the town. We went through similar terrain as we did yesterday, seeing olive trees seventy-five feet high, and walnut orchards ready for harvesting. These were on rather small tracts of land along the base of the mountains. Any streams that were here have been obstructed with dams up in the hills so you seldom see running water. There are a lot of palms and different trees and shrubs that I have not seen before, growing here adding to the interest of our tours. I saw a rubber tree today that measures nearly twenty feet around, the height was over eighty feet and the spread over 100 feet. There would be enough cutting on it to supply Canada for the next fifty years! By a series of canals, they are bringing in the sea enabling people to go out in the front of their homes by car to town and out in the back to the sea. I may add that all through the district they have used windbreaks extensively to protect the different fruit groves, large and small. The weather here is rather warm in the daytime but cool at night near the ocean.

23 September   *Ventura.* Looked around this area this morning and saw lots of plants and trees new to me. Not very hot today but the brush fires up at Santa Barbara are affecting the atmosphere and bringing down some ash. The reports say the fires are serious. Toured around this afternoon and visited the Senior Citizens Club where I played my first game of shuffleboard. Had dinner at my sister's and then played a game of euchre after which we retired for the night as we were all very tired.

24 September   *Ventura.* In the morning we visited a small nursery and saw a lot of material new to me. I had a good talk with the boss and he gave me a catalogue of the nursery stock. This afternoon we returned to the Senior Citizens Club and had a couple of games of shuffleboard with the old 'cronies'. We had our supper in a restaurant on the pier overlooking the ocean and then watched the boys fishing.

25 September   *Ventura.* Had a walk around the district and again saw quite a few new plants and trees. I found out the name of the grass—Bermuda, a close stiff type which would be hard to wear out. Went down to the pier and watched the fisherfolk who consisted of male and female of all ages and types. All seemed to be having fun.

26 September   *Santa Barbara.* Left Ventura in the afternoon and drove to here which is quite a large city about thirty miles north, fronting the Pacific. On the way we passed numerous oil fields, orange and lemon orchards.

The district backing to the mountains is taken up mostly by large estates. Much farther back there has been a large loss of many large residences caused by the brush fires. Millions of dollars in damage but thankfully the city was not touched by the fires. We went out on a very large pier that juts out over the ocean and also visited a large park which contained some wonderful big trees of many kinds but not much in the way of flower beds.

27 September   *Sequoia National Park.* Well, here we are up amongst the big trees and some trees they are! We left Santa Barbara this morning at 9.00 a.m. and went through miles of orange, lemon, persimmon, nectarine and olive orchards, vineries, cotton fields and some farm land. The orchards continued until we entered the mountains where we went into a 'tizzy' over the road. To reach up here, we had to make over 230 hairpin turns! You really had to 'follow your tail', up and up and up. There were some majestic views on the way but you needed a good driver and Jack is one but I would not go down the same way back in the dark for a hundred dollars. We arrived at the park, which is a big plateau stretching for miles on top of the mountains, about 4.00 p.m. The trees are tremendous and so numerous that it is hard to believe that there are such trees in the world. We are booked for the night in a very comfortable apartment. Jack and I went to a camp fire discussion and movie on Nature schemes which was very interesting.

28 September   *Sequoia.* We are staying over another night here, and spent the day walking around to admire all the wondrous sights. The trees I shall never forget.

29 September   *Madera.* Here we are on our fourth night out from Ventura. The last time I was in a Madeira—different spelling, same pronunciation—was in the Atlantic Ocean about sixty-five years ago! Of course this is a different place and here they <u>want</u> water badly. There, it was all around the island. Jack and I went out at daybreak and walked around the big trees before breakfast, after which we went for a long walk right up to the mountain top. It's impossible to describe all that we did see. There were giant trees all around us, some as close as three monstrous ones in a 30 ft circumference, nearly touching each other and rising 250 ft. I stood by one fallen one that was 100 ft from the bottom, out over the bank another 250 ft and 12 ft through. In some places you could count twenty-five of the monsters without moving and they could be seen like this for three miles or more. There were pines mixed through them that were from 1 to 7 ft through and up to 250 ft high, growing as straight as could be. We only saw two small trickles of water in all that walk so what sustains these mighty trees is hard to fathom as in some places there is so much timber standing in

such small areas. The sorrowful part of it all is that nearly all of the largest trees have been badly damaged by fire which, we are told, happened 160–180 years ago! Some were burned at the base on the side, some half-way up, some to the top and still standing. Nothing is being done to help them as the idea seems to be in keep it like Nature has done. I do not agree with this idea as nowhere in the world would we have such wonders. The place is full of cabins and other buildings for which they have laid a lot of black top that will not help the health of these trees. We left the top at noon and came down the back way to Fresno and through the wonderful stands of pines. As soon as we left, on a mile or so, I saw the large pines—down from the top 2,000 ft—more than I have ever seen in my life. They were truly wonderful. After that there was not much until we reached the flat lands where we again saw olive, lemon, orange, peach, pecan, nectarine groves, grape vineries and cotton. From the foothills to here it was one long level valley with good land. Also saw fig orchards and alfalfa growing. A nice part of the west coast.

30 September   *Laytonville.* We left Madera early this morning for Alameda which is across the bay from San Francisco. My youngest sister, Lottie, lives there but unfortunately is in hospital where we went to visit her. On the way there we went through many wonderful valleys and mountains. We saw grapes by the hundreds of acres, orange, lemon, apricot, peach, olive, walnut and fig orchards, and cotton. Also saw some corn and other vegetables growing. Thousands of acres of lovely flat land but all must be irrigated and if not, it's all burned up. No timber through that country, just scraps at times. I did notice places that had been ruined by fire. After we had our visit with Lottie—too short, because of her illness, but an enjoyable reunion—we made tracks for my brother Charles' place which is in the hills where there is not much good land. We travelled a long way today, the last part in the dark which prevented me from seeing much.

1 October   *Laytonville* at brother Charles' place. Another day when we awoke in new surroundings. Charles has quite a fancy log cabin on the mountainside with woods and bush on all sides. The cabin—really a large house built in cabin-style—overlooks a river which at times swells enough to become a lake if a dam was built. With work and money, the possibilities are here for a wonderful place as it is off the beaten track and very quiet. I tried to do a little fishing, unsuccessfully, as now, like all other places here, the water is very low and the surroundings very dry. Jack and I walked around the place which is extensive. Charles has collected everything here in his home from 'a needle in a haystack', all in a western theme—a really marvellous collection, including a letter signed by Jesse James, the notorious outlaw. I had to go a little easy

today because my legs were not good, a result of the climb up into the big trees, I'm sure.

2 October   *Laytonville*—my brother's place. Jack took me for a walk north of the house and we saw where the possibility of a dam was on Charles' river. If done it would make a beautiful lake below his home. Now the river is low, showing a lot of river bottom in places. To bring out the beauty of the place, the river bed needs to be covered with water. This place certainly has lots of possibilities for a beautiful spot. It is lovely now but with time, work and money the potential is unlimited. In the afternoon we went to a 3,000-acre ranch owned by a wealthy man from San Francisco. On this ranch I saw the most wonderful barn that I have ever seen, 60 ft across, 35 ft high, with an aluminium roof. They have their own dam on the river for irrigation. Their cattle were Herefords crossed with an imported Scottish breed. This gave them black cattle which matured early. I was told that the farm hands were paid $100 a week and board, a far cry from what I earned as a lad. The land is cleared by ridding it of the scrub and bush but now the part outside of the irrigation, is all dust dry. Here in most places on the hill tops where there has been no cutting, there seems to be lots of soil which accounts for the big trees. I am told that this ranch is run more for getting rid of extra cash than making money and it's obvious that the owner has spent lots of money on it.

3 October   *Laytonville*—brother Charles'. This morning, Jack and I toured over the rest of Charles' property on the south end. He has lots of nice trees down that way and lots of land which is more level than the upper part. Also visited his stables although there are no horses kept now. In the afternoon Jack took us for a nice ride through part of the redwood district towards the ocean, about twenty miles from here. We saw a lot of wonderful stands of redwood and pine, one quite different from the other. I noticed a redwood that had broken off 30 ft up and around the base there were from 8–14 trees growing up, second growth and part of them big enough for timber, up to 200 ft high, all in the space of 20–35 ft across. The pine was 6 ft through and up to 200 ft in height and in some places, it was so thick with timber that it was hard to understand how they lived, having had no rain for six months we're told. It is said that they have more rain up here than down in southern California but now everything is parched dry through they expect rain any day. After viewing the Redwood Forest, which is part of Government Preserves or Park, we went on west to the ocean and came out at Fort Bragg. From there we went up the coast for several miles and then turned back inland. Again we passed through miles of the Redwood Forest and pine. This sector is truly a marvellous sight, part of the marvellous trip all through the mountains and valleys. Sometimes we were away up thousands of feet with so many hair-pin turns in the road that we were

nearly dizzy. This were no protection on the low side and no nervous driver should attempt the driving. Again we were lucky in having Jack for a driver and no one showed any fear. Along the way we visited a big lumber saw mill where we could see the huge logs, 5 and 6 ft though, piled up. Going from there we passed a place where they had cut some of these tremendously large trees. Coming home we spied some deer out feeding with the cattle. There are lots of deer around here and they come around Charles' home at night where they eat the roses along with other material. It was a most interesting afternoon.

4 October   *Laytonville at Charles'.* Bad news today as we heard that sister Lottie, though home now in Alameda, is not well so Jack and sister Ede have left to go down to her. Thus we have lost them and it may be the last time we shall meet, as we are all getting old. The dog and I took a stroll around and surveyed the landscape in the morning. In the afternoon we looked over Charles' Trading Post where he has an 'anvil to an anchor' in a tremendous assortment too numerous to mention. I had a talk with his caretaker about trees and places, spending an interesting time with him. The balance of the day was quiet.

5 October   Went for a walk with the dog and met neighbours who promised to take us up to the main Redwood district, which is distinct from the ones we have seen. This is an entirely different direction so we are looking forward to that trip. We enjoyed an evening of slides which one of the neighbours brought in showing scenes of Death Valley and areas of that part of California, accompanied by a descriptive talk. An interesting evening for all.

6 October   *Laytonville,* 1,400 feet above sea level. Again this was such an interesting day. The good neighbours, Roy and Lillie Butterfield, took us for the tour of the main Redwood district as promised, 20–30 miles north of here. The things we saw were, to us, almost unbelievable. We were able to walk amongst the trees at different points enabling us to view them

52. Father in California, 1964.

from all different angles. The journey was a most scenic one all through the mountains, away up and then away down, needing a good driver like Roy who knew the roads well which gave one a feeling of confidence.

7 October   *En route to Vancouver.* Today we readied ourselves early for our departure from Laytonville. We left at 4.00 p.m., after a most delightful stay and were sorry to leave the peaceful surroundings but with plans made, we had to be on our way. A friend took us to the bus and then—what a ride we had through the mountains! We are still on the bus heading north.

8 October   *Vancouver.* Travelled all night and day! It sure takes good drivers for those roads—up and down, in and out. We did not have much chance for any sleep on that rocky ride for eighteen hours, with the drivers changing every six hours, well needed. Arrived safe but tired in Portland, Oregon, a large fine city. It had admirable buildings with large tubs on the sidewalks in front of them containing hawthorne trees and in some places, I saw a fine ground covering which looked smart. After a two-hour wait we were on our way again to Seattle, Washington, where we arrived about 6.30 p.m. This also is a very large city which seems dominated by the Boeing Aircraft Company with their large buildings and grounds, although there are also many other industrial works in the city. Leaving Seattle, we began to see much more water and a lot of it would be from the sea. Sighted lots of young timber about 25–60 years old. As we progressed north there was good farm land, levelled out in large areas. Nice looking country until we nearly reached Canada where there was more broken and uneven bush land up to the boundary. No more could be seen as it was then dark for the rest of our journey to Vancouver. We had a little trouble locating our friends as we had the wrong phone number but finally contacted them and they came to drive us from the bus station to their home. We've made it OK but both very, very tired from the travelling and lack of sleep.

9 October   *Vancouver, BC.* We woke up to our first day in Vancouver still tired, with no pep, so took it quietly today with no tours of the city. I did go for a little walk and noticed that the grass and evergreens sure do well here with the trees putting in a tremendous growth.

10 October   *Vancouver, BC.* Recovering from our last trip but on the look-out once more for different types of Nature lore. Our hosts are moving so I helped move some of the shrubs, thus did not get out any distance.

11 October   *Vancouver, BC.* Rick took us up the high road of the Squamish on a sight-seeing tour on the outskirts of the city. This was a road between the mountains and the sea—truly a wonderful drive for viewing

and we went quite a distance. There is no shortage of water as it is seeping out of the rocks all along the side of the road, which accounts for all the timber here. From there he took us to the British Properties, financed by the Guinness Company. This is a large district of first-class homes built on the mountain side. Very many beautiful homes but must be hard to maintain because of rock and position although they do have some wondrous views over city and sea. Same people also built one of the main bridges, at a cost of seven million dollars, now taken over by the city, so Rick tells us.

12 October   *Vancouver, BC.* Thanksgiving Day. Today Rick drove us up to the Headquarters of the RCMP where he is in charge of the grounds. It is a nice place and well maintained. From there, he took us to the Queen Elizabeth Arboretum which is run by the Parks Board. This is truly a beautiful spot on top of a mountain, set in a deep cliff of the rock—a natural setting for such a scheme. The material there was fair as the season is well on but the grass was wonderful, clean and well cared for, but for an arboretum there were not enough names listed on the materials for the benefit of the public. Leaving there, we went on a ride through Stanley Park which covers many acres with a lot of fine trees and look-outs. A very marvellous park.

Emily and Father took the train back to Toronto after their stay in Vancouver but this end of their journey is not recorded by him in the trip book. From Emily's reports, Father spent most of the train trip up in the observation car, not wanting to miss a thing, to the extent that she was forced to ask the porter to go up and tell Father when it was time to eat or sleep!

His recording ends with the notation to himself to 'explain the mountain trip, the prairies and the sights seen in northern Ontario', but apparently he never did complete it. He did record the names of some of the newspapers in the larger cities of California, probably intending to write to them later giving his views on water conservation, and so on, as he did frequently to the papers here. I also noted that, in his daily write-ups while at Laytonville, he never mentioned Aunt Margaret's name although he spoke well of her upon his return, when talking of the trip. I often felt that he was secretly rather embarrassed by the situation there, although he never said so, but then he never had a bad word to say about anyone in the family.

Father had enjoyed every minute of the trip, more so than Emily, I believe, because of his greater interest in Nature. Emily had begun to suffer from arthritis and must have found so much travelling painful at times. The rest of us found it amazing that the two of them, at their age, could have kept up such a continuing fast pace for the length of time

they were away. We were all glad that he had been able to fulfil his desire
to see that part of the country, with its horticulture, both cultivated and
wild—so different to any he had seen before. Once home, he enjoyed
his favourite 'Westerns' more than ever, having travelled through the land
pictured in them, and had even managed to bring back a few stalks of
pampas grass that he himself had cut out west: a prized souvenir. During
visits to Weston, we enjoyed hearing him recount details of the trip,
details that only he would have kept in his still very active mind. I'm
sure that no one else would have absorbed so much of Nature as he did.

On 1 November that Fall we held, at Jim and Wilma's home, a big
birthday party for Father to celebrate his eightieth birthday. We did not
feel that at his age it should be a surprise entirely but we did keep from
him the names of all those invited. There were the Trimbee relatives,
neighbours, old friends including as many of the gardening associates as
we could contact. Father had a wonderful time, talking constantly to one
after another, when they made their appearance at the party. Some of
them he had not seen for years and many were the happy memories
recalled. He was the recipient of numerous presents to mark the occasion,
and one that greatly amused him was a mechanical monkey made up to
toss dice, for a reminder of his stay in Las Vegas on his way to California!

The afternoon was topped-off with him cutting a huge birthday cake,
made as always by Eileen, this time enjoyed by many more than usual.
It was a happy afternoon that he enjoyed thoroughly and reminisced about
for quite a while.

CHAPTER 8

Once rested up from the trip and the party, Father returned to work at the greenhouses, age not stopping that. During this period of time, a stray cat appeared one day, and it was a wild one! No one would, or could go near it and it was more like a mad dog than a cat. Father, possessing a great feeling for animals, took it upon himself to tame it. He would stand back, throw some food to the cat and then back off, talking to it all the time, and gradually the cat would approach the food to eat. It took a while to tame the cat but even after that, Father was the only one who could approach him. Later, though, the cat would walk along the wood shelves above, following Father as he worked his way along, watering the plants. When Father was disbudding, he had a wooden box to hold the discards and Tom, the cat, now named by Father, would sit in this box. As Father moved along the path, he kicked the box to move it too, and Tom remained in the box, like a trusting friend. Father continued to talk all the time to the cat and it answered in its own fashion to the point where, sometimes, customers in the store beyond would question as to whether there was a baby in the greenhouse, hearing the goings-on. Tom seemed to know when Father was to arrive for work and would sit at the front of the property waiting for him to show up. And when Father left to go home at the end of the day, Tom would just go crazy; so upset that Father was gone from him.

Early in the new year of 1965, Father decided to lessen his working hours. They were to be from 10.00 a.m. till 3.30 p.m. but his day usually stretched out until 6.00 p.m., seven days a week. Once he started to work, time meant nothing to him. Tom sensed the change in hours and adjusted himself, so that he was waiting to greet him at the new starting time. One could tell it was 10.00 a.m., by Tom's appearance right on time and, when Father left for the day, Tom was never seen again until the same time next morning.

One day, before Father made his appearance, Tom was found with a very bad three-inch cut on his thigh, which laid the flesh right open. Apparently he had attempted to go through a hole in the glass, ripping the leg. Jim decided the cat must be taken to the veterinarian and so Rob and the driver somehow managed to put Tom into the back of the truck where he was absolutely wild, bouncing off the walls. When they arrived at the Vet's, Rob finally got hold of Tom with both hands, but when he let go with one hand to open the door, the cat took off, somehow leaping over a 10-ft fence, making a fast escape. Rob and the driver searched the district without success. Tom was gone. Rob's birthday was coming up and he says he felt then that he should ask for a shotgun to use in self-defence, as he knew his Grandpa would be very angry that his beloved Tom was missing and suffering also. Father was indeed upset and told Rob that there had been no need of taking Tom to the vet, as he could have sewn up the cat! He even had Emily prepare a sterilised kit with needle and thread to keep on hand if Tom returned. In later years, Rob's wife asked Father how he could get so 'close' to all these different animals he had known. The reply was that, if you paid attention to anything or anyone, it would pay attention back in return, whether it be animal, plant or person! At the same time he told her of a cat named Jimmy that was his pet in England many years before. The story was that the cat had given birth to kittens on the Master's daughter's bed which was not at all appreciated and of course, it couldn't be called 'Jimmy' any longer, either!

Coming events pushed Tom's disappearance into the background. That Spring, Father suffered a serious heart attack. Emily phoned Wilma to say Father was ill and immediately Wilma rushed to their home where, as soon as she saw Father, she phoned for an ambulance in which she accompanied him to the hospital. Wilma later reported Father's remark to the doctor who checked him in the Emergency Department. He looked up at the doctor and said, 'Well, Sonny, I hope you've been reading more than comic books 'cause I really need some help!' The doctor assured him of his expertise, with a smile, and Father was admitted for a prolonged stay in hospital. He was very ill for a few weeks but gradually improved, though never to be as strong as before, due to the damage done by the heart attack. Once he was feeling slightly better he again became a favourite patient of the nurses. His great sense of humour amused them, all were amazed at such a sharp mind for his age and they enjoyed tending to his needs. He was undemanding and grateful for any attention given him.

He was discharged from hospital at the start of the summer, which he spent recuperating, fussed over by Emily who gave him constant care and comfort. Visitors helped to pass the time, such as Alice and Harry Worth whom Emily had known since her youthful years in England. Harry, retired, had been employed also in gardening so there was a common bond between him and Father. The neighbours came by, relatives visited and members of the family called regularly—Jim to discuss greenhouse business, Bill to tell of his work—so the summer passed uneventfully, with Father content to supervise the tending of his garden by others.

By September Father was eager to return to his work at the greenhouses and did so part-time again, confining himself to light work, leaving the heavier chores to others. However, once the cold weather set in, he found the strain on walking up the street to work too hard on his breathing, and decided that the time had come for him to take full retirement. Thus, nearing age eighty-one, he finished working, after starting at age twelve. Quite a work span for any man!

The family gathered once again to celebrate his eighty-first birthday on 1 November more appreciative than ever to still have him with us after what he had been though since his last birthday. We often remarked that we were so glad Father took the trip to California the previous year as such travelling would no longer be possible, due to his health.

Around the same time as Father's birthday, brother Jim put the Trimbee name into the news in Weston. He was fairly well known in the area because of the business, a member of the Weston Parks and Recreation Board for two years and at that time, President of the Lions Club of Weston. The time was nearing for the Municipal Elections and in Weston this included six aldermen on the council and a mayor. Only six nominees entered for aldermen, and rather than have them acclaimed, someone 'twisted' Jim's arm and suggested that he, 'just put his name on the ballot to cause a contest: let people have a choice.' Acceding to this plea, he entered his name, informing his family immediately, though he did not expect to win. Father thought this was great and took a keen interest in his son's campaign. He went to all the candidates' meetings and, never taking a back seat or showing favouritism, questioned all the candidates, including his own son, on different issues of the day, much to the amusement and enjoyment of all present. I'm sure that if he had been able to run for office himself in his earlier life, he would have been a lively candidate. I worked on the campaign daily in Weston for a few weeks. One final job was to move down to Father's house to use their phone, leaving the phone lines in the campaign office free for others to use. With a list to follow, I phoned as many voters as possible, in the time left before the polls closed, to offer rides if they had not already voted. This was entertainment for Father and Emily as they listened to my 'pitch' and I then conveyed to them the answers received, some of them humorous, some of them strange, but all enjoyed by my listeners.

Jim was victorious in the election and to his surprise, received more votes than any other candidate, with the result that he was also Acting Mayor during any absence of that official. The whole family gathered on the evening of election night to watch the returns tabulated and, later, to celebrate the victory. One more happy night for the Trimbees!

To everyone's surprise, Tom the cat returned to the greenhouses in December. He had been given up for dead months earlier, so it was with great relief and pleasure that Rob rushed down to inform his Grandpa of the good news. Father was overjoyed to hear of the cat's return and remarked to Wilma shortly afterwards that he had just received his first and best Christmas present. He even had the thought of bringing Tom down to live at the house but soon dismissed that idea, knowing that the cat was not tame enough. Sadly, six weeks later, the cat was found dead in one of the greenhouses, lying under a slow-dripping tap. He had died of distemper and apparently had sought to cool his fever under the water dripping out. Who knows, maybe Tom just couldn't get along without his buddy, Father, around any more?

By the next Spring, Father was prepared to start working in his own garden but soon found, much to his chagrin, that he was not able to do all the work required. A man was hired to do the digging, under Father's direction, of course, and others would help out. Father felt confined by his health restrictions but had no choice so once more he was in the role of supervisor of any help given. Martha remembers him sitting in a chair in the garden, explaining to her how to thin-out his white turnips, tie up the tomatoes and other like jobs. She was glad to do these things for him but always felt that she would never do them as well as her Grandpa. Sometimes, though, he did put forth more effort than was wise, not willing to give in completely. David recalls one time when his Grandpa came up to the greenhouses to get bags of soil which he would drag home for use in his garden. He was forced to stop and rest at the end of the driveway and then warned David not to tell Emily as she worried about him. David was very young at the time and wondered why his Grandpa had to rest. Father had always been strong and self-reliant so David took for granted that he would be that way forever.

Father's interests were taken slightly farther afield when cousin Jim Flack built a new home on a lovely piece of property in Streetsville. He was 'Jamie' to Father even though by now he was a school principal, a married man with four growing sons. His contact with Father had continued over the years and now he invited him out to see his new home, the landscaping he had done, and to ask advice on further improvements. Father was happy to hear of Jim's new acquisition and willingly accepted the invitation.

Jim recollected:

Uncle Jim was very impressed with the location of the property and its proximity to the river, which meant good drainage. He toured very carefully all my planting, questioning me as to what I had done, telling me various things to do and that I hadn't done but basically commended me on what I had accomplished. I do recall that, as we walked along the back, he asked me, 'When did you have the argument with your neighbour at the back?' I thought to myself, 'Now what's coming?' but replied that I had not had an argument and that the neighbour was a friend of mine. He said, 'He's no friend of yours—he's got those weeds growing there along the property line, robbing your land of nourishment and water and the sooner you cut them down, the better!' Those 'weeds' were big poplar trees. My neighbour had been there first and, when I moved in, he had planted them for privacy—but—the trees are down now: they died—the neighbours are still there and still good friends.

I also took him for a walk up to where there were no houses, up on the escarpment, and he loved it. He stood on the banks viewing the Credit River, gave me some history—why the water was so low and why we had to do something about it or the whole world would go down the drain! I can recall an article in a newspaper one time—'Conservationist James Trimbee of Weston, saying (and he always said this), Every farm or every field needs a pond.' He was quite concerned about the drainage on our property but, by and large, he was pleased with what we'd done.

My boys were fascinated by Uncle Jim. They hadn't had as much contact with him as I and one of the greatest fascinations was the nail on his right index finger which was long and carved downwards. It was gnarled and rather strange looking but he enjoyed showing the boys how he could use it to pinch leaves off trees, bud off plants etc. He always had some little game or trick to show them.

He was into his writings earnestly by then, having more free time in his retirement. I used to tease him and tell him that he wrote just like Plato because his titles always began with 'On Conservation', 'On Pollution', and so on, like Plato's had.

I was impressed with Uncle Jim because of his 'presence', and he had the capability of being a 'centre'. He didn't try to be but people would ring around him with a sort of space between him and them. When he came to visit us, it was like an 'Earl' or 'Duke' appearing amongst us, although he carried on in his own way.

In the long winter, Father did keep busy with his writings about pollution, water conservation and the likes. Remembering his Grandpa, David pictures him sitting in his little TV room writing away with all sorts of paper around him and, though busy, he was never too busy to make you feel welcome for a visit. A neighbour once told David that his Grandpa was twenty years ahead of the times in his obsession with pollution. Time proved the neighbour correct. In those days, no one wanted to pay attention to him on the matter but now it is headlines in the papers.

Father always looked forward to the CNE so that he could go to see the Flower Building displays. Emily did not relish the thought as she feared for his well-being when he went on these outings alone. She could not accompany him as the arthritis she suffered prevented much walking. Nevertheless, he would not miss it and would walk to the end of the street, take the bus, transfer to a streetcar which took him into the 'Ex'. He went on a Senior Citizens' Day to get in free, after using his Senior's pass on the TTC. One year, looking very dapper in his navy blue suit contrasting with his white hair, he went to the gate of the CNE, where he was asked if he was a Senior Citizen. This filled him with pleasure and he replied, in his joking way, 'Just look at the back of my neck where it's stamped—made in 1884!' His time there was spent mainly in the flower building but he gradually became disillusioned and remarked that he thought it had become more of a display area for the Parks and Recreation Department. He did not think that there were any exceptional displays, by private companies, as had been seen in earlier years.

One Fall, Father asked Martha to take photos of his runner beans to show how high they had grown. He told her that when she was older, married and with children of her own, she would be able to show them photos of the beans growing up the back of the house, right on up the TV tower, and that she should tell them they could believe in stories like 'Jack and the Beanstalk'! Another Fall, when the beans were up so high, he insisted I climb up to pick them as he was past doing the job himself. I protested going up as high as the TV tower, expressing my fear of electricity, to which he replied, 'Get up there, don't be so silly!' Needless to say, I carried out his orders without any further argument.

He was very proud of his garden and the fact that he could grow anything which was seemingly true. His perennial border in the back yard was a joy to behold and, knowingly, from his delphiniums and other plants, he would take seed at the right time for further use. As a teacher, he excelled and, if you expressed interest, he was happy to show you all the growing methods he used.

Martha remembers her Grandpa telling her that he once considered becoming a minister but had to forget that in a hurry as it was a financial impossibility. This shows what a deep thinker he was in all areas, a very intelligent man who, unfortunately, did not have the resources to further himself in school. When Martha grew older, she was informed by her Grandpa of the dangers of pollution and other like issues. He showed her his drafts of letters he had written to the authorities about this, and asked her to read them to check the spelling and grammar for him. A dictionary was always by his side when writing; he felt very badly about his lack of formal education and sometimes in letters he would write, 'When I was a young man at Cambridge . . . ' Martha questioned this and he replied, 'I was in the town of Cambridge once,' with a smile on his face, 'they don't have to know the difference!' He never went so far as to put that in a letter sent but, sadly, he learned over the years that the people to whom he wrote his letter did know the difference and paid no attention to him. He was not a man with letters after his name and, therefore, they probably assumed he could not know anything pertinent to the subject. One year, he wrote a letter to Inco complaining of their new high

53. (& 54.) The runner beans reach the top of the house.

54. Runner beans continue up TV tower!

smokestack, which he felt would just send the pollution that much farther. The company did reply, which pleased him, as many other never had the courtesy to answer his letters. History has proved that he was a forerunner in his fear for the future of our water, forests, etc. Acid rain would be an added burden to him these days.

In 1967, Trimbee Florists opened a temporary small lot on Jane Street, near John Stret, to sell annuals for spring planting. One of the employees hired for this was Paul Fini, a young lad who worked there after school and on weekends and, after the lot was closed, he continued to work off-school times in the greenhouses. He was to become more important

55. The delphiniums in full beauty.

to us than just an employee as, in a few years hence, he and Martha were to marry.

On 29 October that Fall, we held a Trimbee family reunion with a dinner which took place in a private dining room of a local Weston restaurant. All the Trimbees in the Toronto area attended, as well as cousin Ethel, her husband Jack, who came down from their home in Barrie and, unexpectedly but happily, cousin Lottie and her husband Fred who were visiting at the time from their home in New Jersey. Father was, of course, the honoured guest, not only because he was the head of the family, the oldest one there and the only remaining one of his generation in Canada, but also because his eighty-third birthday was coming up shortly on 1 November. After dinner, Jim acted as Master of Ceremonies, with a few well chosen remarks about the joy of the occasion, bringing the family all together and giving Father birthday greetings, in which all present joined. Greetings were also extended to Ethel and Jack, who would be celebrating both their birthdays and wedding anniversary also on 1 November. Following the dinner and greetings, we continued the reunion at Jim's home where family stories were recounted once more, to everyone's enjoyment, with Father as the 'star' of the evening!

56. Father and Emily at Trimbee family reunion, 1967.

CHAPTER 9

E lection time came around in the fall of 1967 and changes were made in the Municipality of Weston when it was incorporated into the Borough of York, which is part of Metropolitan Toronto. Jim ran successfully again for Alderman and, as before, Father attended all local meetings, questioning the candidates, his son included, on current issues. Fortunately Jim always had the answers! Whatever the weather, Father never missed voting, which he considered to be every citizen's duty. There was always a campaign sign on the lawn of his house for Jim, and his interest in the campaign never waned. Another happy family gathering took place on election night to celebrate Jim's second victory.

Early in 1968, another branch of Trimbee Florists opened on Maple Leaf Drive at the corner of Jane Street. This, it was hoped, would catch the passing trade, being in a more travelled area than the store at the greenhouses. It was obvious that the business was steadily improving. Though Father was not working any longer, he and Emily helped out in their own way. During busy times in the flower trade, such as Easter and Mother's Day, Emily would prepare food for Jim's family, who by then were all engaged in working in the stores or delivering at those times. She packed the food in a wicker basket and Father delivered it, said, 'Hello,' had a look around at the stock in the stores and then disappeared to let them get on with their work. By this time, there was other full-time help employed, with extras for special days. Father and Emily kept up their food service for as long as they were able.

In the spring, news was received of another intended visit by Uncle Jack and Aunt Ede for the coming summer. They planned to stop in and see us all on their way to the Rideau Lakes, north of Brockville, where my cousin Lottie and husband Fred operated a summer tourist lodge. They expressed a hope that Father would take the trip down there with them, knowing Emily's arthritis would prevent her from going. Father showed interest in this prospect and in the meantime gardened as best he could, which was still very good for his age and health.

57. Father's twenty-fifth anniversary shoes.

He often walked down to Frank's fruit market on Jane Street to shop for Emily and would stop to talk with the Italian owner. One day Father queried him about the high price of garlic and Frank told him that it was because it couldn't be grown properly in Canada. Father bought one clove each of red and white, went home and grew a whole crop of this garlic over the summer. He returned to Frank's fruit store with a six-quart basket of each type, put them on the counter saying, 'There you go, don't tell me these things can't be grown in Canada!' He knew he could grow anything and Frank's statement was a challenge to his knowledge.

On 31 July 1968, Jim and Wilma celebrated their twenty-fifth anniversary with a party at their home, given by their children. Another family gathering was enjoyed, Father and Emily highlighting the party with their presence. At one point of the evening, Father 'stole the show' when, with a sly smile, he commented that his shoes were also have their 'twenty-fifty anniversary'. Yes, he was wearing the shoes that had been purchased for him to wear at Jim and Wilma's wedding! They were his dress-up shoes and obviously he didn't dress-up to go out very often, though I'm sure the shoes had been soled and heeled more than once over the years. As I have told earlier, Father was a man to whom the essentials in life, including clothing and footwear, were fine if adequate—more than that was never sought. Luxuries for himself were never desired. To mark the occasion of the shoes, Martha took the silver medallion that decorated the party cake, placed it between Father's shoes and took a photo to record the event!

Uncle Jack and Aunt Ede arrived in August and Father was feeling well enough to go to cousin Lottie's. He did not travel with them for they had planned an extensive visit; longer than Father wanted to be away, so he accepted an invitation from cousin Ethel and husband Jack to go down with them for a weekend. The lodge was situated on Brothers Island, accessible only by boat, so there he was at eighty-three, heart attack and all, riding the waves once again! He enjoyed his stay there, walking all over the island, seeing another different part of the country, but then

58. Father in the greenhouse, 1968.

he had always enjoyed any outing made possible. We heard later that all there, including the paying guests, had found him 'a joy to have in their midst'. As usual, his personality delighted eveyone!

Sadly, Uncle Jack took ill on their way back to California, two days after leaving Toronto, resulting in his admission to the local hospital, and Lottie and Fred flew out to assist the older couple in their time of stress. In time, Fred drove Uncle Jack's car to California and the other three flew back. Uncle Jack died shortly after his return home and, after his funeral, Lottie and Fred returned to Brothers Island to close the lodge for the winter, after which they drove home to New Jersey. It was another sad loss for Father, especially as he had seen more of Uncle Jack and Aunt

59. Jean and father, 1 November, 1968, on his 84th birthday.

Ede in the past ten years than in the previous thirty, and felt grateful to them for the wonderful trip to California they had made possible for him.

In 1969, Father had another setback with his heart trouble, requiring a short stay in hospital, but he recovered well enough to recuperate at home and then continue with his writings and gardening at his own pace. As usual, his property was the showplace of the street with its many varieties of colourful flowers.

That spring I had cause to give him pleasure with respect to his garden. As he wrote in his story, he had brought a new variety of dahlia, the Jean Trimbee, on to the market when he ran his dahlia gardens while living in Lambton Mills, before we moved to Glenalton. He had disposed of his stock before moving and, over the ensuing years, the 'Jean Trimbee' had disappeared from the market. I now met a dahlia grower who was interested in my story of the dahlia, searched other sources and finally located another dahlia grower, who did have some Jean Trimbee tubers. With great anticipation, I contacted this second grower, obtained some tubers and gave them to Father to grow, using his magic touch. He produced a fine ornamental show of them with beautiful blooms from summer through fall. The 'Jean Trimbee' had returned to the family! In later years I acquired them and still grow them with pride and pleasure, doing my utmost to follow his instructions for their care. One great belief of his is outlined in the poem below which I found in his possessions later. It covers not only gardening, but also life.

> 'Fore the soil begins to bake,
>   Cultivate!
> Stir it up for culture's sake,
>   Cultivate!
> Tillage hinders 'vaporation,
> Tillage works weed 'radication,
> Tillage helps food 'laboration,
>   Cultivate!
>
> If it rains and lays the dust,
>   Cultivate!
> If it pours and forms a crust,
>   Cultivate!
> Save the moisture hygroscopic,
> Help the microbes microscopic,
> Talk to neighbours on this topic,
>   Cultivate!
>
> If your head begins to swell,
>   Cultivate!
> Harrow, crush it, pound it well,
>   Cultivate!
> Cultivate a humble heart,
> Give 'Big I' a meaner part,
> Let the germ of culture start,
>   Cultivate![1]

[1] Source unknown.

60. "Jean Trimbee" dahlias.

During the summer, my husband Merv and I took Father up to Keswick to the farm of 'Whipper' Billy Watson, the well-known Canadian wrestler. He had a large property on which he grew mostly corn, and kindly gave Father the 'grand tour'. It had been years since Father had visited a farm and he thoroughly enjoyed the day, and meeting Whipper.

By now, grandchildren of the Trimbee family were marrying and Father and Emily were always honoured guests. Some of these brides and grooms were marrying mates of varied ethnic descent and Father passed the remark that the family 'was getting to be quite the League of Nations', but accepted it all, knowing that it was a changing world in which we were living, far from life in little Upham. He did not modernise his term of reference, though, to 'United Nations'!

Jim ran again in the fall elections, this time for the position of Controller, stepping up from Alderman, which meant that he would represent the whole Borough of York instead of one Ward. This entailed a stronger effort in a bigger campaign to reach all the voters in the Borough so, as before, I went out daily to help work done in the office in his home. Because of this, I saw Father and Emily more frequently than usual. I remember one day, when driving up Church Street on my way to the office, I sighted Father coming down the street with a small trailer, made from a child's wagon, attached to a wheelbarrow which he pulled behind him. He was busy gathering up the neighbours' leaves, left out on the roadside for him to make compost for use in his garden. Again he was practising his 'earth to earth' theory, ignoring the hard work involved, his decreased health and his age of nearly eighty-five. Stopping my car, I jokingly inquired of him how much he gave for 'old rags and rummage'. He grinned, well able to take a joke as well as give one, and explained his mission. I complimented him on his ingenuity in the transportation of the leaves, cautioned him not to tire himself and drove on, smiling, thinking of what a marvel he was.

Jim not only won his election but gained the majority of the votes for the two Controller seats which meant that, as well as his duties with York Borough Council, he also sat on the Metropolitan Toronto Council. Father's pride was obvious in his son's victory and Jim would often, on his visits to Father, discuss the issues of the day, recounting the topics of the meetings he attended, bringing Father up to date on the happenings at both Councils. Father's interest in politics never lagged and often we would see letters of his on current issues printed in the newspapers on the 'Letters to the Editor' page. To mark the distinction, Father was always

61. *The family at Jim's inauguration, 1970. Rob, Martha, James Jr, Wilma, James, David.*

62. *Mr and Mrs Trewin, 1970.*

'James W Trimbee, Sr' and Jim 'James W Trimbee Jr'. With Jim in politics and Father active in his writings, this distinction was a necessity.

The dream trip of my life finally came true in August 1970 when, after years of hoping, I visited England and Scotland. Merv and I, his brother Gordon and wife Marion, and our youngest daughter Janis made the trip together. Before we left, I spent time with Father querying him about Upham, his birthplace, which was a 'must' on our planned trip. He was so pleased to know that we would be seeing his old village and gave me a vivid picture of the way he remembered it. After touring the northern part of England where we visited with relatives on Merv and Gord's side of the family, we drove through Scotland and down the west side of England, finally arriving in Cornwall at the home of dear old Mrs and Mrs Trewin, our old neighbours from Glenalton. I had written to their daughter Marion, my old pal, of our impending visit, so they were excitedly awaiting us. Our busy time schedule only permitted a short but sweet visit with them but, after all the years that had passed, it was good to see them again. Many were the questions asked of me, about my dear Mother, Father and his new life with Emily, my brothers and sisters and cousins they remembered. Poor Mrs Trewin was so overwrought with emotion that she was in tears for our whole visit, pouring tea and putting out cakes while wiping her eyes! Glenalton to the fore again as the happy days there were recalled once again. From there we made our way to Plymouth, Devon, where the Trewin's daughter Marion lived with her husband John and son Peter. Another similar visit, hugs and kisses, tea and tears! It had been thirty-five years since I had seen her though we had always stayed in touch by letters. Onward again to what would prove to be the highlight of the trip.

Following the map anxiously, we entered the little village of Upham about 6.00 p.m. on a Sunday evening. Upham at last! We stopped at the local pub, the Brush Makers' Arms, to inquire about lodgings for the night, and were advised to go up around the bend to the home of Mrs and Mrs Ken Freemantle, who sometimes took in guests for 'Bed and Breakfast'. Merv, Gord and Marion drove round to there while Janis and I walked, anxious already to see the local sights.

What a delightful little village and, eerily, just about the same as Father had remembered it from when he left sixty-five years ago. The reason for this, we were told later, was that the area had been declared a 'green belt' and no further building could be done, to keep the village historically as it was many, many years before. Any repairs or alterations would have to follow the original architectural lines. How lucky for me personally! As Janis and I walked up the road from the pub, passing the houses and

63. Jean at Upham sign, Manor House in background.

64. Janis outside the family home – old cherry tree still there.

areas described by Father earlier, I felt as if I had been there before!
Everything was just as Father had described it. The only place missing
was the old schoolhouse, which had been across the road from Father's
home. Unfortunately, it had deteriorated with age until, beyond repair,
it was torn down.

Mr and Mrs Freemantle accepted us as guests but regretted that they did
not serve evening meals, suggesting that we drive into Winchester, seven
miles north, for dinner. But after I recounted for them my family's con-
nection with the village, their hospitality was extended to include an
invitation for supper, if we didn't mind a short wait. Tea was served
immediately and, while they prepared the meal, we settled into our rooms

65. Jean outside the Trimbee family home.

which meant them giving up their own bedroom, going into Mr Freemantle's Mother's house next door to sleep. Such hospitality for strangers,
but the Upham tie had brought extra consideration for us. In the meantime,
we took advantage of the daylight left to walk around the village, taking
many photos to show Father when we returned to Canada. At Father's old
homestead, we knocked on the door to explain the reason for our pho-
tography to the lady owner, to satisfy any curiosity she may have had, after
seeing her look out the window. She was kind enough to invite us in and
showed us all around the house. Of course, there had been modernisation
and changes but basically the layout was just as Father remembered. In the
front garden the old cherry tree, of which Father had often spoken, still
stood proudly, though now gnarled and showing its age.

66. Mr and Mrs Freemantle and Merv outside "B & B". House was Blundell's in Father's childhood.

After a delightful supper, in which everything offered had come fresh out of their garden, except the ham, we were advised to go round to the pub, hopefully to meet some old timers who might remember the Trimbee family. Janis stayed with the Freemantles while the four of us made our way back to the Brush Makers' Arms, where once, it is claimed, Cromwell stayed. The name came from the fact that over a hundred years ago the old schoolhouse nearby had been the site of a small brush-making factory and so, for decor, the pub walls were decorated with brushes of every type and size. The pub itself had been in existence since then. We were greeted by the locals in a very friendly manner and we did meet one man, a Mr Stubbington, who, though

67. Jean outside the Brush Maker's Arms.

slightly younger than Father, remembered the young ones of the family. The Stubbingtons were always, and still are, the bell-ringers of the Upham Church Father attended. It was a delightful evening, topped off by the owner removing one of the tiny brushes from the wall, to send home with me for Father.

Before making our departure the next morning, we visited the Church, took photos of it both inside and out and found the tombstone marking my Grandfather's grave in the churchyard. I also sent Father and Emily a card from there, so that it would be postmarked 'Upham'. The Freemantles were excellent hosts and the five of us wished we could have spent more time in the village, one of the most picturesque places we visited in our entire trip. Little did I know then that I would return in later years.

68. Janis at Upham Church.

As soon as possible, after we arrived home in Canada, I hurried out to Weston to give Father a descriptive account of our trip, especially Upham, to which he listened avidly. I was so happy that I could truthfully tell him of our very high opinion of the village, which I am sure pleased him immensely. My regret was that, when time and finances finally permitted him to make a return visit himself, his health prevented it. A look of nostalgia came into his eyes when I spoke of his old home. Memories, I'm sure, came flooding back to him. He was very appreciative of the tiny brush sent home to him as a gift from the pub-owner and displayed it prominently in his home from then on.

69. Grandfather's tombstone in Upham churchyard.

The following Christmas I gave him a present of an album containing enlargements of all the photos taken in Upham, and Emily said later that it was the best present he received that year. She also told me that it became such a frequent habit of his to look through the album, that she kidded him that he was going to wear it out! I don't think I did anything for my Father that pleased him more.

The 20th of November was Father and Emily's twentieth anniversary and the family gathered for a quiet celebration in their honour. Quite an achievement for two people who had married in their later lives, never dreaming that time would treat them so well.

70. Janis at signpost of places Father knew.

CHAPTER 10

On 7 December 1970, Father became newsworthy again when he attended a meeting held at the Royal York Hotel. His attendance there was arranged by Greg Clark, a well-known Toronto writer who, after reading some of Father's 'Letters to the Editor', thought he deserved a chance to air his views at the meeting. The write-up of this meeting, which appeared in the next day's *Toronto Evening Telegram*, is shown on the next page.

I was unaware of this event until the day after the meeting. I had phoned to inquire how they were and Emily told me that they were both all right, although Father was nursing his sore knee, and then gave me the story of the meeting. This Father of mine was really a wonder! After reading the write-up, I went over that night to hear his side of the story. As I entered the room where he was sitting, leg propped up, he looked up with a smile on his face, whereupon I said to him, 'I'm just so proud of you,' and I certainly was. The write-up had omitted two things, the first being no 'Sr' after his name, which caused Jim some kidding at the next Council meeting. Someone remarked to him that he really didn't look elderly whereupon Jim enlightened them quickly saying, 'That was my Father.' The explanation was easily accepted as the Council members knew of Father's interest in current issues. The other omission, which I thought would have highlighted the article, was that after being called a 'dirty Limey hireling', Father told his opponent to meet him out in the hall at the conclusion of the meeting! Here was Father, with a heart condition and at age eighty-six, issuing such a challenge. Luckily the challenge was ignored and Father returned home safely but limping, having cut his knee breaking the plywood sign. No wonder Emily worried when he was out of her sight. I think he almost enjoyed his sore knee, as he was the hero of the day in his defence of the Monarchy. He received many laudable comments from friends and neighbours over the story, which was also featured in the local paper. Within two weeks the knee was healed and life returned to its previously orderly fashion.

The following passage is printed by permission of Canada Wide, a Division of the Toronto Sun Syndicate Corporation.

Grab-bag of complaints greets constitution probers

The joint Senate-Commons committee on constitutional reform turned into a public forum for complaints yesterday as the committee opened its two-day hearings in Toronto at the Royal York Hotel.

It took the committee four hours to wade through the first five briefs presented as members of the audience took to the microphones to complain about mental institutions, sky-rocketing taxes, pollution and other topics not within the committee's terms of reference.

A minor skirmish developed within minutes when Zoltan Szoboszloi, a self-styled traffic summons consultant, entered the meeting carrying a large wooden sign reading "God Save Everyone From the Queen—Behind the Limey Curtain."

James W. Trimbee, an elderly Weston resident, rose to his feet, grabbed Szoboszloi's sign and smashed it in two pieces, shouting: "You don't bring things like that in here." Szoboszloi accused Trimbee of being a "dirty Limey hireling."

Szoboszloi has repeatedly and vainly argued in court that summonses issued in the Queen's name are invalid because Canada has no Queen. An immigrant from Hungary, Szoboszloi has been refused citizenship because he won't take the oath of allegiance to the Queen.

Three Metro politicians—Mayor William Dennison of Toronto, Metro chairman Albert Campbell and Toronto alderman Karl Jaffary—told the committee that a new constitution should provide more autonomy for large urban centres.

Only Jaffary made a formal presentation to the committee which is holding public hearings across the country. Dennison and Campbell were merely welcoming the parliamentarians to Toronto but said they hoped the city and Metro could agree on a brief before the committee completes its Ontario hearings.

Chairman Mark MacGuigan, the Liberal MP for Windsor-Walkerville, said the committee may make a special trip back to Toronto to hear the Metro brief.

Jaffary said large urban centres must be given the constituitonal powers to "levy our own taxes and conduct our own schemes" in addition to the property tax base which now exists.

He was content, though, that he had been able to put forth his views at such a meeting and was proved right on at least one point, about the Humber Sewage Plant thirteen years later when, in the summer of 1983, all the beaches at Sunnyside were closed to the public because of pollution from the plant. Unfortunately, at that time, though, his suggestions were not taken very seriously, as shown in excerpts from the minutes of the meeting which follow. Only the ones quoting Father's name appear.

71. *Father on his eighty-sixth birthday, 1 November, 1970.*

e No. 19	**Fascicule no 19**
ınday, December 7, 1970—Toronto, Ontario	Le lundi 7 décembre 1970—Toronto, Ontario
nt Chairmen: **Senator Maurice Lamontagne**	Coprésidents: **Sénateur Maurice Lamontagne**
Mr. Mark MacGuigan, M.P.	**M. Mark MacGuigan, député**

nutes of Proceedings and Evidence
the Special Joint Committee of
e Senate and of
e House of Commons on the

*Procès-rerbaux et témoignages
du Comité spécial mixte
du Sénat et de
la Chambre des communes sur la*

⌐onstitution
▸f Canada

Constitution
du Canada

ITNESSES:

;ee Minutes of Proceedings)

TÉMOINS:

(Voir les procès-verbaux)

7-12-1970   Constitution du Canada   19 : 3

MINUTES OF PROCEEDINGS

Monday, December 7, 1970.

(23)

[Text]

The Special Joint Committee of the Senate and of the House of Commons on the Constitution of Canada met this day in the Royal York Hotel, Toronto, Ontario, at 2:10 p.m. The Joint Chairman, Mr. MacGuigan, presided.

Members present:

Representing the Senate: Senators Cameron, Ferguson, Haig, Quart and Forsey.—(5).

Representing the House of Commons: Messrs. Allmand, Asselin, Breau, Brewin, Dinsdale, Fairweather, Gibson, Lachance, Laprise, MacGuigan, Marceau, Osler, Prud'homme, Ryan and Whelan.—(15).

Also present: From the House of Commons: Mr. Givens.

The Chairman made a short introductory statement and introduced the Members of the Committee to the public.

Mayor William Dennison of Toronto welcomed the Committee to Toronto and spoke briefly on the problems of large Metropolitan areas.

Alderman William Kilbourn and Alderman Karl Jaffary of Toronto spoke briefly and presented a brief on behalf of their statement and responded to questions thereon. (See Appendix "T")

Messrs. A. Tuchel, Thomas Blanchard, Bruce Magmuson and Reginald Babooblal were invited by the Joint Chairman to make statements from the floor.

Mr. Albert Campbell, Chairman of Metropolitan Toronto, welcomed the Committee to Toronto and made a brief statement.

Dr. Albert Abel of the Faculty of Law, University of Toronto, presented a brief to the Committee and made comments thereon. (See Appendix "U")

Dr. Abel responded to questions by the Members.

Messrs. Thomas Blanchard, Zoltan Szoboszloi, Art Dean, James Trimbee, M. Lutczyk, M. Kilgore, Ted Rotenburg, J. L. Lotchell, J. L. McCormick and Miss Renee de Jong made statements from the floor.

The Chairman thanked Dr. Abel for his presentation.

The Chairman introduced Mr. Ernest Benedict representing the Union of Ontario Indians who presented a brief and responded to questions thereon. Mr. George Bevan commented on the brief.

Alderman Tony O'Donohue of Toronto presented his personal views on the Constitution to the Committee and responded to questions. Mr. Trimbee commented from the floor.

23210—11

[Texte]

Mr. Szoboszloi: I am commenting that always by Supreme Court of Canada and by the Supreme Court Canada, June 17, did witness my appeal Szoboszloi Regina and in Canada does not exist the right, does exist this Bill of Rights and this is impossible to cont the society, social control without courts. Every jud swore allegiance to the Queen. This means that eve judge is outside of jurisdiction. This is so clear if som body learned the law in criminology outside of the Lim Curtain. Thank you very much gentlemen. We are livi behind the Limey Curtain. I fled from the Iron Curta now we are living behind the Limey Curtain. Thank you

The Joint Chairman (Mr. MacGuigan): Order please.

(After the "skirmish")

Mr. Art Dean (100 Church St., Weston, Ontario): M Chairman, ladies and gentlemen, first I want to thank t Chairman and the Committee for at least providi facilities for the public, much better than the job th you did with Paul Hellyer. You really did a snow job him when you had the Task Force on Housing here Toronto. You had no facilities whatsoever but I thai you for giving us fair seats in nice surroundings.

Mr. Abel, sitting here, if I close my eyes I would swe I was listening to Justice Rand when he was trying implement a strait-jacket and shackles for the labo movement. You say to us you want gods from ea province and I assume each province would appoi retired judges of the calibre of Mr. Rand because th are always considered the super gods of each country a of each province it seems in Canada. I would like to the question, how do you propose to develop these peop and where do you expect to get them to fill this position

Professor Abel: I think they exist. I have not giv myself the appointing power, but I think I could useful advise the government on choices to be made.

Mr. James W. Trimbee (231 Church St., Westo Ontario): Freedom—I think we pay far too much and tal it too literally when you consider just what that friend mine just put over on us. Here we have gone on fo hundreds of years to try to get freedom. We have pa far too much for it. We go to work, we elect members the House and the first thing they do when they g there, they put the wages right up. The next thing is, th labour unions see that they can get away with it an they do the same thing and the same thing runs all th way down the line until we do not know where we ar going today with regards to wages. That is freedom.

I have watched events in Canada now for 65 yea since Laurier's day all along the line and I have come the conclusion after living those days and watchin events, and listening today to you people here, our big gest trouble is that we are allowing too few men handle our destiny.

If you go back in history right to the beginning yo will find that all of our troubles from the beginning hav been caused by one or a few.

Listening to these gentlemen today especially I think we are going to change the charter the first thing we should put into it is that any big event, either by th federal government, provincial or right down to th school trustees, after they have worked out what the

A TRAIL OF TRIALS

: 46 Constitution of Canada 7-12-1970

[*Text*]

...sh to do, it should be put to a vote of the people before it goes through. The whole thing is getting out of hand all over the country, and all over the world, but all over this country today. We are getting taxed to death. Where are we going to finish? Everything is getting out of hand.

The Joint Chairman (Mr. MacGuigan): Mr. Trimbee, are you relating this to the present question?

Mr. Trimbee: I am relating this to the meeting we are having here. If we are going to change anything in the constitution, the biggest thing we could do would be to bring in a clause that any big issue should be voted by the people before it is spent. This is just to show you what has happened, we received a notice last week where a neighbour of ours up the street a little way wants to put a back room on his house. It is going to cost about $1,200 that he is adding to his bungalow. We got that notice, did we want to make any complaint. At the same time, a month ago, after we had put down a street five years ago with a nine-inch base, along come the roads people, or whoever had control, and sliced the thing in two and put in a new sewer. We were not asked about it. Just before that, a high school in Weston that was only put up in my time was considered obsolete and another $6 million high schools goes up. Nobody is considered about it.

The Joint Chairman (Mr. MacGuigan): Mr. Trimbee, could I ask you to bring your remarks to a conclusion?

Mr. Trimbee: All right. The same thing happens to the government. The Ontario government goes to work and they put this monstrosity in the lake. You talk about where your money goes. Why do you not watch where it goes? The next thing is the federal government says we will have another $100 million for biculturalism and bilingualism.

M. Gibson: Bon! Bonne idée.

Mr. Trimbee: What is the matter with you? You are all crazy.

The Joint Chairman (Mr. MacGuigan): Thank you, Mr. Trimbee.

Mr. M. Lutczyk (59 McGillivray Ave., Toronto, North York): Mr. Chairman, I would like to point out concerning the laws we are talking about today how here in Canada in what we call a free country. I cannot sue a government of the British here in Canada. I have been investigating a few cases with a lawyer and the lawyer tells me you cannot attack the Crown. As we are living here in Confederation and we have so many problems here we cannot move freely, especially ethnic groups here. We cannot express ourselves, like myself, in fighting for freedom but I do not receive my freedom here in, as we call it, a free country, Canada. I have been a prisoner myself and have been sent to a penitentiary as a mental case for 30 days. The court was held in Ottawa. They released me, dismissed. Then what happened? Thirty days I was in the mental hospital. I have investi-

[*Texte*]

other words, I think the International Joint Commission would have policing authority as well. I would go for that.

Mr. Gibson: You would be in favour of policing empowered in the Act.

Mr. O'Donohue: Yes, I would.

The Joint Chairman (Mr. MacGuigan): The gentleman at the microphone.

Mr. James W. Trimbee Sr. (Private Citizen, 231 Church Street, Weston, Ontario): How could we ever expect to get anything better while we keep doing the same thing? I started 40 years ago. I reported to the government 40 years ago about the Humber River and I have been fighting it in different ways ever since.

Today, Mr. O'Donohue is speaking about a new incinerator for the city. Etobicoke is talking about a new incinerator out there. As long as we do the same things, how in the name of God are we ever going to do anything better?

When the Almighty created this earth, He created it in the way that so much had to be used and the rest funnelled back into the earth to keep it going. Over the years as I have watched Toronto, we have wasted millions of tons of garbage, as they call it, or waste, which should have all went back to replenish poor land and build up poor land all the way back and go back and back. All that is necessary to keep this world going.

It is all so simple if you would only follow the proper rules of life. It is the same with water. I have an article here that I put in the Toronto Star before they put in the filtration plant for the Humber River and warned them what would happen. I told them that the other one had never worked, which it never has done—and Mr. O'Donohue knows I am telling the truth. They cannot purify it. It is impossible, for the simple reason that every time there is a storm the effluent goes out in the lake both ends. Am I telling the truth or not, Mr. O'Donohue?

An hon. Member: We are working on it.

Mr. O'Donohue: As far as I am concerned, with respect to sewage, we have treatments now available. We give primary and secondary treatment to our sewage.

Mr. Trimbee: But you know it does not go out clear enough to drink.

Mr. O'Donohue: We treat something like 289 million gallons of sewage every day.

Mr. Trimbee: It is impossible. The proper place to purify the water is on the land. All filth is made on the land and it should be purified in the land before it goes into the water in the air. Until we get down to that system we are going to pollute ourselves to death.

The Joint Chairman (Mr. MacGuigan): Thank you. Mr. O'Donohue?

Mr. O'Donohue: I would like to make a comment on the federal aid to cities with respect to research on

23219—5

Uncle Charles wrote in the following summer, 1971, suggesting that if possible, Father go for a visit to Vermont, where he and June were working at the Green Mountain Track. They had hoped to come up here for a short stay but their work schedule prevented this, as they worked six days a week. I willingly offered to drive him down and he agreed, much to Emily's concern as she worried about his health. However, he was determined to see his brother again and we left on a Sunday morning in July accompanied by two of my daughters, Kerry and Janis. Kerry took her turn with the driving and rated Father's approval thankfully. It precluded any nervousness on his part so that he could relax and enjoy the ride.

We headed east and crossed the border at the Thousand Islands Bridge into New York State. This is a very scenic area and Father missed none of the sights to be seen. The trip took us most of the day but we made frequent stops along the way, so that Father could get out of the car to stretch his legs which cramped up if he sat too long without moving. Following the map that Uncle Charles had sent, we arrived safely at the motel where Uncle Charles and June occupied an apartment for the season and where he had made reservations for us. We had time to check in, unpack, and for Father to have a rest before they arrived from the track about 6.00 p.m. There were fond greetings between all, as we had not seen each other for fourteen years, when they visited Toronto in 1957. Uncle took us out for dinner, after which we returned to their apartment for the evening. Then, of course, Father and Uncle Charles had a great discussion about the visit to California, including the ranch, in 1964.

The next day, their only day of the week off work, Charles and June drove us all over the outlying areas, showing us so many interesting sights. One of these I remember clearly was an old church, one of the oldest in that part of the country, a beautiful, white, history-laden building. Uncle Charles was giving us the history of it when he looked around and saw Father gazing up into a big tree nearby. Uncle Charles said, 'Good Heavens, here we are at a place steeped in history and what is he doing—staring at a tree!' It wasn't just a tree, it was a tree new in species to Father and that really interested him, though he was listening to Uncle Charles. Yes, Nature came first, wherever he was.

We also saw the home of Grandma Moses, the famous artist and that did interest Father, knowing the story of her fame coming late in life. Uncle Charles and Father were patient enough to stop at a woollen mill for some shopping. It was a full day, enjoyable every minute, ending with dinner out again in an unusual restaurant converted from an old train station. Back at the apartment, another discussion about conservation, the state of the world and other like things, ended the evening when Father

72. Father blowing out birthday cake candles with Caroline, youngest grandchild.

and Uncle Charles retired for the night. June then joined Kerry, Janis and I in our room for some 'girl talk' and entertained us with stories about some of the celebrities she and Uncle Charles knew through their connections with the racing world. Kerry and Janis, of course, had become much more mature since they had last met June, whom they found to be a kind, beautiful lady.

Early next morning, we met for breakfast in the motel restaurant and then said our goodbyes. It was a rather sentimental farewell as, without saying so, I'm sure the two brothers knew it was probably the last time they would meet.

On the return journey, there was much to talk over, after all the sights we had seen on our tour the previous day and our visit with the relatives. So that Father could stretch his legs, we made frequent stops, some of these at plant nurseries he wanted to look over. He relished seeing the stock, and having short chats with the owners about the various flowers, plants and shrubs. For Father's benefit, we came home a different route, this time crossing into Canada at Niagara Falls, from where we took the river road through the Niagara Park to Niagara-on-the-Lake. In the park we stopped, so that he could see the beautiful flower beds and greenhouses run by the Niagara Parks Commission, one of the highlights of the trip to him. Kerry, Janis and I enjoyed the trip with him, his great sense of humour often bringing forth our smiles and laughter. One incident is clearly remembered by us. Leaving Niagara-on-the-Lake, we turned a corner, passing a green of the local golf course on which four golfers were putting cautiously. At that moment Father leaned out of the window and in a loud voice shouted, 'FORE!' Looking back, the girls saw fists raised in anger towards us which sent us into gales of laughter, thinking that at age eighty-six Father could still pull such a trick. Shortly after we made another stop so that he could get out of the car to examine the grapes growing close by the road: another 'Nature study' for him. When we stopped for dinner, Father requested that I call Emily to inform her that we were on the last part of our journey and would soon be home, thus relieving her of any worry about him. She was happy to see him home and feeling well, his travelling over. Surely no man was ever better cared for or loved.

Jim once made the remark that he didn't know how one man could be lucky enough to have two such good wives and it was true, as both women cared for him so well. He was the number one concern to both of them.

The store on Maple Leaf Drive was closed that year, when the property was sold for redevelopment, concentrating the flower business at the greenhouse store, though plans were developing for another store to be opened in the near future on Jane Street.

Father's and Emily's health gave us cause for concern. Emily, because of arthritis and Father with increasing heart trouble. His visits to and from the Doctor increased as his activities lessened and we were informed by the medical men that Father's heart was weakening progressively. It was a subdued birthday gathering for him that 1 November, when he turned eighty-seven and, though we did all visit them on Christmas Day, no one lingered long as he tired very easily.

One Saturday in the latter part of February, my daughters and I drove out to visit Father, who was in bed most of the time by then. Shortly after our arrival, he took ill and I immediately phoned for an ambulance in which I accompanied up to the hospital, thankful that it was such a short distance away. One girl, Marilyn, stayed with Emily and the other two went up to the store to notify Jim and Wilma. Father was immediately admitted and the doctors began treatment, aware of his condition from previous stays in hospital. He was placed in the intensive care unit, hooked up to monitors, and we were told that he had suffered another serious heart attack. After a few days, he rallied enough to be taken from the intensive care unit and placed in a room near the nurses' station, where they could keep close watch on him. However, our hopes for his recovery were dashed when the cardiologist told us frankly that Father's time was running to an end: his heart was just worn right out.

Word was spread to the other members of the family, who in turn visited him. I'm sure Father knew the situation but his weakness allowed no fight. Quiet and sad were the times spent with him, though we did our best to comfort him. Even though he was eighty-seven, he had been so active mentally and, until lately, physically, that I think we had all felt he would go on forever.

He had been sharing a semi-private room but on Friday 3 March, he was moved down the hall to a small private room. I visited him that afternoon and remarked that the private room would be better for having visitors. He looked up at me knowingly and said quite calmly, 'They've moved me in here to die.' I tried to deny this fact but knew in my heart that his wisdom that had shone forth throughout his long life had prevailed again. The next day I took Emily in for a visit and left them alone for a while. It was a touching moment when they said their goodbyes, and I has to muster all my control to avoid tears. I returned to the hospital a short time later and met brother Bill there visiting Father. It was the last time I saw my Father alive.

In the evening, when Jim was visiting Father, cousin Jim Flack arrived and his memories of the evening follow.

> At that time I was very involved in kids' hockey but thinking of Uncle Jim in hospital. That night I said to my wife Sue, 'I think I should go in and see Uncle Jim. I've been so busy I've not seen him lately and I feel that I should go in tonight.' It started to snow, I was tired from working at the arena all day and gave the proposed trip from Streetsville a second thought but decided to go ahead and see him. We had a nice visit and as he lay in his bed he told me that from there he could look out the window and see the high smoke-stack of the hospital which perturbed him to see the pollution belching out into the atmosphere. It was like purgatory for him to see that. I felt very fortunate that I had not let my laziness overtake me which would have kept me from my visit,

as he passed away early the next morning. I have fond recollectins of
Uncle Jim, I always thought he liked me, I liked him, we had good jokes
together. I was 'Jamie' to the end and still feel now that he is always
teaching me.

I think all who knew Father also feel that somehow he is still teaching
us, as sentiments such as that were echoed over and over by many who
came to pay their respects at the funeral home.

Father had outlived most of his gardening associates and all the Toronto
relatives of his generation, but it was still a largely attended funeral. Many
people who came told us that Father had touched their lives in some way
by word or deed, and they wished to pay respect to his memory. The
York Borough Council attended as a body, not just for Jim's sake as a
member of that Council, but out of their recognition for Father's active
life. The day he died, Martha's husband Paul, at my request, hoisted
Father's beloved Union Jack flag out the front of 231 Church Street to
half-mast, which I thought appropriate to mark the sad occasion. After
the funeral, Emily gave me the flag, which I proudly accepted and use
now, in Father's tradition, to mark special days.

I finish my Father's life story in this year of 1984, the one hundredth
anniversary of his birth, as a tribute to him. He gave us all a fine example
of living, never giving up in times of stress, failure or setbacks. Thankfully,
he lived to see success in his florist business, flourishing as it was before
he died.

An excerpt from something he wrote typifies his principles in life and
the struggle he fought for future generations:

> The warnings are coming more rapidly and, maybe like others, I could
> ignore them, thinking I get by, why should I worry about what is to
> come? My time on earth will soon be over but my belief is that anyone
> coming into this world should try to leave it just a little bit better in some
> way for having lived in it.

Epilogue

Since Father's death in 1972, many changes have taken place in the Trimbee Family—some happy, some sad.

In the spring of 1972, another Trimbee Florists store was opened, on Jane Street, Weston, followed by another branch at Mississauga Square One Shopping Centre, in 1973. By now, Jim's son Rob was in the business full-time, exercising his ingenuity in enlarging the operation. 1974 brought about another expansion, when Trimbee Florists moved into Gerrard Square, a shopping mall in the east part of Toronto, not far from where Father began his first greenhouse operation, soon after his arrival in Canada in the early 1900s.

Father's remaining relatives in California died within a few years of each other soon after Father's death, and our dear Emily joined them in 1979 aged ninety-five, still a joy to all who knew her.

Rob took over control of the flower business while Jim was busy with a successful political life. On 4 September 1982, brother Bill's death occurred after a short illness, and sixteen days later Jim died suddenly, at a Council meeting. Father's two sons followed him ten years after his death: sad losses for the family.

I have returned to Upham twice since my original visit. I have seen the places Father wrote of, and attended service at the Upham Church, where he sang in the choir. I was greeted there warmly, as one 'returning to the fold'. One feels a great sense of peace in that tiny village, and I understand the nostalgia Father felt for it. I put it to Fate that I visited there once shortly after my Grandfather's tombstone was found broken. I had it repaired, to stand upright again to his memory in that ancient churchyard. There is now a Visitors' Book inside the entrance to the church, which I donated in memory of the Trimbee Family, who at one time were all members of the Parish.

When visiting Upham in 1980, I checked on some family 'roots' and, quite by accident, discovered a cousin, a grandson of Father's sister Rose, who, until he met me, did not know he had a single living relative. I had with me a copy of Father's story and, by comparing details mentioned in it, proof was established as to our relationship. He is Raymond Hitchcock.

Twice, also, have I visited the ground of Didlington Hall, Norfolk, England, from where Father emigrated to Canada. Unfortunately, the great house had been demolished, but when my desire for a photograph of it was made known, many kind people of the area sent me photos, write-ups and their personal memories of the Hall. The history of the estate makes very absorbing reading.

In April 1984, the official opening was held of 'Trimbee Court', a housing development in Mount Dennis, adjacent to Weston, named to honour Jim who had actively participated on the Ontario Housing Authority in his political days. Obviously the Trimbee name will be recognized in more than one way.

The flower business carried on under Rob's guidance for a number of years. Now although the business still goes under the Trimbee name in 1995, it is no longer under family ownership.

The following narrative is added at the request of William (Bill) Farr, now a Vice-President of York University, Toronto. After reading the manuscript, he wished to add his personal memories of James Trimbee. I gratefully accepted his offer, thinking it would give the reader the reflections of one other than a family member.

Pop Trimbee

It's a privilege to be able to append a few lines to Pop Trimbee's auto-biography and the loving continuation of his story by Jean Trimbee McKenzie. I am grateful to Mrs McKenzie for this opportunity to remember Pop and to reflect upon what his friendship meant to me at the time, and what it means now.

I worked for James Trimbee Florist from 1957 to 1963, while in high school, first during summers and on Saturdays, then after school every day as well while I was in Grades 12 and 13. After my first winter at University, I came back to the greenhouse for a couple of months in the summer of 1963, and continued to visit on and off for a long time after that.

The job was hard and sweaty and dirty and hot. People often said that it must be nice to be 'working with flowers', and in a way it was; I think we all respected the flowers and found them beautiful. But the work was mostly with dirt, and glass, and manure, and pipes, and boilers, and cinders and coal and wheelbarrows, shovels and digging forks. I worked hard. Everybody at Trimbee's was expected to work hard. I started at thirty cents an hour my first summer, and worked my way up by the end of my time there to the same pay that the regular grown-up men made. I learned to do a man's job, to take responsibility, to set my own standards of work, to do complete jobs. I haven't learned much about working that I didn't learn at the Greenhouse.

The people you spend your time with when you are becoming an adult have huge influence on you. Sometimes it's football or hockey teams, or gangs, or classmates. In my case, it was Jim and Wilma Trimbee, Eddie Seery and Tommy MacDonald, Bill Jennings and Tom Kennedy . . . men that I worked alongside, learned to like, sometimes imitate, sometimes judge.

Most of all, however, the Greenhouse was Pop Trimbee. He was the first Trimbee I met when I went looking for a summer job prior to starting high school. I edged my way into what seemed a deserted greenhouse, finally found someone and asked for Mr Trimbee, was sent into a labyrinth of pathways and benches, and encountered Pop, who told me I'd have to come back when Jim was there. I was disappointed, but I came back later and I got the job.

The first day after school was out, I reported for duty, full of anxiety, and was set to work with Bruce Trimbee, then about eleven or twelve, whose first day it also was, pulling out what seemed to be an endless bed of snapdragons, in heat worse than I had ever imagined in my sheltered life. And Pop drove us crazy. He simply would not let us alone. He harassed us terribly, visiting every few minutes to hurry us up, correct our mistakes (which only he could see), stop us from talking too much, drinking too much water, or a hundred other temptations which he assumed that teenage boys would be prey to. He was a tyrant, a spy, a terrorist, a slavedriver. We lived in fear of his surveillance and his tongue. It wasn't just us new kids either. No one escaped. It was probably worse for Bruce, since Pop expected more of a Trimbee. But generally, all the workers were terrorized alike, without mercy if they erred. Even Pop's favorites, Bill Jennings, who was about seven years older than I and whose family had once owned the greenhouses, and Tom Kennedy, who moonlighted at Timbee's from a full-time job at the TTC, had to hustle hard to avoid his wrath.

I don't know how long it took me to prove myself to Pop. sometimes he was so sharp and caustic with me, and so difficult to please, that I wanted to cry; on those occasions the victims would pull together to complain among ourselves and offer comfort, or Jim would intercede once in a while. But, however hard he was as a taskmaster, Pop had a way of challenging you to beat him, to beat yourself, to do better than you thought you could do, to get more done, to do the job as well as it could be done . . . thoroughly, quickly, carefully (no plant should ever be damaged, no matter what) . . . and clean up afterwards. He was infuriating, because he could do so many of the jobs well himself, even in his seventies, that he just made you determined to show him that you could do the same.

By the start of my second summer, I think, things improved a lot. Pop started to talk to me at tea-time and coffee-time or when we were on a job together. He would spring the *Reader's Digest* 'Improve your Word-power' on me, and when I started to show that I could do a man's work in the greenhouse without surveillance, and that I had a *Reader's Digest* vocabulary (my grandmother's collection of hundreds of *Reader's Digest* was stored next to my bed at home, and I had read them all by the time I was fourteen), Pop began to lecture me. He had a lot to say, too, about almost anything; politics, government, the economy, education, music, sports, fishing, the monarchy. He read all the time . . . newspapers, maga-zines, old papers used as wrapping . . . and followed radio and TV news avidly. He was full of scepticism and opinion. He took it as obvious that the world was running downhill, that no one worked hard enough anymore, and that public figures were almost certainly corrupt or foolish or naive. Yet he persisted in his view that living by honest hard work, and respect for nature and one another, was the way to life, and would see you through. The values and experiences that Pop wrote about in *A Trail of Trials* were the things he talked to us about. Although Pop's language was as salty as anyone's, and some of his insults so outrageous that they should have been recorded, I don't recall ever hearing smutty talk or hurtful gossip from him. Most surprising to me, as I think back, is that I didn't ever get any real sense of the many hard times that Pop and the Trimbees had been through until I read Pop's life story. He may have railed against politicians and time-wasters and laziness, but I don't think I ever heard him complain about what his life had been or the troubles he had seen. He loved being alive, doing his job, having a good argument, tormenting his grandchildren, loving his Emily (about whom, in my association with the Trimbees, I never heard anything except praise and admiration and affection, from even the roughest of the workers), finding out what 'nutsy-ness' was abroad in the world today, and what advice he could offer to the unwary.

Pop had a great respect for education . . . probably more than education deserved. None of his children had been able to go to university, because of money needs, I now realize. But he had instilled respect in them for books and learning, and they were smart, and knew how to think; Jean Trimbee McKenzie's completion of Pop's story is carefully crafted writing and a joy to read; Bill Trimbee was a hugely funny and outrageous and exasperating character. Jim Trimbee, like his father, had a large influence on me. He was a relentless hard worker, and an insatiable reader; I used to think during high school that I was pretty hot stuff in the reading department, but Jim was almost always ahead of me on anything new or important in the Weston Library. He and I had some great talks about things we were reading when I worked in the Packing Shed or the Store. I doubt that I would have needed much encouragement to go on to university after high school . . . I was doing well at school and my parents were keen . . . but if I had ever had doubts of that kind, Pop and Jim would have set me straight. They both, especially Pop, lectured me endlessly on the need to get a good education, to read widely, to learn facts and how to think for myself, to avoid pitfalls laid by clever rascals. When I graduated from high school, Pop was proud of me, and cut my picture out of *The Telegram* and put it on the shed wall by the telephone for a while. He even warned me once, in a short but serious talk, not to get too interested in the greenhouse business; he thought that education was a better and safer way.

And through this time, we became friends, and I guess I came to love him in a way. One of my grandfathers had died before I was born, and the other when I was very small, and Pop fitted into that role pretty easily for me. After I bought a car, in 1962, I would take him for drives on Sunday. These would be long, rambling excursions into the farm country around Toronto, while Pop searched for landmarks of places he had been, and things he had seen when he was young. He would drive me nuts, with instructions like 'turn left or right somewhere up ahead'. For a long time I would assist him by editing and typing the long letters and opinion pieces he sent off to newspapers and politicians, mostly about water conservation. He had ideas, and schemes and proposals, most of them doomed to failure at the time because they were based on conservation of natural resources and the Golden Rule as an operating principle. In this most ecological era, he might have been more successful. But, as Jean McKenzie has described, he loved these disputes and arguments, and pursued them to the point of great excitement. I felt that they kept his spirit alive, and that the lively spirit kept him going through some of his difficult illnesses.

I have read and re-read *A Trail of Trials*, and Jean McKenzie's completion of the manuscript. The kinds of memories I get from it are the ones above: affection, nostalgia, backbreaking hard work, and the fun of learning how to do that work and do it well. What I make of it all, from where I am now, from having known and cared for Pop, and from learning what the book has told me about his life, I am not so sure. The closest I can come to a summation is that it was indeed a trail of trials; whether Pop's life would have been counted a success by most success-counting measures, I don't know. But as a man, full of contradiction and vitality and trouble and passion and anger and fury and love, he was a marvellous success. He never surrendered his love of beauty, or integrity, or toil, or determination, or nature. He was a force in the lives of the people he knew. He challenged them; I think he made them better than they were; I think he was a great man.

William D. Farr
York University
26 December 1990